KAZAN ON KAZAN

in the same series

WOODY ALLEN ON WOODY ALLEN
edited by Stig Björkman

ALMODÓVAR ON ALMODÓVAR
edited by Frederic Strauss

BURTON ON BURTON
edited by Mark Salisbury

CRONENBERG ON CRONENBERG
edited by Chris Rodley

DE TOTH ON DE TOTH
edited by Anthony Slide

FELLINI ON FELLINI
edited by Costanzo Costantini

GILLIAM ON GILLIAM
edited by Ian Christie

HAWKS ON HAWKS
edited by Joseph McBride

HITCHCOCK ON HITCHCOCK
edited by Sidney Gottlieb

KIEŚLOWSKI ON KIEŚLOWSKI
edited by Danusia Stok

LEVINSON ON LEVINSON
edited by David Thompson

LOACH ON LOACH
edited by Graham Fuller

LYNCH ON LYNCH
edited by Chris Rodley

MALLE ON MALLE
edited by Philip French

POTTER ON POTTER
edited by Graham Fuller

SAYLES ON SAYLES
edited by Gavin Smith

SCHRADER ON SCHRADER
edited by Kevin Jackson

SCORSESE ON SCORSESE
edited by David Thompson and Ian Christie

SIRK ON SIRK
conversations with Jon Halliday

KAZAN ON KAZAN

edited by

Jeff Young

faber and faber

For Annie

First published in the United States in 1999
under the title *Kazan – The Master Director Discusses His Films: Interviews with Elia Kazan* by Newmarket Press: A Division of Newmarket Publishing and Communications, 18 East 48th Street, New York, New York, 10017, USA

First published in the United Kingdom in 1999
by Faber and Faber Limited
3 Queen Square London WC1N 3AU

Printed in England by Clays Ltd, St Ives plc

A CIP record for this book
is available from the British Library

ISBN 0-571-19217-3

2 4 6 8 10 9 7 5 3 1

CONTENTS

PHOTO/POSTER CREDITS

A Tree Grows in Brooklyn, Boomerang, Gentleman's Agreement, Pinky, Viva Zapata!, and *Wild River:* Courtesy of the Academy of Motion Picture Arts and Sciences and the 20th Century Fox Photo Archive. Copyright 20th Century Fox. All rights reserved. *Sea of Grass:* Copyright 1947 Turner Entertainment Company. *Panic in the Streets* and *Man on a Tightrope:* Courtesy of the 20th Century Fox Photo Archive. Copyright 20th Century Fox. All rights reserved. *A Streetcar Named Desire:* Copyright 1951 Charles Feldman Group Productions. *East of Eden:* Courtesy of the Academy of Motion Picture Arts and Sciences. Copyright 1955 Warner Brothers Pictures, Inc. *On the Waterfront:* Courtesy of Columbia Pictures. Copyright 1954, Renewed 1982 Columbia Pictures Corporation. All rights reserved. *Baby Doll, A Face in the Crowd*, and *America America:* Courtesy of the Academy of Motion Picture Arts and Sciences. Used by permission of Castle Hill Productions, Inc. Copyright Warner Brothers Pictures, Inc. *Splendor in the Grass:* Courtesy of the Academy of Motion Picture Arts and Sciences. Copyright 1961 Warner Brothers Pictures, Inc. *The Arrangement:* Courtesy of the Academy of Motion Picture Arts and Sciences. Copyright 1969 Athena Enterprises Corp. and Warner Bros.-Seven Arts, Inc. *The Visitors:* Courtesy of MGM Consumer Products. Copyright 1972 Home Free Corporation. All rights reserved. *The Last Tycoon:* Courtesy of the Academy of Motion Picture Arts and Sciences and Viacom Consumer Products.

What the Catcher Said to the Pitcher

An Interview with Elia Kazan

WHEN I WAS A BOY I loved baseball and was lucky to grow up in a town that had a major league team. The baseball diamond remains a place of awe and wonder to me. How does the pitcher get a ball to sink and curve? How does a batter adjust in microseconds to a ball flying at his head? How does a fielder take off at the crack of the bat and race to the exact spot where the ball is going to land? These were mysteries to ponder. But perhaps the greatest of baseball mysteries occurs when a pitcher gets in trouble. The catcher rises out of his squat, takes off his mask and saunters out to the mound. The entire stadium goes quiet, all eyes focused on the two men. A silent question is on every fan's mind: What is the catcher saying to the pitcher?

Many years later and in a very different context, I had the great pleasure of asking that question out loud—and best of all I got the answer. As baseball had been the love of my childhood, movies became the passion and central focus of my adult life. As a professional in the film industry, I quickly learned that, just as the catcher takes the pitcher aside and whispers in his ear, it is the director who whispers in the ear of each of his co-workers.

In the late 1960's I was in film school. I wanted to learn how to direct movies. I was certain it was what I was going to do for the rest of my life. The astonishing success of Dennis Hopper's *Easy Rider* had sent the studios into a frenzy looking for young filmmakers who, they thought, could speak directly to the vast youth market they had discovered. A couple of my prize-winning short films and my receiving an American Film Institute grant to apprentice to Arthur Penn on *Alice's Restaurant* persuaded Paramount that I was just what they were looking for, and so I made a picture called *Been Down So Long It Looks Like Up to Me.* The six weeks of shooting and six months of editing that followed made me vividly aware of how much I didn't know. I'd learned a lot, but I desperately wanted to learn more.

If directing were a learnable craft, I thought, surely the best possible teacher would be the person whose work I most admired. Elia Kazan was my favorite director. He had years of experience facing and solving the thousands of problems and decisions that arise in the making of every film. Why not go to Kazan?

The possibility that Kazan might have something more important on his mind than becoming my personal tutor did occur to me. But I figured what was the worst that could happen? He could say no.

But if I could get him to reexamine his work, if he would tell me what he had said to the writers, actors, cameramen, and all of the other people involved—get him to explain how he made the countless decisions, ranging from the choice of material to the approval of the final answer print, I would indeed find out what the catcher said to the pitcher.

Why did I choose Kazan? There were other great directors. Stanley Kubrick, Joseph Mankiewicz, Arthur Penn, George Stevens, Orson Welles, and Billy Wilder were among my favorites. So what was unique about Kazan's work? To put it simply, his films moved me more than anyone else's. I was transported, taken into the worlds they depicted, made privy to the inner tensions, conflicts, and feelings of Kazan's characters, in whom I'd always found some part of myself—from a ten-year-old girl who longed to become a writer to a tough, semiliterate longshoreman. Kazan's films both forced and enabled me to think about my life and to view the world around me as I never had before. This was artistry of a very high order.

My experience of Kazan's films, though very personal, was hardly unique. For twenty-five years he stood atop the world of American film and theater. That's one hell of a long run by any standard. Arthur Penn, a wonderful filmmaker who also had an enormously successful stage career, once had five hits running on Broadway at the same time. Nonetheless, he remarked, "For years if any director even got to read a play, it meant that Kazan had already passed on it."

What's all the more astounding is that Kazan did it by going his own way. Considerations of box office success didn't influence his choices. It is hard to find in his films or in his theater work material that has obvious or simply popular appeal. Mere entertainment was not his game. For Kazan, filmmaking was a means of self-expression, and if he went at it hard enough, looked deeply and openly and honestly enough, he would find things that were true and relevant to everybody. His job, as he saw it, was not only to entertain but to leave the audience with something when they went home, to change their lives.

Even in the theater, where the director's primary role is to serve the vision of the playwright, Kazan's inner life was always present, front and center.

And what an inner life it has been. A life on the run. He was born on September 7, 1909 to Greek parents living in Istanbul. His father, Yiorgos Kazanjioglou, had fled Kayseri, a small village in Anatolia where for five hundred years the Turks had oppressed and brutalized the Armenian and Greek minorities who had lived there even longer. The running didn't stop. Before Kazan was five the family had moved first to Berlin, back to Istanbul, then to New York City, where his father, now called George, started dealing in rugs, a business so successful that a few years later, he was able to move the family again, to the Westchester suburb of New Rochelle. Elia Kazan was nine.

Already Elia had developed his own version of the "Anatolian smile" that he had inherited from his ancestors. It was a smile that hid everything—fear, rage, resentment, frustration, even love and joy. It was a smile that allowed him to get along in the world, to avoid being beaten up because he was an outsider. It was a smile that hid his feelings of insecurity, of not belonging, of feeling foreign, unattractive, different. It was a smile that defined him as a person constantly at war with himself. Behind that mask he could plot his revenge, develop a means of proving he was better than any of "them."

Elia's father pressured him to go into the family business, as was expected of the oldest son, but Kazan hated the idea. His father never stopped reminding him what a disappointment he was—another stake in the heart. Many boys might have been broken, crawled into a shell of shame and terror and never again ventured out. Who's to say why some give up and others struggle on? Like everything else about Kazan, there are no easy or complete answers.

There is one historical fact, however, that cannot be ignored. His mother, Athena, having come from a better-educated family, encouraged and nurtured her oldest son and protected him from his father's obsession with money and business. Later, the Crash of '29 destroyed his father, but it set Kazan free to accept a scholarship to attend Williams College.

There, to help pay his way, he waited on the tables of rich, Waspy fraternity boys. Again he was the outsider, full of jealousy and contempt for the privileged. The need to prove himself, to become somebody, grew stronger and deeper, but, like many other liberal arts graduates, his drives lacked direction.

He followed a friend to the Yale Drama School, as much because he'd learned he could pay for his meals by operating a dishwashing machine as for any other reason. He had no real interest in drama, only a general feeling that he might find a niche somewhere in the arts. Yale would give him three years to look around. Again there were tables to be waited on. But during those years his ambition began to take shape. While he enjoyed the classes in acting and directing, what he really took to was the scene shop. He thought he might make a living working backstage as an honest craftsman.

The Drama School eventually led him to an apprenticeship with the Group Theatre, which was headed by Cheryl Crawford, Harold Clurman, and Lee Strasberg. Kazan worked his way in, not as an actor as he had hoped, but by being willing and able to do anything, solve any problem, make anything work, and by so doing please anyone he had to and make himself indispensable. He became Mr. Fixit and earned his nickname "Gadg," short for Gadget. By now he was not so much running as hiding. It would be fifty years before anyone knew how he had always despised the nickname he'd once answered to so cheerfully.

By the time the Group Theatre broke up in 1940, Kazan had joined, served in, then quit the Communist Party. He'd also earned his stripes as an actor in plays like *Waiting for Lefty* and *Golden Boy*, both by Clifford Odets. More importantly, he'd made up his mind what he wanted to be. "Everything! A film director as well as a theater director as well as a playwright as well as an actor as well as a producer." Having made a bit of a name for himself as an actor, he went to Hollywood and played small roles in *City for Conquest*, starring James Cagney and directed by Anatole Litvak, and *Blues in the Night*, also directed by Litvak.

He'd already started directing in the theater and had a string of beginner's flops but eventually got a break and was offered a Broadway show when Orson Welles dropped out at the last minute. Thornton Wilder's *The Skin of Our Teeth* was a hit. Hit followed hit, and Broadway had a new fair-haired boy. In 1944 he headed west to shoot his first film.

On a crisp early spring morning in 1971 I rode the IRT subway to 42nd Street. Kazan had agreed to meet with me. His office was tucked in an old building hidden behind the world's biggest billboard—seven stories high, stretching from 46th to 47th Street on Broadway—in the heart of the theater district. The elevator was broken, so I climbed four flights of stairs to his office. On each landing I could see into the open doors of the ticket agents who seemed to be the building's other sole occupants. They were doing a brisk business.

Kazan's quarters, a tiny central room with even smaller rooms leading off of it, fit the funkiness of the building. Eileen Shanahan, Kazan's longtime assistant, offered me coffee and said he'd be right with me. I tried to appear casual as I looked the place over. It was so full of filing cabinets that there was barely room for Eileen's desk. She caught my eyes scanning the walls on which were crammed dozens of theater posters. It looked for all the world like any of the ticket brokers' offices I'd passed on the way upstairs.

"I mounted them myself. Mr. Kazan had them put away. He doesn't like to show off." I nodded knowingly and looked again.

On one wall alone were posters for *The Skin of Our Teeth* by Thorton Wilder, *One Touch of Venus* by S. N. Behrman, Arthur Miller's *All My Son's*, *After the Fall* and *Death of a Salesman*, *Tea and Sympathy* by Robert Anderson, *The Dark at the Top of the Stairs* by William Inge, *J.B.* by Archibald MacLeish, Tennessee Williams's *Camino Real*, *Sweet Bird of Youth*, *Cat on a Hot Tin Roof*, and *A Streetcar Named Desire*.

It was like the entire reading list of my college course on contemporary American drama—and Kazan had directed them all! Incredibly, they represented only a third of his stage work and included none of his films and none of his books. I was at once uplifted and demoralized. How in God's name was he going to find time for me? Why should he?

A door opened behind me. I turned and saw a short, gray-haired man who looked as if on a good day he could still fight middle-weight, smiling at me. I stuck out my hand. "Kazan" was all he said. He doesn't shake. He pulls you toward him, tugging your hand down to his hip, almost behind his back. I was yanked off balance, into his court, and the game hadn't even started. Thank God he was still smiling.

He guided me through the door and gestured toward a low couch, offered a cigar, then sat facing me on an identical sofa. A leg was broken off, and two telephone books propped it in place. The room was warm, comfortable, and unimposing. The only light in it filtered through a fire escape that snaked past a window facing onto the theaters below. A desk stood in front of it.

One wall was covered with family photographs. No Oscars, no Tony Awards. No plaques, no trophies. On the table between us was a phone. In the middle of the dial, where one usually found the number, a small clock was mounted. I wondered if my time was nearly up: Was I about to be tossed out?

Kazan has a greater gift for making you feel at ease than any man I have ever met. I was soon to learn it is a finely honed tool that he uses in his work. But it isn't only a tool. He has a genuine interest in people. (Much later as I walked the streets with him at night, he'd talk to anyone who approached him, more often than not guys looking for a handout. They always got one.) Within moments he and I were chatting as if we'd been best of friends for years.

My timing in approaching Kazan had been extremely fortunate. He was still very actively involved in directing pictures, working on scripts, making the kinds of choices about which I wanted to ask him. Committed to writing his autobiography, he was already thinking closely about his past as well as his future, and he was in a reflective frame of mind. When he asked why I wanted to interview him, the truth just popped out. "I want you to teach me to direct and couldn't think of any way to get you to sit still for it except to suggest that we do a book." There was a long silence. Finally, he said, "We'll start tomorrow at four. What the hell, if you drive me crazy, I can always throw you out. Now get outta here. I've got work to do." I couldn't believe my luck. Fortunately, I'd spent a month at the Library of Congress looking at his films over and over on an editing machine, running them backwards and forwards, studying them frame by frame. I was ready for him.

I don't think either of us knew that we would spend much of the next eighteen months together. But however long this project might take, I knew it was essential to start out on the right foot. The issue of Kazan's "friendly" testimony before the House Un-American Activities Committee would inevitably arise, and I wanted to deal with it right at the outset. I had my own problems with Kazan's testimony. The blacklist was not a political abstraction in my home. My uncle, Ned Young, had been blacklisted and unable to work for years, despite winning an Oscar for writing *The Defiant*

Ones. He would never again put his name on a screenplay. I made my position very clear to Kazan. He was not fazed, or at least he didn't show it.

On one occasion or another, Kazan has been called excessive, stagey, inconsistent, flamboyant, overly simple, overly complicated, almost anything you can imagine, except boring. No one ever called him that. Even Kazan's detractors agree that he is among the most influential directors of our time. His contributions have been monumental, and they have endured.

He took on subject matter that was rarely, if ever, touched by Hollywood. He dealt with the inner lives of his characters in ways that no one had ever seen on film before. And while his films focused on those inner struggles and conflicts, they were set within strong, well-dramatized social contexts. When Kazan chose the material for his movies, they raised penetrating questions about the world we lived in.

Had he done no more than to discover the two most enduring male icons of post–World War II America, Marlon Brando and James Dean, he would have earned a place in film history. But he did a great deal more. Film acting has never been the same since the day Kazan first stepped behind a camera and called, "Action." He shattered clichés and stereotypes. Many actors have done their best work in his films. But he didn't just help them give better performances. He changed the nature of film acting.

No longer was an actor simply to illustrate the thoughts, feelings, and actions that the script and the director required. He was directed *to experience* those thoughts, feelings, and actions. By doing so he would inevitably reveal the character's moment-to-moment truth. The effect was instantaneous and startling. Audiences everywhere knew they were watching something new. They might not have known why, but they certainly knew they were being moved in a different way by the performances in Kazan's films. The revolution in acting had actually begun with Konstantin Stanislavski and the Moscow Arts Theater at the turn of the century. But Kazan was the one who brought it to film.

While Kazan is not thought of primarily as a visual stylist, it is almost impossible to think of a single moment in any of his movies when you wish you were seeing anything other than what he has chosen to show you. For instance there's a key moment in *East of Eden* when Julie Harris tells James Dean that she loves him. It is played under a willow tree, and all that you see of Harris and Dean is their feet. Somehow he knew that was the most interesting way to shoot that scene, and that is the true mark of a man who understands visual storytelling.

As I spent more and more time with Kazan, the objectives and scope of this book broadened considerably. Because Kazan's work has always been so utterly central to his life, the more he talked about his films, the more a distinct portrait of the man himself began to emerge.

These revelations were inevitable, as Kazan is a quintessential humanist. He always describes his characters' experiences in terms of the inner as well as the outer events. When asked about a scene shot thirty years earlier, he is able to recall it precisely. It was not a trick of memory or a matter of technique. His answer went to the essence of what a work of art meant to him. If he asked a cameraman to move a light, you can be sure it was because he thought it would elucidate more about the inner lives of the characters, their relationship to each other, and the circumstances they were facing. His eye was always on what went on in the hearts and souls of his people. As he saw it, *his lifelong task was to turn psychology into behavior*. And, as the twentieth century is man's most overtly "psychological" era, perhaps Kazan's psychological acumen is one of the reasons that his work is as alive and insightful today as it has ever been.

Kazan imposed only one condition on our work. He had promised his publisher he would not be involved with anything that might compete with his autobiography. The transcripts of our interviews would have to sit in their box until his book saw print. It didn't seem like a lot to ask. He expected to finish fairly soon. As it turned out, the autobiography was published seventeen years later.

In the meantime my career had taken a lot of twists and turns. Soon after moving to Los Angeles I was offered a job running a small studio. It was too good an opportunity to pass up. The interviews, meanwhile, stayed in their box. Once Knopf issued *Elia Kazan: A Life*, in 1988, I reread our manuscript with pleasure and regret. The passage of time had made it impossible to include Kazan's insights about *The Last Tycoon*, which had been made in 1976.

However, the famous book of interviews between Alfred Hitchcock and François Truffaut stopped short of Hitchcock's last three films, and it remains, nevertheless, a valuable document. Perhaps so could my interviews with Kazan. I have offered my own views on *The Last Tycoon* and the circumstances leading up to its production and release. I hope that it brings to a satisfying close this discussion of an outstanding filmmaker's career. From 1945 to 1976, Kazan was a long ball hitter across the board. A baseball fan himself, Kazan, the catcher, has been extremely forthcoming and generous indeed in sharing what he said to the pitcher.

A TREE GROWS IN BROOKLYN

(1945)

★★★

SHORTLY AFTER the turn of the century, the Nolan family struggles to survive in their Brooklyn tenement. Francie (Peggy Ann Garner), full of yearning to know everything, has a special love for her father, Johnny (James Dunn), a hopeless, charming, Irish drunk. Full of the blarney, he encourages her to fulfill her dream of becoming a writer, despite the crushing financial hardships they face. It is Francie's practical, puritanical mother, Kathy (Dorothy McGuire), who has to impose order and discipline, while Johnny feeds them the promise that someday it will all be different.

Finances go from bad to disastrous when Kathy discovers that she is pregnant again. They move to a smaller apartment. Francie and her brother, Neely (Ted Donaldson), work harder; Johnny goes on more and more benders. When told by Kathy that he must tell Francie that she is going to have to quit school and go to work to help pay for the new baby, and give up her aspirations, Johnny can't do it.

Instead he fights freezing weather and endless rejection and, finally, dies trying to get a better, steady job. Francie is inconsolable. The outpouring of love from neighbors reminds Kathy of how special her Johnny was. But life must go on.

In the end Kathy accepts the proposal of marriage from Detective McShane (Lloyd Nolan) and with the approval of her children, marries him. Life will be more secure now. When Francie remarks that the baby, Annie Laurie, named after a tune her father

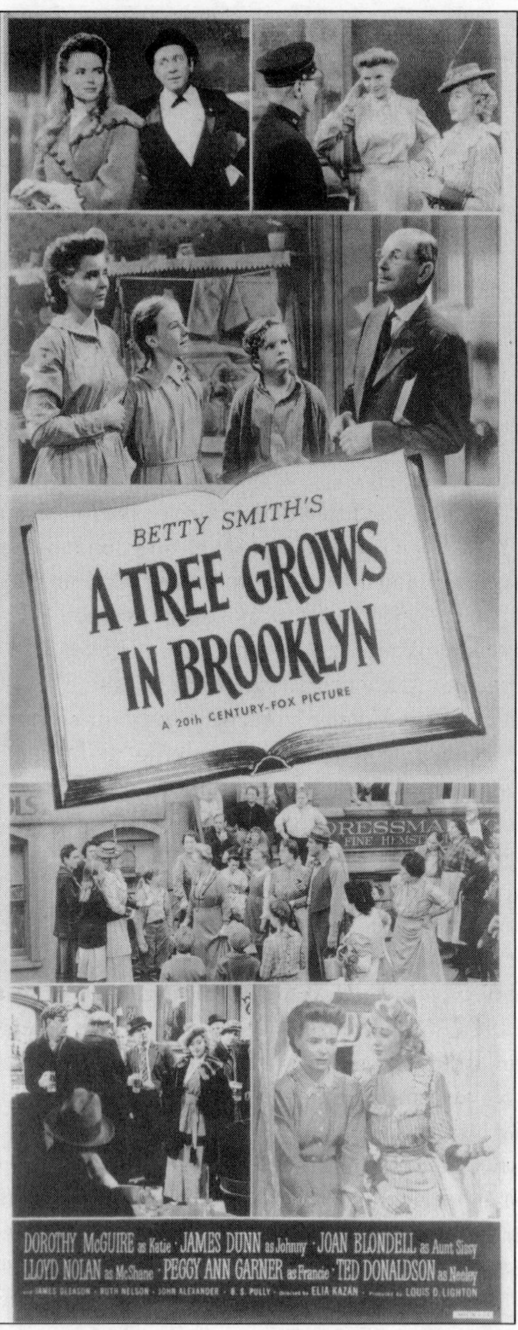
BETTY SMITH'S
A TREE GROWS IN BROOKLYN
A 20th CENTURY-FOX PICTURE
DORESSMA
FINE HEMST
DOROTHY McGUIRE as Katie · JAMES DUNN as Johnny · JOAN BLONDELL as Aunt Sissy
LLOYD NOLAN as McShane · PEGGY ANN GARNER as Francie · TED DONALDSON as Neeley
JAMES GLEASON · RUTH NELSON · JOHN ALEXANDER · B. S. PULLY · ELIA KAZAN · LOUIS D. LIGHTON

used to sing, will never have to face the hardships they've been through, Neely comments that she won't have all the fun they had, either. Francie smiles. For her too, all of the struggles and losses have become cherished memories, a legacy of love from her father.

You've been quoted as saying you don't look back at your earlier films with much affection. Is that true?

That's a generalization. I look at some of them kindly, particularly *Boomerang.* I had a great time on the first film too. I met a wonderful man, Louis Lighton, the producer. We used to have long talks. He told me about a lot of old-time directors. Vic Fleming, who had directed *Gone with the Wind* and *The Wizard of Oz*, had just died. He'd been a particularly good friend of his. We used to talk about our rushes and I learned a lot from our conversations. He did *Test Pilot* and *Captain's Courageous.* I really loved that old man. He was my first bond of affection toward films. So I had a good time. The only miserable experience I had was *The Sea of Grass.* I should never have made that film, or I should have quit.

A Tree Grows in Brooklyn *has an artificial look. Was it all shot on a sound stage?*

Absolutely. Even the outdoor stuff was shot on the backlot. The one thing I really liked about that film was the little girl. By far the most authentic thing about the film is Peggy Ann Garner's face. Nothing compares with it except maybe Jimmy Dunn's face. He was terrific. I did a smart thing or a good thing with Dunn, something I learned from Lighton. In the theater if you needed a guy to play a drunk, you got an actor who probably had some experience with drink, but more importantly someone who you knew was good at playing those kinds of scenes. In film you try and get the real thing itself. Jimmy had been run out of movies for drinking. He was largely unemployable and felt ill at ease at the studio. But he was an awfully sweet, nice man, a hell of a guy. When I met him I said, this is it, this is Johnny Nolan, himself. He's full of watery-eyed Irish affection. He's ebullient. He feels guilty. He slinks. He and the girl are authentic, so I stayed off the background as much as possible and got onto their faces.

The film looks like a photographed stage play except for one transitional scene which is pure film. As Francie starts home from the library, she walks out of frame. The next shot is a long crane that takes us round and round an interior tenement courtyard, finally landing on Francie high up on the fire escape.

That was one piece of scenery construction they did nicely. It reminded me of New York. I was separated from my wife and children at the time, and my own feelings of nostalgia helped me with the picture. That longing to be back with my family. All that was truthful and I had that going for me. When I put my early films down, it's because I think I did better, more independent and more hardboiled work after 1952.

A Tree Grows in Brooklyn *is a very romantic, sentimental picture.*

Yes, but real sentiment is good.

How did you work with Peggy Ann Garner?

There wasn't anything that Peggy had to do as Francie that I couldn't somehow awaken because it was all going on inside of her. In terms of her parents all the psychological material was there. The parallels were strong and there was a lot of affected emotion that had been conditioned, trained, ready for me. As a director, I do one good thing right at the outset. Before I start with anybody in any important role, I talk to them for a long time. I make it seem casual. The conversations have to do with their lives and before you know it, they're telling you about their wives, their mothers, their children, their infidelities and anything else they feel guilty about. You're storing it away. You're getting your material. By the time you start with an actor, you know everything about him, where to go, what to reach for, what to summon up, what associations to make for him. You have to find a river bed, a channel in their lives that is like the central channel in the part. Without their knowing it you're edging them towards the part so that the part becomes them. The story of the part is the story of their lives or an incident in their lives. You're weaving these associations in all your conversations. The work you do before you start shooting is the most important work you do. Before you shoot any big sequence, you go to dinner with them, you lay around with them, you go to lunch with them. I know all my actors very thoroughly before I start. You're in a position of trust, and the actors who trust you continue to tell you more. They work with you in an internal way. Peggy was that way with me. She made another father of me. We used to play together like kids. I loved her. She was a marvelous little girl—so filled with longing, with unfulfilled, unrequited, and unsatisfied love. Her father was in the air force and she was always scared to death that he was going to get killed. She loved her father more than her mother, so there was a constant worry about her. One day I played on that. I didn't come straight out and say that her father could get killed, but I talked to her about where her father was and how she missed him, and I got a very good scene from that.

The actors seemed to bring an emotional quality into each scene. The scenes would then take all sorts of turns but would always resonate off of those original emotions. For instance when Johnny comes home from a night of being a singing waiter. For a moment he looks utterly beat. But he quickly shifts gears and spins a long, celebratory description of his evening to his family. After the kids go to bed, the scene turns very quiet and sad. "Someday it's all going to happen," he says, and Kathy starts to cry and berates him for being nothing but a dreamer and a fake. You watch Johnny slowly give in to the quality of suppressed desperation he walked into the room with but which he had hidden in order to make his family feel that everything was just fine. How do you get the actors to go through all of those twists and turns?

You call attention to the turns within the scene. You tell him what he thinks before he goes on to the next "beat" as they call it in the Method. Without making it a technique, you mark the turns, the developments, the stages of the scene, and it is best if you mark them with some piece of business or something else they can hold on to. In this scene I made Johnny cross to the window and do something physical so that the physical act would be associated in his mind with the psychological movement. Later, when Kathy's mood turns dark, I had her walk away from him. That way you keep the actors, who have read and reread and rehearsed and re-rehearsed the scene, from jumping ahead to the next "beat" before they have truly experienced the last one.

How specifically do you prepare a scene like that? How do you get them started on the right note?

That depends on the kind of training the actors have had. Part of the Stanislavsky Method as it was developed in this country has to do with "given circumstances." You not only talk about them, you create in the actor the given circumstances with which he comes into the scene. All good actors try to do something about where they are coming from. If they're in a hurry or have been having an argument or whatever. In the Stanislavsky Method you do more. You couldn't talk any "Method" to Jimmy Dunn. He was just a sweet Irishman. But what I would do is walk him around and talk to him about what had happened in his life. He'd tell me and before long I got him going. I'd do it informally, indirectly. Later in my career with actors like Brando or Malden, I'd very often improvise the scene that took place off camera just before the one we were about to shoot. That way, the actor comes into a scene having actually played the scene which theoretically occurred off camera. But with Jimmy Dunn I would just talk to him about it. He was very open. He'd hear me cuss somebody and before you knew it, he was in the right mood for the scene.

Would you talk to him about what the off-camera scene might have been like—his night as a singing waiter, for example—or would you go into a personalization taken from his own life?

You never do it directly. If he catches you dealing with his own life, it will create a block. You do it ostensibly on a purely made-up basis, you create a fantasy, but you tie in elements from the actor's life. You bring it as close as possible, so that the person's emotions are affected. It's very easy. It's part of play. With Jimmy all you had to do was mention a producer who fired him and you were away. You use very simple, naive techniques like that. It was the same with Peggy. They were both like children. Jimmy Dunn was a beautiful child. He was, I thought, a wonderful man. He felt deeply guilty. So did Spencer Tracy, except he controlled it. Tracy was another Irish drinker, but he was able to defend himself because of his position in the industry. Jimmy Dunn had no position. With Tracy I did none of this. Tracy worked by himself. He was very good with the activity within the scene without any of these techniques. Anyway, going back to Jimmy Dunn, I treated him and Peggy the same way. I also threw them together a lot. I would tell Jimmy about her father being away and how much she missed him. I got him concerned about her. And I would tell her she was important to Jimmy and got her to love Jimmy. I have often tried to create something behind the scenes, that was close to what has to be in the scenes. For instance, there is a scene later where Johnny and Kathy decide that he must tell Francie that she has to quit school and go to work. There is no other way to afford the baby that's coming. Johnny goes in determined, but before he can get to it, Francie tells him how much she wants to be a writer and his resolve melts. I didn't need to do a lot of schmoozing before we shot that scene, as important and emotional as it was. The values were obvious and by then Jimmy loved Peggy as if she were his own. How could any feelingful person not want Peggy Ann Garner to be anything she wanted?

Did you rehearse the film before you started shooting?

Yes, but like a play. It's very well staged in the sense that there's constant business which makes the scenes in the kitchen seem particularly real. It is also much more intricately staged than films I did later.

Did you improvise much during rehearsal?

Very little. I never improvise except with actors who are trained to a certain extent in the Method. During my career I changed my whole way of working several times. I did *A Tree Grows in Brooklyn* like a stage play. I always varied in one way from the so-called Method. I didn't work with every actor in the same way. It depended on their individual training. If you make someone feel like they are lacking, or out of it, all of a sudden their confidence is gone. You mustn't score off an actor—or anyone else—for your own favor. You've got to keep their confidence up. If their method is good, you respect the way they work. And you must be careful about the actors you pick. The more power I got in the business, the more I chose just the actors I wanted. For a while I was very lucky. In *On the Waterfront* every actor was someone I had known and worked with. The same with *Splendor in the Grass* and *Wild River.* There's one actor in *Tree* I always admired: Lloyd Nolan. There was nothing to do with him except let him roll. He played the Irish cop. He had a clear and definite role in the community and in the end courts Kathy, asking her children for their approval. I like the Irish a lot. My best friend in college was an Irishman. I love their dignity and respectability. The way Nolan sat in the parlor and talked to her was beautiful. So you see I like the film. It's just that I think later I did much more ambivalent work, which is more in keeping with the way I see life actually, without villains and heroes.

There aren't villains and heroes in A Tree Grows in Brooklyn. *They're all heroic—even Dorothy McGuire.*

Kathy is the first of my puritan characters. There is a strain all through my pictures dealing with puritanism.

There's a puritan and an intellectual, and often they are the same person.

Dorothy McGuire was a puritan intellectual. Puritans often have problems with their own rigidity. They're touching to me because they're trying to make the world over and it's always a gallant but hopeless fight. My first wife was that way.

Were you involved with the editing?

Somewhat, but not really. The producer supervised it. I was always consulted, but it was being cut at the same time that I was shooting. The producer was boss in those days: he engaged the director who directed the scenes and the actors but he always functioned as an arm of the producer. The producer would then engage an editor who would take the director's rushes and cut them as he was told to by the producer.

Did that seem strange?

Strange! It's totally inorganic. Cutting is as much a part of directing as any other process. But to me as a young guy coming out to Hollywood from New York to do my first film, it seemed like a cooperative, decent way to work, and Louis Lighton was very square with me. The system seemed strange and outrageous only when I got to *The Sea of Grass*, which Pandro Berman produced. In those days the producer controlled everything. He prepared the script. He usually wrote it along with a writer, but he didn't put his name on it. Bud Lighton wrote *A Tree Grows in Brooklyn*. I never met the guys who signed the screenplay.

If many directors were pretty much restricted to staging the scenes with the actors, the cameraman must have played an even bigger role then than they do now in the "look" of a picture.

Absolutely. When Louis Lighton engaged a cameraman, he chose one specifically who would help me—Leon Shamroy. Although I'd studied filmmaking a little, and made some documentaries in New York and Tennessee, I had no experience with this kind of feature film. Lighton kept everything well organized. We were a good team. There was a very warm, gentle harmony between us. We never had a harsh word, but the system itself was terrible.

It took a while to develop a visual style of your own.

I didn't do that until *Panic in the Streets*, my fifth film. I forced myself to do it on that one. The first time I used a visual style to speak thematically was *Viva Zapata!*

In Tree *the photography was very simple, old-fashioned, and straightforward. The lighting was used as visual underscoring. If there was a tender, sentimental moment, there would always be a highlight in the eyes. There's one interior scene where it's raining outside. The light comes pouring in through the raindrops on the windowpanes, casting a shadow on Francie's face as if a tear were running down her cheek.*

Every trick to try to make things sentimental, romantic and affectionate.

Did you participate in those choices?

I wasn't even really aware they were choices. I thought it was just camerawork. I was learning about making movies while I was making one. Only when I looked at it later did I think, "This is really mushy and not like me."

Speaking of mushy, let's talk about The Sea of Grass.

THE SEA OF GRASS
(1947)

LUTIE CAMERON (Katharine Hepburn) goes West to marry Jim Brewton (Spencer Tracy), an enormously rich cattle rancher. En route she meets Brice Chamberlain (Melvyn Douglas), who warns her off her fiancé and tells her to go back home.

But Lutie is full of pluck and loves her man. They marry, she wins over all his friends and builds her nest. Then Jim takes her out to meet his true love—the Sea of Grass. He's obsessed with keeping God's grasslands as He made them and keeping the settlers out. Though her heart is with her husband, her sense of justice, constantly stoked by Chamberlain, is with the settlers.

Lutie has a baby girl, Sarah, at the same time a terrible storm wipes out the few settlers Jim had let stay. Jim and Lutie have a terrible fight and she goes to Denver where she has a brief fling with Chamberlain.

After she returns to Jim, the couple tries to make things work. But Lutie's pregnancy causes a question of paternity to hang in the air. Several years later, the law states that the prairie is open to the settlers, and Chamberlain, now a judge, means to see it enforced. Jim threatens to kill any settlers who come near his prairie. Once again Jim and Lutie have a horrible fight. This time the marriage is torn irreparably. She leaves her children and goes back to St. Louis.

Jim backs away from committing mass slaughter and the settlers move in. Lutie comes to visit and possibly to reclaim her chil-

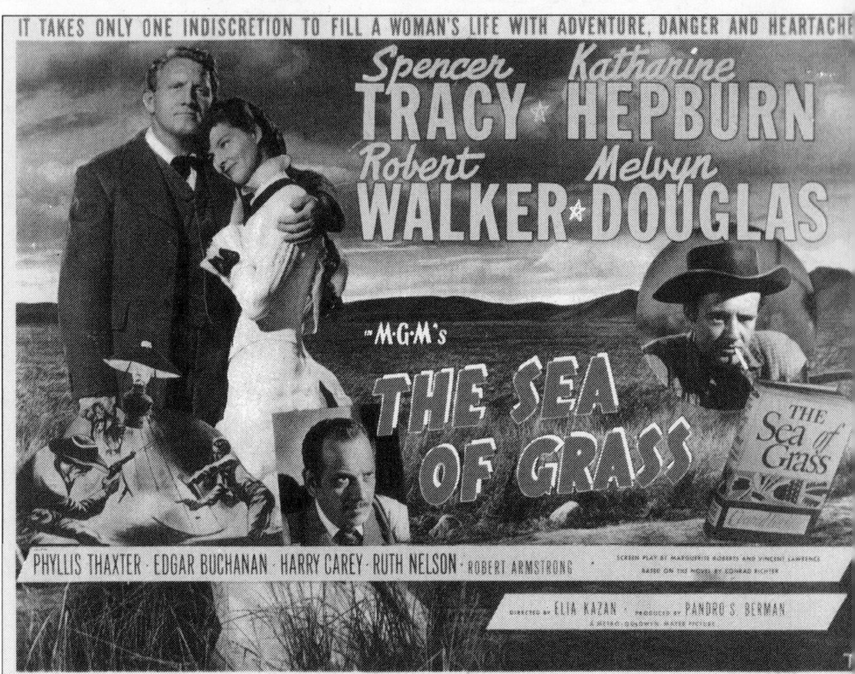
IT TAKES ONLY ONE INDISCRETION TO FILL A WOMAN'S LIFE WITH ADVENTURE, DANGER AND HEARTACHE
Spencer TRACY
Katharine HEPBURN
Robert WALKER
Melvyn DOUGLAS
M-G-M's
THE SEA OF GRASS
THE Sea of Grass
PHYLLIS THAXTER · EDGAR BUCHANAN · HARRY CAREY · RUTH NELSON · ROBERT ARMSTRONG
SCREEN PLAY BY MARGUERITE ROBERTS AND VINCENT LAWRENCE
BASED ON THE NOVEL BY CONRAD RICHTER
DIRECTED BY ELIA KAZAN · PRODUCED BY PANDRO S. BERMAN
A METRO-GOLDWYN-MAYER PICTURE

dren. But Sarah and her son, Brock, hardly know her. Jim is ice cold. Though it breaks her heart, she goes back to St. Louis alone.

Years later, droughts have ruined the land. Brock has grown up to be a wild and violent young man. He flees after killing a man who questions his paternity. In turn Brock is killed in a shootout with the law.

Lutie reads about her son's death in the papers and heads West again. Finally, she and Jim are reconciled. Life has not worked out as either had hoped or planned, but they will face whatever is left of it together.

The Sea of Grass *is the first of two films you made in 1947. You said it was the one miserable experience you had. What happened and how did it all go so wrong?*

Bud [Louis] Lighton had spoken to me about the novel by Conrad Richter. When I read it, I was very moved. I thought it was terribly romantic in the good sense of the word. I like romantic things. They express an aspiration, a dream that's not realized, something that people are reaching for. I like that feeling in any work of art. The book was owned by MGM and was in the hands of a producer named Pandro S. Berman. The first day I arrived at Metro I should have quit. When I walked into Berman's office he said, "I've got great news. We've got ten thousand feet of the most wonderful stuff for you." I said, "What do you mean?" I was so inexperienced that I deceived myself, and incidentally deceived him. I didn't realize that that footage was a clear indication as to how they had decided the rest of the film was going to be shot. I thought he was referring to stock footage that I might use here and there. But what he showed me was the background footage from which they would make the plates for rear projection. I should have realized Metro's intentions: we were never to leave California, and my whole idea was to shoot the film out where there was still tall grass—Wyoming, Colorado, wherever. I was looking forward to being on location and instead I was stuck with the opposite approach to filmmaking. It was terrible, just awful.

I agree. On the other hand, how wrong can you go with Spencer Tracy, Katharine Hepburn and two hundred violins?

About as wrong as possible. In the first place, I should never have cast Spencer Tracy, who I hardly knew, because Spencer was not an outdoor man in any sense of the word. He just wasn't a man that liked to leave Beverly Hills and the comfort of his home. He was a good actor, but he was not the sort of person I would have cast. And then the idea of a Tracy-Hepburn starring vehicle—I should have investigated that a lot before I went in for it because while they were good at comedy, they were limited in other areas.

And the fact that *The Sea of Grass* was not going to be shot on location by people who liked and fitted into the outdoors, meant that a whole side of the creative process, what you get from the day-to-day confrontation with your environment was going to be missing. I wasn't going to be out there, see something, and be able to say, "I want to shoot this scene here, I want to photograph this, I want to get this on film," and so on. During the shooting there was no creative process at all. Jack Ford had had it right. When I first went to Hollywood, I talked to him a lot because I really do admire him above all American directors, since Griffith and Chaplin. Nobody is in a class with Ford for male poetry in his best films. I asked him, "Where do you get your ideas for how to direct each scene?" He said, "Go out and walk around the set. It'll give you ideas." He was absolutely right. That's what I was able to do on *On the Waterfront*. I used to get there at dawn all alone and walk around the waterfront of Hoboken. I got ideas from the docks, the river. Even the cold gives you ideas. Everything stimulates you, whereas nothing is stimulating on a sound stage, and that's obvious in *The Sea of Grass*. It was a phony. One of the reasons I feel so resentful was that I felt that I should have quit and I didn't. I had clues but I really didn't understand them until later. Spence and Hepburn were lovers, and she was very protective of him. She'd watch him shoot and say, "Isn't Spence wonderful?" And I'd think, "He's only giving a tenth of what he's got." In one scene he was supposed to come in from the open plains where it was snowing and he'd take a little water, throw it on his face and make an entrance. His shoes looked like they had just been shined. I never could get him to stretch himself.

Did you try?

Some. You can't just give up, but it didn't work. Do you know Irishmen well? They have this great inertia. I don't know if he thought I was a wise, fair-haired boy from New York. You know, I was a fair-haired boy at that time. At any rate, he wasn't very friendly toward me. And Hepburn had a star complex and believed in "personality."

Is it different working with stars?

Absolutely. You can't criticize stars as freely. They'll say, "You just don't like me in the part. We're just not getting along," and put up a block. They'll use their status as a weapon and protect themselves with it. They did it subtly; they were never mean. But you couldn't press beyond a certain point because if you did, you shook their structure, and you got nothing. Spencer Tracy was great in take one, okay in take two. About take four he began to go down and by take six he was not very good. After take seven he just wouldn't do any more. He'd say, "What do you want?" Once I was directing Ethel Barrymore and I said, "Let's do it again." And she said, "What do you want another one for, your collection? Wasn't that good?" Now, I'm not putting her in a class with Spencer. She was a wonderful woman. But that was what it was like in the old days. The stars did as well as they could.

So the story about one-take Spencer Tracy isn't apocryphal?

No, it's true. That's when he was best, spontaneously. He knew it. By the way, he was a nice guy. But the only true test comes out in your work. The point isn't whether he was a nice guy or not.

It was just that he and I didn't jell. A man can have a way of making himself unapproachable. He's a male and not to be tampered with or he'll walk. And she was always saying, "Isn't he wonderful?" I may sound like I'm blaming Tracy and Hepburn but I don't really blame anyone but myself. I really don't. I made some missteps, misjudgments, and I didn't do anything about them. I should have quit or forced things to be done my way. I don't have any grudges. I liked Spencer Tracy. He was a nice guy and had problems of his own. So I'm really talking about myself learning, going through the experience of *The Sea of Grass*, discovering how overwhelming the producer system at Metro was. It taught me a hell of a lot. Seven years later I was ready to fight Sam Spiegel to the hilt on *On the Waterfront.* The major thing I learned from it all was to be myself. If you can't do your own thing, don't do it at all.

The Sea of Grass *might well have been made by any of thirty other directors. Yet, if you compare a scene between Tracy and Hepburn with one between Dana Andrews and Jane Wyatt in* Boomerang, *the latter comes up short. Despite the difficulties you spoke of, Hepburn and Tracy still manage to bring off their scenes together.*

That man was absolutely commanding when he acted on a simple level that he understood. Where the confrontation was direct, Tracy was tremendous. I'm not putting Spence down. When the thing was right for him, he was terrific—absolutely believable. He wasn't like the hero in *Boomerang*, not Dana Andrews.

What do you do when you get stuck with a guy like him?

You don't cast him. You have to make sure that the actor you cast—underneath all of the niceness and sincerity and talent and skill—in some ways shares your sensibility. That doesn't mean he has to agree with you. It's more profound than that. I got much more careful later on.

The Sea of Grass *doesn't have much of a personal feel.*

I don't think it has any. I didn't choose the sets. I had nothing to do with the costumes. I okayed them all, but I didn't like them.

They were star costumes. The things Lutie wore were not the things a girl going out West to marry a cattle rancher would take out with her, even if she was from Boston, let alone St. Louis. They were not even period things. They made her look pretty. Every time she went into the bathroom, she'd come out with another dress on. I look at the film now and think I must have been out of my mind. And the thing is, I knew it at the time. It was embarrassing to me. There is a big theme in that material somewhere, very much like the theme in *Wild River* but in *Wild River* I did it right.

Were you able to work on the script?

No, in the studio system the script was given to you.

But you still chose to make the film.

Correct. I did. It's a little like taking the first step in a very seductive process. Even when part of you knows you're being seduced, that things will not all turn out as promised, you still let yourself go along. You get beguiled and flattered, you mention the problems and they say, "That's right. Brilliant. We'll work on it." So you sign on and then discover that by the time you're brought on, things are already frozen. A lot of people have been committed on the basis of that script and you can't change it. It was as good as I could get at that time. I didn't like it much. But once you got on that particular roller coaster, control of the movie was no longer in your hands. That was the Metro system: you always had a producer over you. Fox was the same. It was all in Zanuck's hands. My whole drive was to get enough power myself so I could say, "Now we'll do the picture. Now the script is ready. Now I've got the right actors, etc." That was a big fight in those days. It isn't anymore. This generation is resting on stuff that we had to fight for years ago. Also, the producers collapsed. By and large they showed themselves unable to meet the challenges of a new day, and they don't have anything like the power they once had.

It's never clear what it is about Jim Brewton that attracts Lutie Cameron except that he is played by Spencer Tracy and she by Katharine Hepburn.

That's exactly right. You took it for granted that if the guy was played by Spencer Tracy, she was going to be attracted to him. You didn't battle with the complexities of relationships. If there were a male and a female star in a film, the audience not only knew, but they expected them to be attracted to each other. That's the star system. Even Hepburn. At first I thought it was great that I could get this cold Yankee broad to cry. It turned out she was very proud of crying. I'd say, "action," and she'd start to bawl.

How did you get her to stop?

That was the problem. It had nothing to do with what Hepburn was like in real life. She'd committed herself to a particular tradition of acting. Personally, she was a marvelous woman, absolutely independent, fearless, funny, smart—but she was out of another world. Because she was out of the old Theater Guild, she aspired to be like Katharine Cornell or Lynn Fontanne. Stars of that ilk had a duty to their audiences to uphold a certain image of glamour, heroism, and bravery. A star never did anything wrong. It's completely artificial. People are not like that at all. Essentially, it's the tradition of the 19th-century theater carried over, milked down, and transposed. It was still going on in the '40s with certain directors. Hitchcock and Howard Hawks continued even longer. But I think I had a lot to do with changing it.

Were you aware of the power of the star system? The way it not only affected the way you worked but how it also bent the requirements of dramatic structure?

Not nearly as much as I should have been. Learning about filmmaking was very seductive and I knew I had a lot to learn, but still I had a terrible feeling that something was wrong the morning Berman showed me that ten thousand feet. How could I not have understood? It's like a guy is walking down the street and a safe falls from the fortieth floor and hits him on the head. He gets up and says, "I think something's going wrong here!" When I look back on that era, I laugh but at the time I thought, "This is dreadful."

In the Hitchcock/Truffaut interviews Hitchcock remarked, "When a film has been properly staged, it isn't necessary to rely on the player's virtuosity or personality for tension and dramatic effect."

In his films that's true.

Hitchcock essentially made cartoons. Your films have always been based on a theme. It's true even in the most purely cinematic of your films (probably less in Panic in the Streets *than any other). Though the inner story may vary from film to film, some inner story is always being told. As a result it's essential for you to rely on the specific behavior of your actors.*

Where else does an event take place except within people, really? You have external things, but the event, the drama, as I see it, takes place within people. You cannot really sit here and tell me, Jeff, that there is such a thing as a picture that's about nothing. You can't divorce content and form, right?

My interest in Hitchcock centers around visual storytelling.

I think that's true of Truffaut too. I think there are two strains in Truffaut. One of deeply personal autobiography, and another of tricky cleverness. I know Truffaut and he's a far more complex and interesting personality than his films with Jean-Pierre Léaud show him to be. I think Truffaut, as all of us, is ambitious, uncertain, has a sex problem, and is middle class in many ways. He is a complex being and I think he has settled for the superficial mechanics of storytelling. There was much more in the guy and it got lost. He conceals from you what is really in his heart exactly as Hitchcock did. Hitchcock's whole technique was a way of concealing who he was. It was a smoke screen. He threw that up, and you never saw Hitchcock. You saw Hitchcock manipulating.

Whereas all of your movies seem to express something about you.

If we start with the first one, *A Tree Grows in Brooklyn*, what's best in that film is the emotion between the father and the daughter. There is something in that film, sentimental and conventional as it is, that dramatizes and evokes true feelings. I'm not praising myself. I'm trying to explain what I believe a performing art is, or should be. Experiences from your own life are in one way or another played out, and you relive them and understand them through seeing them played out. As a result, you experience a deep feeling. You're affected and left with something. The best films I've done and the films I like all have that. They all have an emotional effect on people and stir them in some way. That's what I think is so great about a lot of Ford's pictures such as *Young Mr. Lincoln*. Ford took the mythological figure of Abe Lincoln and made you understand the terrible pain of being a plain man with a mission that he felt inadequate to deal with. The audience admires Lincoln—he seems like a hero, not a conventional hero but a real hero. If you're going to talk to me about life, talk to me about life. Don't talk to me about technique.

Since you want to affect the audience directly, you almost had to try and make the mechanics invisible.

I don't agree with that at all. I'm not looking for a way to move an audience. I try to tell a story that has moved me. I try to tell it as truthfully as I can so that I re-create what moved me. After that I rely on the faith that's implicit in any artist's work—if I like it, if it's what I meant, it's going to move an audience. That doesn't mean it always will. What I object to in Hitchcock is the absolutely smug belief that if he has a "McGuffin," it's going to get me. It doesn't. I just see it. Hitchcock did some absolutely brilliant things. I thought that the scene in *Psycho* where the woman's blood comes out from the shower was terrific. But that's all it is—a stunt. I don't actually shake from it. I say, "What a good stunt." He was a master of stunts and tricks.

I'll tell you how I like to think of myself. As a mythmaker. In other words, I hope the story that I am telling has so many overtones that it becomes symbolic of our time, of our issues, which is to say mythic.

Which is based on the assumption that what goes on inside you, goes on inside other people: What interests you, will interest an audience.

What else can you do? It's not necessarily true for all artists but most artists work that way. For instance I wrote a book called *The Arrangement.* I got a lot of letters from women saying they identified with the male lead and that they shared his problems. It was amazing to me. I think the book is terrific because it describes universal truths. I don't care if anybody else likes it or not, the book is absolutely true. How do I know? Because I lived through it, I know what I'm talking about. I don't know what value it has artistically or superficially, but that book speaks the truth.

In that book you got right down into primitive feelings very quickly. That's also true of your most successful films. On the other hand some of your earlier films like Boomerang *or* Gentleman's Agreement *or* Pinky *don't have any personal feelings in them. That's why I didn't like them.*

It wasn't a matter of technique though. It was a matter of personal development. Later on I got much more involved in psychoanalysis after having gone through a lot of grief, a lot of pain, and criticism. Now, I'm much more open about myself. I'm not ashamed. Even some of the earlier stuff was okay. If you notice, *Boomerang* is much harder.

Let's go on to Boomerang.

DARRYL F. ZANUCK presents
DANA ANDREWS
in
BOOMERANG
20th CENTURY-FOX
with
JANE WYATT · LEE J. COBB
Cara WILLIAMS · Arthur KENNEDY · Sam LEVENE
Robert KEITH · Taylor HOLMES
Directed by ELIA KAZAN
Produced by
LOUIS de ROCHEMONT
Screen Play by Richard Murphy · Based upon an article
by Anthony Abbot, Published in The Reader's Digest

BOOMERANG
(1947)

OVER ESTABLISHING shots of Stamford, Connecticut, a narrator explains that the film is based on actual events. A priest is murdered, shot in the back of his head, by a barely visible assailant. Despite the pressure put on the District Attorney (Dana Andrews), the Police Chief (Lee J. Cobb), and other reform politicians, particularly by the owner of a conservative newspaper, they are unable to turn up any leads.

Finally, a suspect, John Waldron (Arthur Kennedy), is found. He is identified by an old girlfriend as having been near the scene of the crime. Seven eyewitnesses say he was the man that pulled the trigger, and police ballistics reveal that the bullet that killed the priest came from his gun.

The reformers are overjoyed. At last they have their man. But the District Attorney, despite all apparent evidence, believes they've got the wrong person. Instead of trying for an indictment, he sets out to show that the man is innocent. He persists even when the governorship is dangled before him as a rather obvious bribe. Not even the threat of a scandal that may touch his wife (Jane Wyatt) is enough to persuade him to go along with the boys and seek a conviction.

Piece by piece he destroys what seemed like an airtight case. He does it so masterfully and with such determination to see justice served that even the Police Chief comes around to his side and is glad to see an innocent man set free.

At the end, the narrator's voice returns to tell us that the District Attorney did not go on to become the governor of the state of Connecticut. Instead he became the Attorney General of the United States.

After shooting two films entirely on sound stages, I had a strong feeling that this was not the way I should be working. A script was offered to me. The story was just okay, but what excited me was that we were going to shoot it all on location in Stamford, Connecticut. I felt, now I'm going to really learn what making pictures is about. We all knew what the neorealists had been doing in Italy—De Sica's *Shoeshine* and other movies. It's not that I was really influenced by them so much as that I shared the appetites of the filmmakers: Let's get out in the street.

Some of Boomerang *feels like a documentary, and some of it is very stagey. The styles kept clashing, and it bothered me.*

Unfortunately, a lot of *Boomerang* is the same studio machinery—brought outdoors. Most of the actors were stage actors, like Jane Wyatt. She plays an oversweet version of what a wife should be. Dana Andrews was actorish. He was not like a real lawyer, right? The same thing with Ed Begley. He was a terrific old hand and a wonderful man, but he was again, an "Actor." It's not just that they were stage actors, they were actors not out of my training, but out of another world.

What is the essential difference between an actor and, as you put it, an "Actor?"

It is finally a different view of humanity in the theater, in film, in art, and in life. Ours is an unartificial view. It's a realism of personality. It's an ordinariness in people. It's a feeling of ambivalence within people. It's a non-hero and non-heroine tradition. There are a lot of elements in it, but it's a plainness, a hominess. In our school individuals are people first and actors second. Dana Andrews was an "Actor." He looked like a Broadway leading man. I can't explain it. They dress up. Their ties are always in place, they always have their hair combed a certain way. Dana had a form; he was very much in a mold, the Dana Andrews mold. That was him. Even his suits looked alike.

There was no way you could crack that?

Maybe. Maybe some other director could have. I didn't. I didn't try. He fit generally into an unaccented, uncomplicated style. Ambivalence wasn't a part of the nature of that material. If I had an actor in that role who had doubts, beyond those explicitly expressed in the script, the audience would have wondered, What's going on with this guy?

Did you work with him differently?

A lot. There was very little you could do with Dana. He could learn three pages in five minutes. He had a fantastic memory, even though he'd been up late drinking the night before. He'd come to work, dress up and we'd roll him out. His style was okay in that movie because he was playing a lawyer, and essentially there wasn't supposed to be too much going on inside him. But unfortunately that kind of acting leaves you with the feeling that there was nothing really personally at stake. When you're not really touching something within the actor, you're not conveying the feeling that "This is life."

Did you try to touch something inside him?

I tried a little but not a lot. I was mostly concerned with making a film on location with non-actors. The best scenes are in the police station where the cops are third-degreeing Johnny Kennedy.

A lot of my buddies are in the line-up scene, friends that just happened to be visiting. Arthur Miller's in it. There are real faces instead of actors' faces, and you sense the difference immediately even if you're not exactly sure of what it is or what's causing it. Nowadays the technology is advanced enough so that you can use fewer lights, lighter cameras, etc. We were out there with twenty huge arcs lighting up the street. I wanted to find a new way to make films, and this picture gave me the opportunity to use the real street, real people, real environment.

The major thing that bothered me about Boomerang *was that it was too simplistic. The bad guys are such bad guys and the good guys are so good. There's no specific detailed behavior that suggests a life outside of the film.*

That's right. If I did it now, not only would Harris (Ed Begley) be guilty, the mayor would be guilty, and probably the lawyer would be getting a payoff, too. The corruption would not be centered in one bad person whose identity you hold back until you suddenly reveal it. That's an old, worn-out theater technique.

Boomerang was made a very long time ago. A lot happened to me as I went along. My name is ambivalence now. In my 1972 novel *The Assassins*, there are no villains at all, although people murder each other all through it. I can't even think in terms of pure heroes or pure villains anymore, but in 1947 I was out of the theater and that was more or less the tradition. Anyway, I was offered a script and a job. I'm not as fond of *Boomerang* as I might be.

You used rather obvious narrative devices like newspaper montages and radio speeches. Why? For instance as the film opens you pan the streets of a city. A portentous voice-over says something like, "This could be any town, USA."

That technique was popular in the late '40s, and it was also a part of the technique of the producer, Louis de Rochemont. So was the ending where a crawl tells you as an afterword that the lawyer became the Attorney General as though that were a big deal. It was a very stand-up type film, but I got a lot out of it. The cameraman, Norbert Brodine, was not a classic Hollywood cameraman who knew nothing except exactly how to light every scene from the standard Hollywood point of view. On *Boomerang* I learned a lot of techniques, a lot of little tricks, but more importantly, ever since then I've felt, I can do a film anywhere. I don't need sets or movie stars. In *Boomerang* is, I think, the basis for *Panic in the Streets* and in *Panic in the Streets* is the basis for *On the Waterfront*. If you see those three films together, you'll see the development. There are no sets whatsoever in *Panic* or *Waterfront*. They were shot entirely on location. I get a lot of stimulation from the environment I'm working in. I feel the same about living in New York City. What you see on the street everyday is stimulating. That's why I stay in New York, and why I don't live in Beverly Hills. Everything happens here.

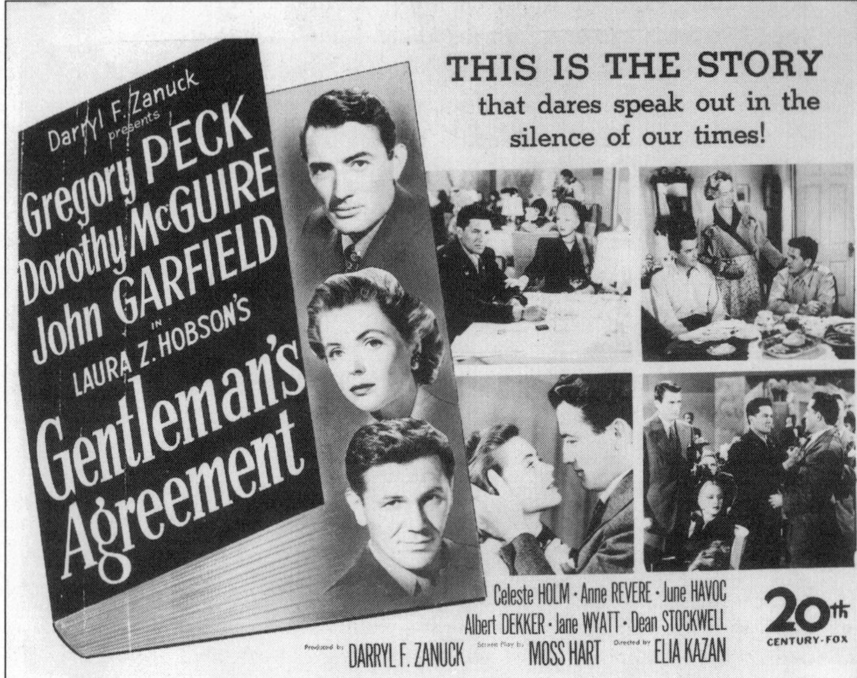
Darryl F. Zanuck
presents
Gregory PECK
Dorothy McGUIRE
John GARFIELD
IN
LAURA Z. HOBSON'S
Gentleman's
Agreement
THIS IS THE STORY
that dares speak out in the
silence of our times!
Celeste HOLM · Anne REVERE · June HAVOC
Albert DEKKER · Jane WYATT · Dean STOCKWELL
Produced by DARRYL F. ZANUCK
Screen Play by MOSS HART
Directed by ELIA KAZAN
20th
CENTURY-FOX

GENTLEMAN'S AGREEMENT *(1947)*

STAR JOURNALIST P. Schuyler Green (Gregory Peck) is given a special assignment by his publisher, John Minify (Albert Dekker): He's asked to write an expose of anti-Semitism in America. Not just about the obvious, ignorant, redneck type, but about the much more insidious, unconscious as well as conscious prejudice among America's middle and upperclasses.

Green, a widower, meets Minify's niece, Kathy Lacey (Dorothy McGuire), falls for her, and their courtship blossoms as he struggles for an angle on his story. He's about to throw in the towel when he stumbles onto an approach. He will pretend to be a Jew for six months and see what anti-Semitism feels like from the inside.

When he tells Kathy, she is alarmed by the whole idea. She agrees to keep it a secret, though she blows it time and again when it is inconvenient or might make trouble. As Green proceeds with his work, he grows increasingly aware of anti-Semitism in all of its ugly forms, including that of Jews for other Jews. Not only does Green suffer at the hands of anti-Semites, his son (Dean Stockwell) gets beaten up in the schoolyard. Kathy's behavior reveals her to be an unconscious anti-Semite. Her family members are conscious ones. The relationship with Green strains and almost falls apart.

The tension is heightened when Green's oldest and dearest friend, Dave Goldmann (John Garfield), a real Jew, comes to visit.

Just discharged from the Army, he's been offered a great job and has come to find a place for his family to live.

Dave thinks Green's idea is foolish, but supports him. Sadly, he finds that he is going to have to give up the job offer because no one in the area will rent a home to a Jewish family, a situation which finally opens Kathy's eyes and forces her to confront her own anti-Semitism. This paves the way for her and Green to reconcile. Green goes on to write a scathing, highly acclaimed series of articles.

You got all kinds of acclamation and awards, including an Oscar for Gentleman's Agreement. *My parents, being Jewish, naturally saw the film when it was first released. They loved it—called it terrific, shocking, staggering. Having seen it only recently, I felt it was dopey, simplistic agit-prop. Your work is best when the characters are fully developed, real people, full of colors and hues. You mentioned before the necessity for an actor to find the character within himself. In* Gentleman's Agreement *Gregory Peck never got to me at all. I didn't believe him for a minute. I think the nicest scene in the picture is when he tells John Garfield what he is doing. Garfield looks baffled and bemused, as if he can't believe what a putz Peck is being.*

It's disgusting. The whole idea of a gentile pretending to be a Jew is a cop-out to begin with. You should really make a picture about a Jew and what he goes through. But it was the central plot device of the novel it's based on. Your parents' experience had some validity in 1947. When that picture was released, it was the first time the word "Jew" had been put on the screen. But whether it has more merit than that, I don't know. There's one good scene in the picture when Garfield says to Dorothy McGuire, "What did you do in the face of anti-Semitism?" And she says, "Oh God, I just burned up. I hated it." She didn't do anything, of course. In that circle, in the upper middle class, they're still that way.

One of the big problems with that film was that I was aware way before Gregory Peck was that Dorothy McGuire was a twit. As a result, instead of being involved, I found myself sitting back waiting for him to realize it too and wondering what took him so long. It's always a problem when the audience is that far ahead of your central characters except in suspense scenes, which depend on the audience knowing about danger that the character is unaware of.

That's good criticism. I agree with you. That's the conventionality of it. There's no ambivalence in the film at all.

Tell me about Gregory Peck.

He came out of the Neighborhood Playhouse and was trained by Sandy Meisner, an excellent teacher. But Greg's nature was very closed off and rigid. He's tried to deal with it. He's tried to open himself up, and he has to a certain extent since that picture. He didn't have an artist's nature. He had his own way, and that was always correct. He was logical and listened. He was cooperative. But it was hard to light a fire in a guy like that.

Since he was trained in the Method, couldn't you use any of the techniques you've described?

I don't think so. I don't think you could touch him.

Was he your choice?

No. *Gentleman's Agreement* was the last picture I made—except *Pinky* which was a special case—where I worked for a producer.

Did you explain what it was all about?

In that script it's obvious.

Which is one of its shortcomings.

It would be a shortcoming in any work of art. It's precise and explicit, but there's nothing more there than meets the eye. Everything the film is about is articulated clearly and simply. There's some value in that way of storytelling, I suppose. It is agitprop on a middle-class level. It said, "Anti-Semitism is everywhere, all through America and especially among decent people who don't believe they're anti-Semitic." At that time this was an important thing to say—loudly and clearly to as many people as possible. So I don't feel like you do about the film. I feel that with all its limitations, it was valuable. Remember, it was just after the war and the war had infused the country with an antifascist idealism. One of the first things that had to be cleared up was American anti-Semitism. It had been rampant in the army. One of the next things that directors all attacked was racism which also ran all through the armed forces. You were probably born about then, so it's hard for you to see the value of that picture. But at the time it was important—the same with Edward Dmytryk's *Crossfire* and *Pinky* and Joe Mankiewicz's *No Way Out.* There was a lot of pressure from the rich Jews in California to not have that picture made. And there was terrific pressure from the Catholics not to have a divorced woman as the heroine.

I don't think Dorothy McGuire is nearly as convincing in that role as she is in A Tree Grows in Brooklyn.

I think she is more convincing. In *A Tree Grows in Brooklyn* she didn't really look like someone married to a waiter. In *Gentleman's Agreement* she was distasteful, but she was perfect.

One of the things I like about most of your films are the contradictions within the characters. Kathy doesn't seem to have much of a contradictory nature.

You're right about that. There was no inner conflict. I guess the essence of drama really is when within a person there's conflict between two sides, two impulses, two desires. She had it in some sense. She wanted to be liked, to be decent, to be liberal. Many, maybe even most, liberals still have the same kind of problem she had. Their goals are abstractly one thing, but they're all in the middle class. And they do everything they can to protect the system that their vision and intelligence tells them must be destroyed. Right?

Ultimately, even a liberal has to take sides.

Taking sides hurts. It exposes you to rejection, to being fired.

Were you in on the script?

To a certain extent. It was done by an excellent playwright, Moss Hart, whose background in the theater, I believe, turned out to be one of his biggest problems with this particular screenplay. He was a great pro, but he was thinking in terms of an Act I, Act II, Act III form, which is what he knew best from the theater, and here he didn't know what Act III was going to be. When he got the idea of Dave saying to Kathy, "What did you do?" that became Act III. The third act should have had something to do with Peck but there was no way to do it. It was nice to have the Garfield character in the film, but in the end it was a half-assed solution.

The film became totally silly to me when at the end Peck rushes back to Dorothy McGuire. Especially since you took great care in making the Celeste Holm character far more interesting.

That was all done terribly. In the old stage tradition the leading man never gets mixed up with the character woman. Green should have gotten involved with her, if she meant something to him, but there was no confrontation. The only real confrontation in the film is between Dave and Kathy.

But you were in on the script. Why did it develop that way?

Partly because of the nature of the book that we started with. We needed to find clarity and form within the material. I think we would have had to throw the whole book over, which I was ready to do later in my life. I don't know how to explain it, Jeff. There were so many people involved in it that although you're in on it, you're talking about it on the premise which is common to all—the book is not to be destroyed. Sam Spiegel and I did a great thing with *On the Waterfront*. We did a lot of variations of the script of that movie.

[Budd] Schulberg [the screenwriter] and I were satisfied with what we had, but Sam was never satisfied until the last draft. He kept saying, "Let's open it all up again." I always appreciated him for that, although we had a lot of conflicts, very ugly ones, about other things. We could never do that with *Gentleman's Agreement* because Laura Hobson's book was a best-seller and Zanuck was very firm about sticking to it. So all the script conferences were within certain limits. I accepted them, and went ahead and tried to direct the picture as well as I could. I think the picture is well directed mechanically. It's done like stage directing. It has good detail that has some meaning and it's not overstressed.

I disagree. I think the details were not well done at all. The party scene at Celeste Holm's apartment is full of clichés and stereotypes.

Gentleman's Agreement is certainly more conventional than any film I ever did. There are no rough edges to it at all, nothing that's not easily and readily digestible. Nobody can believe it now, but at that time, it was considered to be a daring picture. I remember the feeling we all had that we were breaking ground. When it came out, *P. M.*, a liberal paper of the era, praised the film extravagantly because of its message.

Is there a trap in making a film that is so important politically that you don't push yourself creatively?

No, what you do is perhaps even worse. Our whole task was to use a conventional form to force people to listen to ideas that were, at the time, unconventional. At the time of *Gentleman's Agreement* people weren't used to hearing those thoughts and feelings come out on the screen. There is no way to explain to you or anybody at this time what that film was when it was made.

Isn't there a way to combine clarity and simplicity with a richness of detail and ambivalence?

It's deeper than that, Jeff. It's nontechnical finally. It's to tell the truth. In the first place as a creator, get in touch with your own truth, not the truth of your thoughts, but the truth of your experience, with all its contradictions and ambivalences. Then express that truth without crippling it, without doing anything to oversimplify its complexities. And you have to involve yourself in the sense that you don't exclude yourself from the blame. That's why *The Arrangement* was written in the first person, so there never would be a sense that I was excluding myself from the guilt. That's why Mailer writes in the first person. He doesn't want to exclude the narrator by giving him a point of view. Instead he involves him in what's happening.

Did you do any of that on Gentleman's Agreement*?*

Not at all. All I did was try to make the message come across in a form that the middle class, whom I was accusing of anti-Semitism, would accept. They accept the story and thereby the guilt. Then hopefully they'll take on the responsibility for making things change. *Gentleman's Agreement* is thin intentionally. There is nothing in it that will mess up an audience psychologically. I was saying, "You, sitting out there at the premiere, with your fine clothes and fat bank balances, are anti-Semitic. I'll make it so familiar to you that there won't be any way for you to not accept the guilt."

For me it was oversimplified.

You're from another era. And the Jews are not like they were then. All the rich Jews in California were concealing they were Jews. Was your name always Young?

Mine was. My father changed his name.

But if it were you today, you wouldn't change your name. That's the difference. That's my point about *Gentleman's Agreement.* The whole issue of genteel anti-Semitism was much more alive during your father's time. That's why your parents responded to it.

PINKY
(1949)

PINKY (Jeanne Crain), an apparently upper-class white woman, returns to a small southern town, having spent years up north training to be a nurse. She walks through a shanty town to the shack of an elderly black woman, Dicey Johnson (Ethel Waters). Dicey is her grandmother, and Pinky's real name is Patricia Johnson.

Dicey quickly realizes that Pinky has been passing. Pinky explains she fell into it accidentally but allowed it to continue because she enjoyed being treated like an equal. Dicey exclaims, "Shame on you, denying yourself, like Peter did Jesus." Pinky learns that an old white woman, Miss Em (Ethel Barrymore), whom she has loathed since childhood, is terminally ill. Dicey works for her for free, and Pinky, ultra-sensitive to anything she sees as a racial slight, despises Em even more for taking advantage. This is not how Dicey sees it.

Pinky has nightmares, full of train whistles and her own voice calling out for Tom (William Lundigan), the white doctor who asked her to marry him. It was his proposal that caused her to flee back home in terror in the first place. She thinks she loves him, but knows she's deceiving him and doesn't know what effect the truth might have.

Pinky goes to a local scoundrel, Jake (Frederick O'Neal), to retrieve some money he had stolen from Dicey. She gets attacked

by another woman. The cops rescue her, assuming she's white. When they find out she's colored, they haul her off to jail, too.

THE BEST FILM OF THE YEAR IS
DARRYL F. ZANUCK'S
Pinky
... SHE PASSED FOR WHITE!
Starring
JEANNE CRAIN · ETHEL BARRYMORE
ETHEL WATERS · WILLIAM LUNDIGAN
Produced by DARRYL F. ZANUCK
Directed by ELIA KAZAN
Screen Play by Philip Dunne and Dudley Nichols · Based on a Novel by Cid Ricketts Sumner
20th CENTURY-FOX

Back at home Pinky finds Dicey inconsolable. Miss Em is dying. Pinky couldn't care less. She's leaving. She only relents and agrees to stay and nurse Miss Em when she learns that Miss Em had moved into Dicey's shack and nursed Dicey when she was very ill.

Pinky goes to Miss Em's, receives instruction from the doctor, and tends her patient. Em is an imperious old dragon but Pinky gives as good as she gets. Pinky goes home to find her fiancé, Tom, waiting there. She tells all, and Tom insists they face their problems together. In doing so, he reveals a hint of his own prejudice.

Em is visited by her racist, gold-digging Cousin Melba (Evelyn Varden). Em enlists Pinky's help to get rid of her. Em and Pinky move toward mutual respect and sincere affection.

Em dies, leaving almost everything to Pinky. Melba contests the will. The trial is utterly rigged, but the judge rules in Pinky's favor.

Tom wants Pinky to sell her inheritance and go west with him where she can once again pass as white. But Pinky has learned that she must be true to herself. As the film ends, Pinky is converting the house that she inherited into Miss Em's Clinic and Nursery School, serving the black community to which Pinky now proudly belongs.

You replaced John Ford as the director of Pinky. *What's the story?*

He pretended to have shingles. Some years later I said to Zanuck, "Jack Ford never had shingles, did he?" And he said, "Oh hell, no. He just wanted to get out of it; he hated Ethel Waters and she sure as hell hated him." Jack scared her to death and he knew she didn't want to work with him. I also think maybe he didn't like the whole project. Anyway, Zanuck wired me and asked if I'd come out. I wired back, "I'll do it as a favor." Firstly, I threw away what Ford had shot. It was poor. It showed a lack of interest and involvement. So, all the footage was mine. The only things that were not mine, which are a hell of a lot, were the script and the cast. It was the last time I ever allowed that. Jeanne Crain was a sweet girl, but she was like a Sunday school teacher. I did my best with her, but she didn't have any fire. The only good thing about her face was that it went so far in the direction of no temperament that you felt Pinky was floating through all of her experiences without reacting to them, which is part of what "passing" is. The most memorable thing about making that picture was the party at the end of shooting. Ethel Waters had been so sweet, kissing me all the time and telling me how much she loved me and how grateful she was to me. She and I got drunk, and I said, "Ethel, you don't really like any white man do you?" And she said, "I don't like any of them. I'd never trust any of 'em." When she got drunk she told the truth, and

I liked her better for it. I thought, "I don't blame her. I can understand that." Again, I learned a lot on that picture. It was the last of a line. Almost everything was shot in the studio. Even the outdoor set, the village, was built indoors. The trees went up just so high, so you had to put the camera at eye level or slightly above eye level and shoot down. You had to frame on things in the middle foreground so that you didn't go over the edge of the set. Naturally, there was no dirt, no sweat, no water, no anything. That's why I say I don't like *Pinky* much. I don't like *Gentleman's Agreement* much and I don't like *The Sea of Grass* at all. The best of all those five pictures by far is *A Tree Grows in Brooklyn*. It's sentimental but the sentiments are truthful.

I thought you liked sentiment.

It's been abused. It's been whipped up from false premises. People are right to be suspicious of it. I mean, don't meddle with my feelings.

There are some things in Pinky *that I like a lot. Frederick O'neal, who played Jake, the black scoundrel, was wonderful.*

He was good. He was the head of Actors Equity.

There's a scene where he comes in to warn Dicey that the locals are saying that Pinky is doping Miss Em and that he knows about Pinky's white fiancé. Right in the middle of the scene he spots a piece of fried chicken, picks it up and scoffs it while he prattles on, without missing a beat.

That sounds like me doesn't it? That's the way I used to direct, I always did that. I'll tell you another thing I like about *Pinky*—Ethel Barrymore. She was a really grand old lady. She really liked me a lot and I worshiped her. I didn't feel that way about anyone else in the cast. I used to hang around her just to talk. It was a privilege to be near her.

Through most of the movie she's in bed, so there is very little physical movement. Yet, Miss Em is a complete, total character.

Like I said in *The Arrangement*, a guy looks at his face in the mirror, and he sees a piece of sculpture he's been working on for forty years. With Ethel Barrymore it was longer. You see a whole biography in her face. She was wonderful.

There are a number of places where the film felt almost like a documentary. For instance Pinky goes to get the money Jake stole from Dicey. She gets attacked by a woman who claims the money's hers. The cops come and arrest the blacks. When Pinky admits she is black, she's hauled off as well. The cops felt like real people, not actors.

They may have been real cops. We shot outdoors a couple of days and I think that scene was one of them. We went to a community with a lot of blacks and filmed in the street. But most of it was done inside.

How did you light such an enormous set so that you could play daytime exteriors inside on a sound stage?

We had a gallery of lights all the way around the stage. In order to keep it from looking like black velvet, they put a dim light on the backdrop. It created a horizon and gave some sense of depth.

You did some interesting things with sound. When Pinky fantasizes about her fiancé, you hear a train whistle over a shot of her in a private moment. Were you involved in the cutting?

We edited every night right there on the lot where we were shooting. So I was on top of *Pinky* more than I had been with my previous films. As for the scene you mentioned, I used to be a radio actor, and that kind of sound overlay was really pretty routine for me. Besides, I'd worked with the editor before, not Harmon Jones who's credited with editing the picture, but with Bobbie McLean who was Zanuck's overseeing editor. She did *A Tree Grows in Brooklyn*. All those studio heads, guys like Zanuck and Louis B. Mayer, had a chief cutter. Those editors held fantastic power in the studios. Mayer would say to his cutter, Margaret Booth, "I don't like that shot. Get it out." And she was empowered to make the cut. All the producers were scared of her. She wasn't a malignant woman, she just had Mayer's authority. Darryl Zanuck had someone named Bobbie (Barbara) McLean, also a woman. Bobbie would sit with him through all the rushes and he'd say, "I don't like that, change that, make him do that one over." And she would convey those orders to the unit cutter or the director or whoever. For some reason she was not around much on *Pinky*, but she was all over *Gentleman's Agreement.* Zanuck was on the spot or felt he was. The rich Jews had a big luncheon at Warner Brothers. They asked Zanuck to come, but Zanuck wouldn't go. He asked Moss Hart to go and represent him. They said, "What are you doing? Why bring the whole subject up? We're getting along all right." You bet they were. They were protected by their money and their position and their place in the film industry. But millions and millions of Jews in America weren't getting along all right. So Moss, in a smooth way, told Zanuck, and Zanuck told them all to get stuffed. He was a strong guy. Within his own style he was a swell guy.

Was Pinky *rehearsed before you shot it?*

I rehearsed more on *Pinky* than on any of the earlier films. By the time I started to work on it, the actors were all terrified. They all felt that they had a disaster. They had expected to work with Jack Ford and he'd quit. He rejected them and they all felt very unworthy. You have no idea how fragile an actor's self-worth is. And if Ford didn't like something, he didn't try to put a good face on, especially in those days. He was already cantankerous. They all felt shunned, so I had some readings. I rehearsed a lot with Jeanne, because the minute I saw her I knew what the problem was. I think I used her quality pretty well. I tried to pass off her strained face and passivity as tension. I tried to at least make her internal movement a little more clear to her. Where it changed, where it developed, what she was seeking, what she was after, what we call the actions.

How explicit did you get?

You don't ever talk about the emotion. All that does is tense an actor up. What you talk about is what they want out of a scene—why they are going into it. You keep them concentrated on the action, what we call the "objective" in the Stanislavsky Method. If you do that, at least you'll have clarity. If you talk about what their character is feeling, you'll get nothing but simulated emotion. That's the danger of it, and that's what Jeanne had been doing. The first thing I did was relax her, made her feel, put my hand on her body a little bit. I don't mean sexually but like you do with a horse, you know, "Just take it easy, calm down. I'm here and you're gonna be all right." I did that with Ethel Waters, too. Ethel was interesting because she had a strange duality—she was religious on the one hand and on the other full of hatred. I was interested in Ethel personally. I liked talking to her. So perhaps I worked more than I would have ordinarily, but I always worked a lot with all the actors. I like doing that and I think that's where my game is anyway. In fact I never do not rehearse. While the crew was lighting in that slow laborious way in which they used to light, I always rehearsed. The best example was on *A Streetcar Named Desire* when I had to break in Vivien Leigh to a whole group of actors who had been working together for a long time. I had a mock-up of the set, not the walls, but an exact replica of the furniture in the same positions put up in a corner of the sound stage. I'd give the actors five minutes to get some coffee, then start rehearsing. Then I'd get them on the actual set and show the cameraman the basic movement of the scene and determine the first shot with him. I'd give the cast another five minutes to go to their dressing rooms and do whatever the hell they did in their dressing rooms and then I'd get them to the other set and rehearse some more.

How could the crew start to light before you showed the cameraman the actual blocking?

There are two stages. In the first you give them enough to start roughing it in. Later you go in and determine everything very precisely. I did the same thing on location. I always had places where I could go and rehearse. It's not that hard, even on location, because everybody is so friendly around movie people. They're so curious about you. They'll give you their homes, they'll give you coffee, donuts, anything. They're flattered that you're using their place.

There's one scene in Pinky *in which I like the staging a lot. Miss Em calls in the doctor to witness her new will. The scene is all shot quite tightly between the doctor and Miss Em. But at the end of the scene, as the doctor walks out, you pan with him to the door. The shot ends on a tight close-up of Dicey, who we realize has been sitting there, unbeknownst to us, the whole time.*

I agree with you, that was good. She's just sitting there patiently, waiting. I've got a lot of feeling for blacks, and you'll notice in all my films they're always either giving the white man more sympathy than he deserves or busting up with laughter at him. In *Baby Doll* they laugh at everything that poor man, Archie Lee, does. He's ridiculous. Also, the old, old blacks are almost Chekovian in their devotion to the whites who don't return it to the same degree. It was horrible in the South, but despite the terrible situation, the blacks behaved with such human dignity that it was heartbreaking.

You see the struggle for dignity a lot in your pictures.

That's what everything I ever did was all about. Whether it's internally through a character's gradual recognition of the truth. Whether it's about a character finding the courage to do something about an impossible situation that's robbed him of his dignity. Whether it's a social evil that is killing him. Whether it's just through the turmoil of human relationships or whether it's a conflict between one side of himself and another.

Pinky *closes the first chapter in your filmmaking—the studio phase. Now on to the real excitement.*

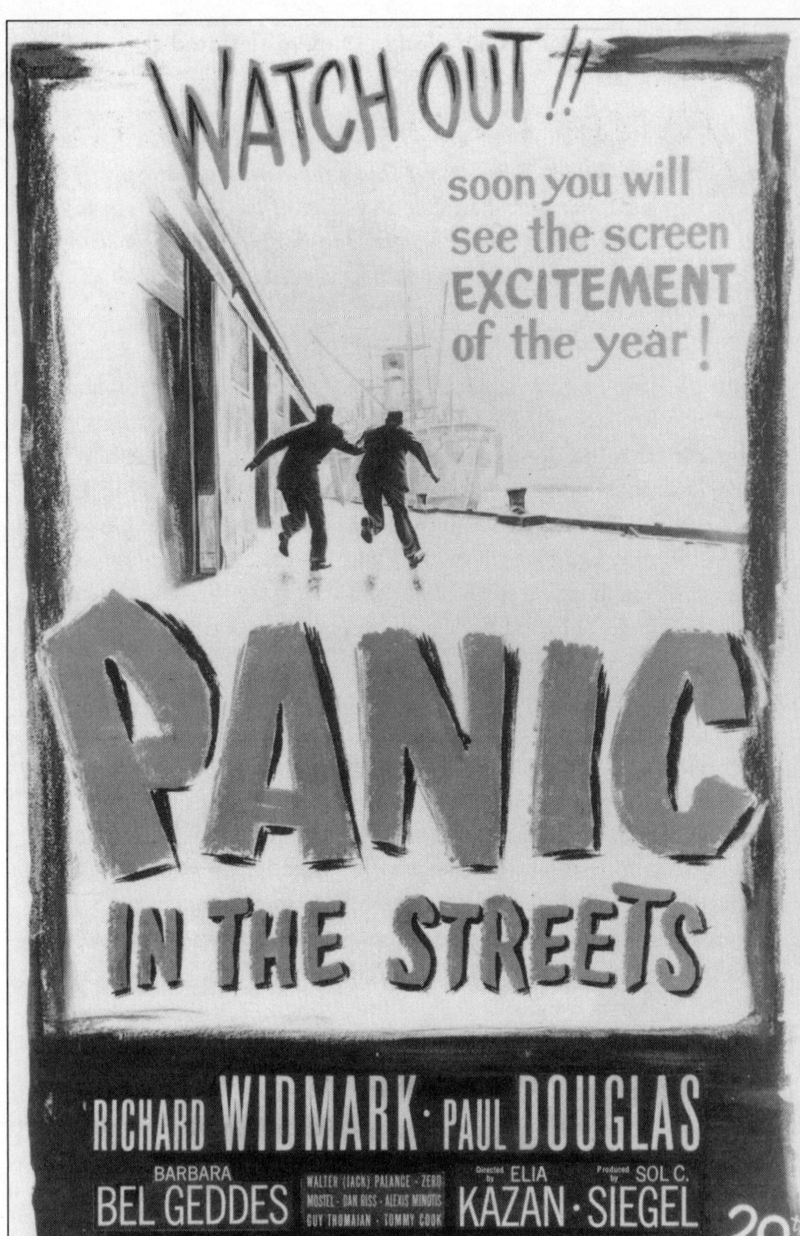

WATCH OUT !!
soon you will
see the screen
EXCITEMENT
of the year !
PANIC
IN THE STREETS
RICHARD WIDMARK · PAUL DOUGLAS
BARBARA
BEL GEDDES
WALTER (JACK) PALANCE · ZERO
MOSTEL · DAN RISS · ALEXIS MINOTIS
GUY THOMAJAN · TOMMY COOK
Directed by ELIA
KAZAN
Produced by SOL C.
SIEGEL
Screen Play by RICHARD MURPHY · Adaptation by DANIEL FUCHS · From a Story by EDNA and EDWARD ANHALT
20th
CENTURY-FOX

PANIC IN THE STREETS
(1950)

A POKER GAME takes place in a run-down hotel in New Orleans. The big winner, Kochak, grows sicker and sicker, and finally bolts when the big loser, Blackie (Jack Palance), a small-time hoodlum, won't let him quit. Fitch (Zero Mostel), Blackie's lackey, and Poldi, Kochak's cousin, give chase. Kochak is shot, his body dumped in the river.

Dr. Clinton Reed (Richard Widmark), a public health officer, gets a call from the coroner's office. He leaves his kid and wife (Barbara Bel Geddes) and heads for what he assumes will be a routine autopsy review.

Instead he finds Kochak's body loaded with pneumonic plague. Reed believes the killer must be caught within forty-eight hours or the plague may spread throughout the city, the country, even the world. After some political wrangling, the unbelieving police, led by their cynical Captain (Paul Douglas), get on the case.

The tension escalates as evidence mounts, supporting Reed's claim. The cops round up petty crooks to no avail. Reed starts his own investigation. It leads to the boat Kochak came in on. Everyone aboard gets inoculated.

The search next leads to a Greek restaurant. At first the owner denies all knowledge, but when his wife dies of the plague, he points them to Poldi.

At the same time, Blackie and Fitch search desperately for Poldi, convinced that he knows where something of great value has been stashed. Time is running out.

Blackie and Fitch get to the dying Poldi first. As they try to remove him, Reed arrives. They dump Poldi and run for it, Reed and the cops right on their heels.

The chase leads to the docks, through a coffee warehouse, and back onto the pier. Reed and the cops corner the criminals, but Blackie gets away. He makes it to a rope which secures a freighter to the pier and falls off trying to get around the rat guard. The plague has been contained, and a very tired Reed goes home to his wife and son.

By the time I finished *Pinky* I thought I was up the wrong tree. I had been doing movies just like I'd done plays. In the first place, I was waiting for material to come to me exactly as I'd been doing in the theater. I was getting all kinds of offers. "You want to do this script?" Finally I realized that the first step towards making a good movie is to develop the script yourself. It took me longer than it should have to understand and deal with that. Maybe because, I had great, great uncertainty about my own writing. I couldn't write anything. I couldn't even write an article for the Sunday *New York Times*. My wife Molly would help me or write it for me. I was in great awe of writers. But I knew in my heart I had to face my insecurities and get involved in the writing. I had to collaborate, even if I did it secretly, behind a mask. I could at least make myself do that.

Another thing I realized was that up until that time I had shot every film in medium shots and closeups exactly as if they were plays except viewed a little closer. Technically, I was telling everything through the interplay of characters rather than the interplay of people and environment or through nature.

I was still hitchhiking in my middle years, and I went down to Galveston, Texas. I remember I was down by the harbor which was full of fishing boats. There was a wonderful wind blowing, one of those spring breezes that are both cool and damp, and I thought, this can't go on a sound stage, what am I doing? This is out of doors, that's what movies are. They're environment. I'd been missing all that. I'd made five pictures and none of them had anything in them that I couldn't have done on stage. And then it occurred to me that the most interesting people I know are not "actors." It's about time I got some of my own people on film who are actors or non-actors, but who have human faces. I've nothing against actors. I really like them a lot, but you know so many of them had a soft, velvety look on screen. It's not quite human. It's not in trouble, it's not committed, it's not in danger, it's not frantic, it's got no tears, it hasn't got a hard-on, it's just a walking mask. I began to look at John Ford's pictures again. At least he had roughnecks in them. He got the weather in them, he got poetry in them. I always liked poetry. I like music and there was no music in my pictures. I really had a big revolution. I turned on myself violently and angrily. I said, I'm going to do a picture that's like a silent, where I tell it all pictorially, and I'm going to co-write it. I won't think too much or analyze too much or keep notebooks that somebody will ask me for years from now. I'll just go in there and enjoy being a film director, enjoy having a camera, enjoy winging stuff. Like Jack Ford said, "Get it out of your set. It will inspire you, just look at it." It's also true that the richer a script, the more complicated the characters, the less you can fool around with it. If it's real, like *A Streetcar Named Desire*, you can't wing it. If it's worthy of respect, you respect it. I'm thankful *Panic in the Streets* was very superficial, conventional, and corny. Still, anywhere I went in that city, it got me. I moved my family down to New Orleans, and I brought a lot of my sort of hooligan friends with me. We used to box in the afternoon. We used to toss a baseball or football around. I used to go down to the French Quarter. I made myself throw off all my stage inhibition and training. I had a great crew and a very funny cameraman, Joe MacDonald. Everyday life was going on all around us, and for the first time I fully enjoyed the pleasure of making a film. So in a technical way it was a development, but also from a personal standpoint *Panic in the Streets* was a big change for me. I ate a lot of New Orleans food. We were close to a guy who ran Owen-Brenners, one of those little French Quarter restaurants, and he used to send us up ostrich eggs and oysters. It was a wild time.

Panic in the Streets *is a genre picture which it seems both enabled and forced you to make the film exceed the limits of the text.*

There was no tether on me. I could do anything as long as I carried the plot forward in each scene. I could play any scene anywhere. I used to wander around that city night and day so I knew it well. I wanted to exploit the environment. It's so terrific and colorful. I wanted boats, steam engines, warehouses, jazz joints—all of New Orleans—in that picture. That was the first picture I truly enjoyed making in the sense that I was in control—not a script, not a story, not a producer, and not a star. There were no deadheads on that picture. I had a great cast. It was a treat in itself just to have Zero Mostel around. I had Jack Palance, making his first picture. And I had Richard Widmark, who was a jewel, as nice a guy as there was in the world. Barbara Bel Geddes played his wife. I cast like a man should. I handpicked everybody just because I liked them. The only one I didn't like that much was Paul Douglas. He wasn't really an actor, you know. He'd been a football announcer. He was a front man. He should have been the host of a steak joint.

He played the police captain and all through the film you showed greater affection for the villains than for the good guys.

Why sure. They're more colorful. I never had much affection for good guys anyway. I don't like puritans. I don't like guys who are rigid and have one point of view, who squeeze the complexities out of life. I like hoodlums and gangsters. Not only that, I like athletes, I like dancers, I like show business people. I like women who leave home, men who leave their wives, and people who express the impossibility of living in a constricted eighteenth- or nineteenth-century religious bind. Propriety, religion, ethics, and the middle class are all murdering us. We're just breaking out of it, or trying to anyway. When you see Jimmy Cagney pushing a grapefruit in Mae Clarke's face, you think, I've often wanted to do that. Why the hell didn't I?

Did you have the plot line totally worked out before shooting?

Got pretty poetic for a minute didn't I? Yes. there was a complete if episodic script. I thought we could improve every scene, and every morning I'd get to the location ahead of everybody, as usual, and figure out what I wanted to do with that day's material. The author would show up about a half hour later, and I'd rewrite the scene with him or get him to rewrite it, so that it fit my plan. Then the actors would come around and we'd get started.

Did you have a cinematic style in mind when you started?

For the first time I said to myself, don't feel you have to jump in all the time with a medium shot or a close-up. Start using long shots. Try to tell the whole story through pictures. Try and get the feeling of the air and the climate into the film. The photography should have been better than it was. Whether it was the film stock or the lab or the camerawork or whatever, we lost some texture, some gritty graininess that I wanted. Everything came out a little velvety. I think it had to do with the bath they developed the film in.

A lot of the climactic chase scene is done in big wide-angle shots which require lighting an enormous indoor area. How did you do it?

It was a problem, naturally, but we had a lot of equipment on hand. Also in the early '50s the labs were just beginning to force-develop film so you could under light a little. The labs would compensate by leaving the film in the developing bath longer or pushing more light through the film in the developing or printing process. I was constantly trying to get as much of a feeling of space as I could into the film.

The music in Panic *is almost all functional: radios, jukeboxes, and so forth. It's a far cry from your earlier pictures where there were 1,700 violins in the background all the time.*

I got to know a lot of jazz musicians down there. Naturally, I used their music. It was the music out of my own taste, not the music of *Gentleman's Agreement.* The overinflated music in Hollywood films was disgusting because what it said was, "This scene is much more dramatic than it appears. Oh, if you only knew how dramatic this scene is. This scene is really very deep. Oh God, what emotion!"

The picture opens on a long tracking shot through the streets. You stop in front of a seedy hotel then cut to a room on the second floor where a poker game is going on.

That opening shot was made from a car.

Why did you start outside where nothing was happening rather than opening inside on the card game?

My whole feeling was to keep moving pictorially—to constantly saturate the picture with the feeling of New Orleans.

In a scene much later, Blackie and Fitch have finally caught Poldi.

They throw him over the rail. What a mess that picture was. That was a good shot. I was really getting the feel of the camera—beginning to know what I was doing. I put mattresses all around the camera and just left a little hole and they threw poor Poldi off the steps. In the scene just before that, Palance kept beating up poor Guy Thomajan, the actor. Everybody enjoyed that picture. As you can see, I feel entirely different about that film than I feel about the first five.

Poldi and Fitch chase Kochak, who's run away from the card game. Kochak crosses a railroad track, and a train almost hits him. It's done in a very wide shot so there was no cheating with a cut. If the timing weren't perfect, you'd have had a bad shot or a dead actor.

I wouldn't do the shot until Lewis Charles, who played Kochak, almost couldn't get across. Everybody was saying, "You're trying to kill us. You're a murderer." I did stuff like that a lot. I really learned that if a man is supposed to be wet in a scene, like he's been in the river, there's only one way to do it. Throw him in the river. Turn a hose on him. I stopped playing games. Movies are not like plays. I was cursed with the fact that I came out of the theater.

At the end of that chase, when Kochak is trapped, he gets shot off screen.

I learned that it's twenty times better if you have violence that suggests further violence than if you're explicit. What you imagine is much more frightening than what you can show on screen. There's nothing as dreadful as the fantasies of a person that come out of fear, hysteria or anxiety. By the way, I met Zero Mostel in the street years later and he said, "I'm still puffing, you son of a bitch. I never ran so much in my life." Palance got a little insulting with Zero once, and Zero was gonna kill him. Palance used to be a boxer, but Zero underneath all of that comic exterior was one of the toughest guys I ever met. Anyway, in that scene I kept Palance slapping Zero in the butt, making him run. I tried to balance a sense of drama with levity so that the violence would not be taken too seriously. So all of it, villains included, was treated with affection because, after all, you can't take the plot too seriously. You know the plague isn't really going to spread. It's a springboard for a sort of caper.

You set up a classic time clock. The good guys have forty-eight hours to find the carrier, so the antagonist in a sense really becomes time itself.

That was just to keep the plot moving. Actually, I always thought *Panic* was a sort of bizarre comedy.

Did that affect the way you shot the scenes?

Absolutely, not only the way I shot scenes, but the staging of the action as well. In the chase scene for example, I could have just had Mostel and Palance running in separate places, but it was more fun this way. Jack kept whipping Zero's butt and Zero kept complaining. Zero makes those scenes, because he keeps them from being just ordinary thriller chases. Guy Thomajan, who played

Poldi, and Palance were always funny to me. Paul Douglas was a blowhard phony, but I thought that was typical of a certain kind of policeman who never quite gets to be the boss but is always around being cynical, playing the big shot. So I cast him that way. Barbara Bel Geddes wasn't another typical glamorous leading lady. Dick Widmark always has a wry quality. Alexis Minotis, who played the Greek restaurant owner, had played Oedipus and Oedipus at Colonus on the same evening in Athens. He was a famous Greek tragedian, who'd just been kicked out of Greece. I tried to keep this whole thing affectionately amusing and small-scale. *Viva Zapata!* and *Wild River* had deep themes; this didn't, and I didn't want to be caught dead pretending. I was smart about that. It's not a great picture, but I think it's a genuinely entertaining picture.

It reminds me of Touch of Evil. *Did you ever see that?*

Yeah, I liked it. That didn't have as much fun as this. It had more danger. Mine is an affectionate comedy. It shows the way humanity deals with all its foolishness. I think there's a marvelous scene in *Panic.* All hell is breaking loose, and Reed comes home exhausted. He and his wife share a few little jokes, and she just puts him to bed. I think that's very good. It's in the scale of truth. I think *Touch of Evil* is superior in some ways, but inferior, really, inside because it's portentous.

The similarities I was thinking of were in terms of style. Both constantly deflect you from their content because their stories are so thin, indeed barely credible.

Panic in the Streets is the first picture I made that I liked. I don't think you're aware those people are actors, even Widmark had played nothing but heavies before that. He became famous in *Kiss of Death*, in which he pushed an old lady in a wheelchair down the stairs, and he had that wonderfully phony, lunatic laugh. We'd worked in the theater together about four or five years earlier, and I returned him to playing a leading man. He had sort of a minor-league charm. But it was a genuine charm. Almost everything he said was amusing and self-deprecatory, and to me, that self-deprecatory attitude is an essential American quality.

Did you do much character analysis in preparation for the film?

No. In the theater I'd been doing all these heavy, serious, great plays that needed very meticulous psychological handling. *Streetcar*, *Death of a Salesman*, etc. I decided that since *Panic* wasn't deep psychologically, not to pretend that it was. It was a big lesson to me. That's a terrible kind of lie. That's what hamminess is, pretending there is more in something than there really is. There's no harm in saying, "This isn't very deep. It has other virtues. It has lightness of foot, it has surprise, it has suspense, it's engaging." So I decided to depsychologize it. I would always read a scene first, make a few points and try to get some business going so the actor would look anchored in his environment. But I wouldn't go into a lot of analysis. I would have the actors read it to me, and I would tell them how they were going to do it, what was going to happen, where they were, what they wanted, etc. I would go through the whole thing, but I wouldn't dwell on it.

Did you have to make many adjustments during rehearsals?

No. Once they knew what I wanted and how I was going to do it, there wasn't a hell of a lot that had to be adjusted. They were all the right types. Except for Zero, the actors were all either playing themselves or a convention of themselves. Here's the kind of thing I did to keep it light and enjoyable. I cast an actress to play Zero's wife that he detested. He hated Mary Liswood (who played Angie Fitch), but I insisted on her. It was terribly funny because he'd look at me and he'd look at her. In that way they had a relationship almost without knowing it.

There's a nice moment in the middle of a scene where Palance is chewing the hell out of Mostel. His wife says, "But Aggie...," Mostel turns and hollers, "Shut up!" He really lets her have it.

That's the kind of thing I worked out when I was reading it with the actors. Not characterizations as much as the dynamics of the scene, how it moved, what the climaxes were.

Are you saying you weren't certain of the dynamics of the scenes until your readings?

I usually was not. Oh, I'd get a few ideas in the morning when we were rewriting it, naturally. But I think I got that particular idea when they were reading. Zero was trembling at Palance, and I thought he should let it out on his wife. God, Zero was adorable. I just loved him. He was just a marvelous, dear, wonderful man.

Did you always wait for the readings to work out the dynamics of the scenes?

I'd start it beforehand, but I got a lot from the actors. Not from them personally but from the process of working with them, having been an actor myself. I'm basically clear when I start a reading. I've got it marked. I draw a line. Here's where it changes. I'll put an asterisk. Here's the climax. I feel the shape of a scene a great deal, sometimes too much. You don't always get it the way you feel it because you find it may be false for those actors. But I get their equivalent of what I have in mind. And I don't let a scene just drift. Every scene, even if it's psychologically complex and built on the small interplays between people, has an external pattern, which is what I call a dynamic. There's both content and the way the content expresses itself in action and behavior, which can have a pattern almost independent. It's like a deep painting that has a design and a form.

Do you mean that the behavior and the action may be different than the emotional underpinnings ?

No, you bring out the emotional underpinnings by the form you give the scene. One thing I always do, and I think that it's important in films, is stretch climaxes.

How?

Time lags. Intercut. You show what a person does. Then what the other person feels about what he did. Then you show the first person noticing that reaction. Then the second one's determination not to take it, and then you see the first person thinking, "The hell with you." It's all in closeup. You actually make the time longer than it is. It's a false movie time that you pick up. You take certain climaxes that in life go click-click and you stretch them and stretch them.

Does that affect your work with the actors in terms of working out the "real" timing of a scene?

Absolutely. Sure. You can't do anything falsely. You make them go through the emotions in every take. You don't just do close-ups of a face sitting there. They must have a point. There must be a thought. The best close-ups are pictorial records of a change from one attitude to another. They show a transition from one emotion to another. You see a man feeling or doing or about to do something. Instead, he changes his mind and starts to do something else. Or you see a man not notice something and suddenly he notices it. You see a man about to run away with fear, and instead he decides to move in and face what's scaring him. Those transitions are what closeups are at their best. In order to get that close-up and have it affect the other person in the scene, you have to take the time when you direct it, which is hard to do in the theater, to make the actor actually experience each of the moments. For example, you say to one actor, "Tell him to get out of here." You say to the other actor, "For a minute you want to do as he says. You look around to see where you can run, you look at him to see if he means it." Then to the first actor you say, "You know this guy is looking at you to see if you mean it. Just let him know that you do mean it." Then you say to the second guy, "He's looking at you as though he's going to bully you. He's shaming you, see? So you suddenly think, 'The hell with that. I'm not going to take that, and you walk over there.'" You describe what happens internally and you do it in a way that stretches the moments so you can photograph them. You can't photograph nothing. You photograph the moments you create. And you arrive at those moments best in little, quiet, intimate readings where you tell them just what to think.

Do you give them physical actions in addition to filling in their interior for them?

Those words mean different things to everybody. What I try to do is tell them what they want and what they do about what they want, just like in acting in the theater. And what they want often comes from what the other person wants. Usually, emotion is a result of action. You want something. You're balked, you can't get it, and emotion arises. You work all that out in terms of what you know about the psychology of that character or yourself or whatever it is that you do know. That's the test of how much you know about human behavior. Once you've worked that out, make them do it. Don't just say it, make them actually do it. Now then, as they begin to do that, you may see they have little physical impulses. Those are great for the camera because they're photographable. So you stretch them a little bit. Make him do that again, or give him an object that he wants to reach or make him do something with his clothing or make him notice something particular on a person's face. Give him something that's very definite, very specific, and then you've got something you can photograph.

What do you do if an actor is going through the proper internal emotional experience but it doesn't give you the behavior you want to see on film?

That didn't come up on this particular film, since, as I told you, I didn't want to psychologize. If it were a deep picture, I wouldn't have used Widmark, as good an actor as he was. I wouldn't have used Barbara Bel Geddes either, although I loved her and she could do a lot. I'd have had someone like Barbara Loden, my second wife, who had a lot of emotional depth. But for what *Panic in the Streets* was, I think I cast that picture perfectly.

A lot of the film is shot with wide-angle lenses. For instance, the scene you mentioned earlier with Palance, Mostel, and the wife, is set in a very dark room, but you can see all the way back. Did you need special lighting or special lenses to get that very deep focus?

No. There was a time in the forties when everybody, including me, was impressed with William Wyler's *The Best Years of Our*

Lives and Orson Welles's *Citizen Kane*. I'm not impressed with deep focus now. I don't like it because it's not the way we actually see things in real life. If I look directly at you, that picture behind you is not in focus. So deep focus seems like a stagey trick to me now, like trying to make movies into the theater. But in those days that was a big thing. So we were using a 28mm lens all the time or a 30. I'd go as far as a 25, but a 28 lens doesn't distort like a 25—the ends don't curve and you still get great depth of field. It's not flattering to women, but who cared in that picture?

The staging was highly dramatic in the wide-angle shots. You constantly had somebody walk into the foreground to fill the frame rather than cut to a close-up.

I still believe in that way of shooting. A simplification of that technique is putting an object in the foreground that will have some special meaning in the high point or the climax of a scene. As the scene develops, the actors approach that object and, thus, that particular place. It's the most natural way to direct some kinds of scenes. I did it a lot. But you have to remember that that technique assumes that a fixed viewpoint is the one you are going to keep throughout the scene. In those days I was able to work very fast, because having worked a lot on stage, I would do whole scenes in one shot. I was known then not only as a good director but as an economical, swift director. A reputation I lost very quickly with *Viva Zapata!*

There's an early sequence at the coroner's office that you did in almost one long continuous shot. You bring in a group of men pushing a gurney. A dead body is dropped off to the room next door. The camera stays with the men in this room and behind them through a window you see the corpse go off into still another room. Then you follow the actors into the room with the corpse. Why do it that way?

It's interesting isn't it? Fun to watch?

Yes.

Do you need another reason? Also, I was impressed with the

setting of the morgue, the cubicles and the bank of bodies. I never worked that way before. In *A Tree Grows in Brooklyn* the biggest thing I had to sell was Peggy Ann Garner's face. In *Boomerang* there was Dana Andrews chewing his dialogue. Spencer Tracy and Katharine Hepburn, Gregory Peck, John Garfield and Dorothy McGuire all chewing up their dialogue, and little no-expression Jeanne Crain. It was all on so-called acting, people's expressions. But in *Panic* my star was New Orleans. You can smell it. You feel the breeze, you feel the river moving. I shot a lot of it in wide angle so that you can see the environment.

Palance plays a scene outside a Greek restaurant with a midget. The content doesn't come to much. I got the feeling you shot it just because it was fun.

That's a hell of a good reason to shoot a scene in my book. At least in this kind of film.

The chase at the end of Panic *breaks every movie rule for a chase.*

How come? I don't know the rules.

Chases are almost always done in short, tight cuts. It allows you to play with time and space. The simplest example is to have the bad guys run past a tree. In the next cut the good guys run past it. Once you put them all in the same shot, the audience knows exactly how much distance (and time) there is between them, how close they are to being caught and the tension dissipates. Yet, in Panic *the big chase finale is done using almost all wide shots. For instance, Palance and Mostel run inside the warehouse from right to left. They go through some machinery. You pan them all the way around and as they start to go out the door and the frame towards the left, the cops show up. They turn around and start to run back and you pan them around to the right, but there are cops coming that way too. Then you stay with them as they go up a flight of steps. You did it all in one shot. The movie convention for a chase would be pan them in and cut as they run into the next room, cut to the cops outside, etc. The action would have been broken up.*

I understand what you mean. Glad you straightened me out on that.

So why did you choose to do it in long shots?

The full figures of Zero Mostel running with Jack Palance chasing him are much more interesting than their faces. Also the cops in long shot are more interesting and threatening than cops in close-up. They were real cops by the way, but they didn't look like cops when you got close to them. When a bunch of them appear in a doorway in the distance, they're far more menacing. So there was no choice really. I just behaved naturally. I've always liked the last part of that chase.The water was rising all the time while we were shooting. We had these catwalks built but every day we'd come in, and what we could walk on yesterday, was underwater today. We'd have to raise it up a little further. Zero Mostel wasn't afraid but Jack Palance kept moaning, "I'm gonna drown. You're trying to drown me, you son of a bitch." It was funny. He was great when he was up on the rope. He actually looked like a cat up there. I liked Jack a lot.

The whole picture was about the plague, and now the principal villain is trapped like a rat. Is that why you took the climax to the waterfront?

That's the kind of symbolism that appealed to me in those days. The climax of it was when he tried to climb up the rope and he came to the rat guard. I'm saying he's a rat, he's carrying the plague. He gets up there, can't get around that guard, and falls in the water.

Did Palance do that fall himself?

Yes, he was a great athlete.

You didn't use a stunt double?

No, he really did it. Remember how I shot Kochak running in front of the train? I told the actors, "Come on, let's do it. The hell with doubles."

Did you consciously stage for the camera differently in Panic *than in your earlier films?*

I did much more for the camera. I wasn't photographing behavior so much as making a certain type of film. As I said, I made up my mind to make this picture as silent as I could. I remember thinking about Jack Ford and seeing pictures of his I'd liked, over and over. I was influenced very much by *Stagecoach.* It was a fantastic liberation for me because I was such a dutiful boy before that. I was from the theater and I was "deep"—loaded up with the first film that said "Nigger," the first film that said "Jew." I finally rebelled. In this picture I broke out of it, and it saved me...really. Otherwise, I could have been a bore all my life. I can't imagine anything more boring than *The Sea of Grass* or *Pinky.* That amount of righteousness is tedious. It hasn't got the breath of life in it.

Panic *was a strong departure, a very conscious choice to start to talk with the camera. But then you went straight back to the theater and did the film of* A Streetcar Named Desire.

A TREE GROWS IN BROOKLYN

"The faces of Peggy Ann Garner and Jimmy Dunn are the most authentic thing about the film."

"I made Johnny (Jimmy Dunn) cross to the window . . . so that the physical act would be associated in his mind with the psychological movement."

". . .when Kathy's (Dorothy McGuire) mood turns dark, I had her walk away from him."

"The way Lloyd Nolan sat and talked to her (Dorothy McGuire) was beautiful."

SEA OF GRASS

★

"Spence and Hepburn were lovers, and she was very protective of him. She'd . . . say, 'Isn't Spence wonderful?' And I'd think, 'He's only giving me a tenth of what he's got.' "

"The things Lutie (Hepburn) wore were not the things that a girl going out West to marry a cattle rancher would take out with her. . . ."

BOOMERANG

"It's not just that they (Dana Andrews and Jane Wyatt) were stage actors, they were actors not out of my training . . . out of another world."

"The best scenes are in the police station where the police are third-degreeing Johnny Kennedy." Note Karl Malden playing Lieutenant White.

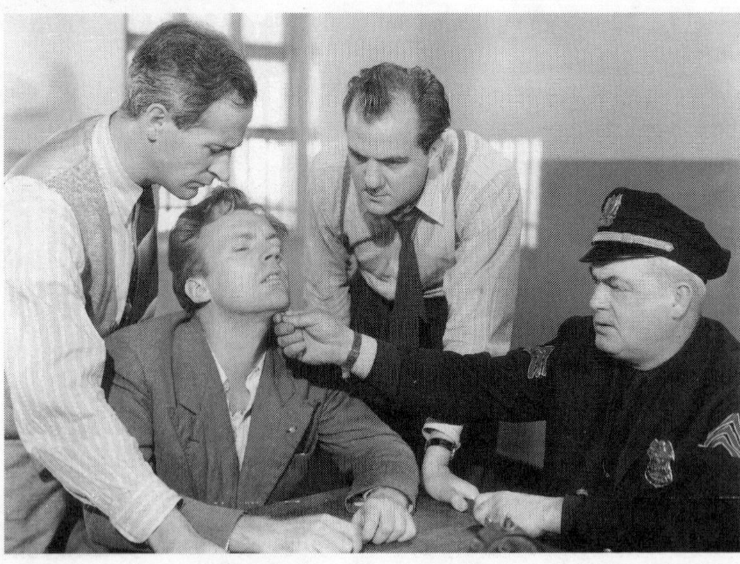

GENTLEMAN'S AGREEMENT

★

P. Schuyler Green (Gregory Peck) telling David Goldmann (John Garfield) that he's "passing" as a Jew.

"There's one good scene in the picture when Garfield says to Dorothy McGuire, 'What did you do in the face of anti-Semitism?' . . . She didn't do anything, of course."

"In the old stage tradition the leading man (Gregory Peck) never gets mixed up with the character woman (Celeste Holm). That was all done terribly."

PINKY

"The only good thing about her face (Jeanne Crain) was that it went so far in the direction of no temperament that you felt Pinky was floating through all of her experience . . . which is what 'passing' is." Jeanne Crain with Ethel Waters playing her grandmother, Dicey Johnson.

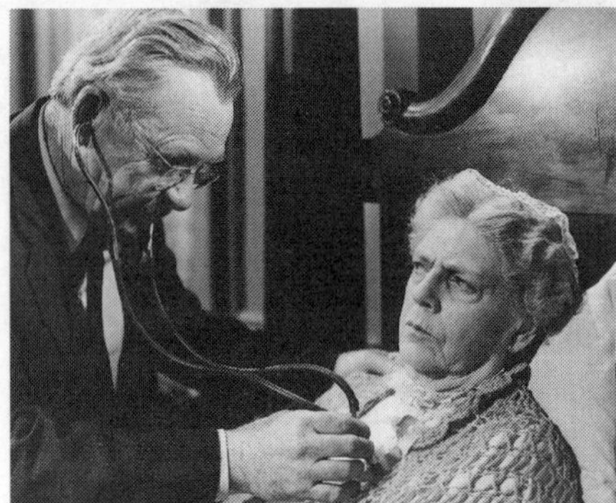

"You see a whole biography in her face (Ethel Barrymore). She was wonderful."

"Right in the middle of the scene, Jake (Frederick O'Neal) spots a piece of fried chicken, picks it up and scoffs it . . . without missing a beat."

Panic is an affectionate comedy. "All hell is breaking loose and Reed (Richard Widmark) comes home exhausted. He and his wife, Nancy (Barbara Bel Geddes), share a few little jokes and she just puts him to bed. It's in the scale of truth."

"I cast an actress to play Fitch's wife that he (Zero Mostel) detested. He hated Mary Liswood (who played Angie Fitch). . . . In that way they had a relationship almost without knowing it."

PANIC IN THE STREETS

"The full figures of Zero Mostel and Jack Palance are more interesting than their faces. Also the cops in long shot are more interesting and threatening than cops in close-up."

"The water was rising all the time while we were shooting. Zero Mostel wasn't afraid but Jack Palance kept moaning, ' . . . you're trying to drown me you son of a bitch.'"

A STREETCAR NAMED DESIRE
(1951)

BLANCHE DUBOIS (Vivien Leigh) arrives in New Orleans to stay with her sister, Stella (Kim Hunter), and her brother-in-law, Stanley Kowalski (Marlon Brando). She has all the airs of a genteel, southern lady, in sharp contrast to Stanley, an uneducated laborer whose idea of fun is to go bowling with the boys, play poker, get drunk, fight with Stella, and then make it up to her in bed. He's a walking libido. Pregnant with his child, Stella is crazy about him. Her loyalty is torn between her extremely delicate sister and Stanley, who loathes Blanche.

Blanche has lost the old family estate. Stanley doesn't believe a word she says, and since the Napoleonic Code grants him community property, he's determined to uncover the truth.

Blanche is badly in need of a safe harbor, and she thinks she has found one in Mitch (Karl Malden), the least boorish of Stanley's friends. But as she drinks more and more, she is haunted by the painful memory of the death of her young husband: a suicide she pushed him to by goading him about his homosexuality. She fancies she's going to be rescued by a wealthy old beau. Her desperate need for love even drives her to make a pass at a newsboy.

Mitch and Blanche's romance grows, but on the eve of Blanche's birthday Stanley reveals that Blanche had been run out of town for seducing a seventeen-year-old. She'd been the town tramp—all the while pretending to be a lady. He's bought her a

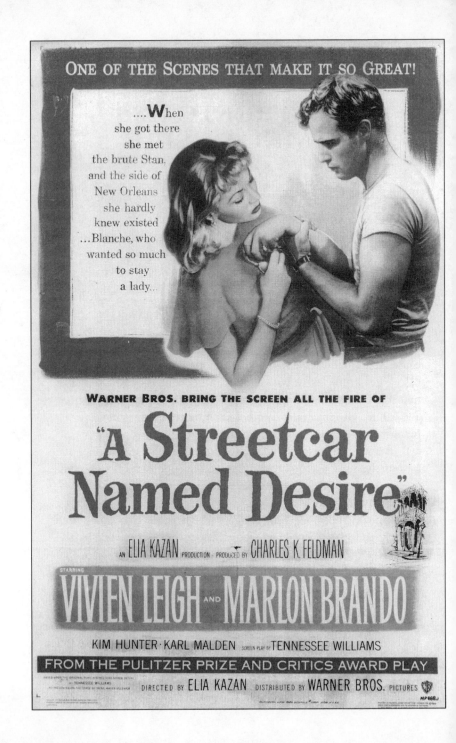

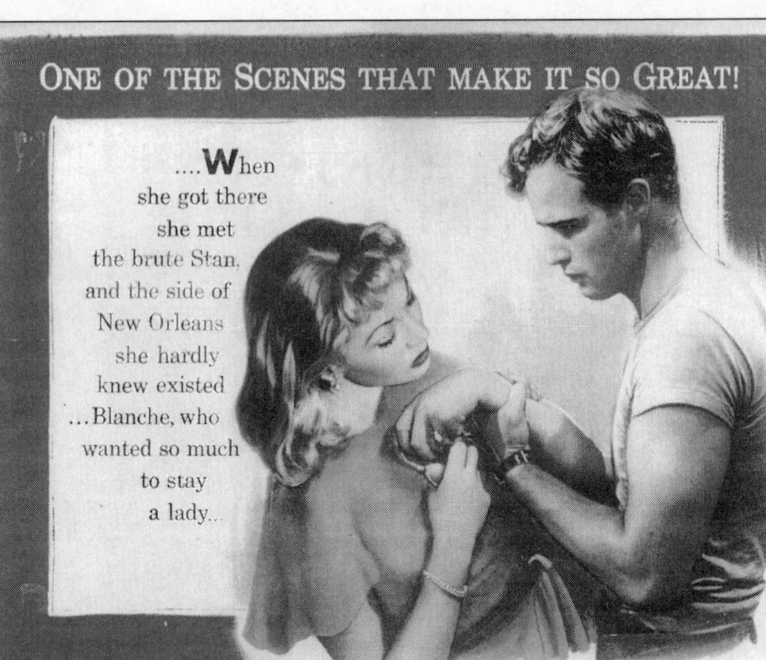

WARNER BROS. BRING THE SCREEN ALL THE FIRE OF

"A Streetcar Named Desire"

AN ELIA KAZAN PRODUCTION · PRODUCED BY CHARLES K. FELDMAN

STARRING

VIVIEN LEIGH AND MARLON BRANDO

KIM HUNTER · KARL MALDEN SCREEN PLAY BY TENNESSEE WILLIAMS

FROM THE PULITZER PRIZE AND CRITICS AWARD PLAY

DIRECTED BY ELIA KAZAN DISTRIBUTED BY WARNER BROS. PICTURES

ticket home as a birthday present. Stella goes into labor, and she's rushed to the hospital.

Mitch confronts Blanche with what Stanley has told him, and she makes a clean breast of it, ending any hope for security through him.

Stanley returns from the hospital. Although repelled by him, Blanche is also attracted. Stanley has sensed this all along, and after playing cat and mouse with Blanche, he rapes her.

Blanche's fragile grip on reality disintegrates. Stanley and Stella prepare to send Blanche to a sanitarium, though Blanche thinks she's going off to her old beau. When the doctor arrives, after first resisting, she takes his arm, and says, "I have always depended on the kindness of strangers."

Had you planned to do a film of Streetcar *next?*

Not at all. I was full of the feeling of liberation and happiness that I got out of *Panic in the Streets*, and my next project was going to be *Viva Zapata!* But Tennessee Williams got after me to do the movie of *Streetcar*, which I'd directed on Broadway in 1947. I really resisted like hell. I had a very sound instinct, which was not to try to get it up twice for the same material. I never did it again, except once—with poor results—when I adapted and directed *The Arrangement*. But *Streetcar* is a masterpiece, and I didn't know as much then about not doing things twice as I do now, so I said okay. But I decided "to open the play up"—I wasn't going to just do it as filmed theater. I hired a screenwriter and worked with him for a long time. We showed how Blanche was thrown out of her home town, how her affairs became complicated before she arrived in New Orleans, etc. When the adaptation was all done, I liked it—thought we'd done a hell of a good job. I went for a vacation, came back a week later, read the script again and realized that we had totally messed up. William's play is a contemporary classic and not to be fooled with. That's a phrase that's used a lot, but in this case it happens to be accurate. His play caught something perfectly. There's only one thing to do, I thought, take the book and just photograph the play. It went against everything I'd just done on *Panic,* and I started feeling that I shouldn't do it at all. At the outset it was like pulling teeth for me. For the first three weeks, I was as miserable as I've ever been. I didn't like Vivien Leigh, though I came to love her by the end. She kept saying, "Well, Larry and I in England..." and I'd say, "You're not doing it with Larry now, you're doing it with me, and I don't like it that way." And she said, "Don't you think it's possible—Larry had this idea." And I said, "I guess it's possible, but we're not going to do it that way." She'd get irritated with me, and I'd get plenty angry with her. But gradually we got to like each other, mainly because I thought she was such a terrific worker. We began to sweat together. By about the fourth week I'd got over my resistance to her and to the whole enterprise. I recognized and accepted the fact that I was just going to photograph the play.

I had a mock-up set in the corner of the sound stage and would rehearse every scene as if it were a play, and then we photographed it. That's the whole story. I enjoyed it because I liked Brando. I liked Karl Malden very much, I ended up liking Vivien, and I loved Kim Hunter—she was another real pet of mine. It turned out to be a pleasant experience working with people I liked. It had nothing to do with what I had programmed for myself. But once having taken on the obligation, I felt it had to be done as well as possible. It's a good record of the play. I think I did an honorable job, and I think I did a good thing, preserving it forever. Later, I wished I'd done the same with *Death of a Salesman*, which I'd also directed on Broadway. Someone else did the film and, I think, botched it terribly.

Why did you cast Vivien Leigh as Blanche, rather than sticking with Jessica Tandy, who had created the role on the stage?

I don't know. It's embarrassing, because I've often wished I'd used Jess. I think in my heart the truth is that I've never really seen any actress do that part as well as I thought it could be done. Uta Hagen was good and Jess was wonderful, but nobody quite touched it. Charlie Feldman, who produced the film, wanted Vivien very much because she was a worldwide star and Jessica Tandy wasn't. I could have balked but I didn't. Vivien was a lovely, beautiful woman, but I don't think she was right for the part. When I look at it now, I think Julie Harris or Geraldine Page should have done it. But nobody could beat Brando. In one sense he was the heavy, but in another he was terribly sympathetic, which was something that was rare and true in Williams. I wanted to preserve those qualities on screen rather than cast a big star in the role.

It's still hard to believe that the role of Stanley was written and that some actor named Marlon Brando came along to play it. His performance is so totally organic, the behavior so believable. All the changes, the mercurial jumps in temperament are dazzling. It's as if he were making it all up as he went along. And yet we all know that he had done it over and over in rehearsal, night after night in the theater and then take after take in the film. Yet it feels as if it's all happening for the first time. What kind of work did you do with him?

There was nothing you could do with Brando that touched what he could do with himself. In those days he was a genius. His own preparation for a scene, his own personality, armament, memories and desires were so deep that there was very little you had to do, except tell him what the scene was about. By the time we made the movie, all I had to do was keep him fresh. That was no problem because Vivien was playing against him and that jolted him out of a lot of the habits he'd formed with Jessica. When I did the play with Jess, I did a lot to break her out of her schooled RADA, Royal Academy of the Dramatic Arts, habits. I once tied her up and had them threaten and make fun of her. I did all kinds of wild things in those days with actors in order to make them feel helpless or whatever the hell I wanted to make them feel.

Let's take a slight deviation and talk about your preparation for doing it as a play.

I did improvisations. A lot of them had to do with making Jessica Tandy feel vulnerable and helpless. Some of the others had to do with making Kim feel drawn, skewered between loyalty to Jessica and loyalty to Brando. We didn't have to do much with Karl Malden. He was very well cast psychologically. He was very polite with women because he was very uncertain. I did much more improvising in other plays.

What kind of improvising did you do?

We improvised the essential elements in a scene so that the actors would have experienced them before they had to learn or get down to the lines. I have improvised, though, in all different kinds of ways.

When you say you get them to experience the essential elements, let's take a specific example. You described doing an improvisation to make Kim Hunter feel being skewered between loyalties.

I'd have Kim taking care of her sister, who was complaining. I'd make up a scene that's not in the play. For instance her sister, Blanche, tries to get her to go home with her, to get her to leave Stanley. Kim is in the position where she has to handle her hysterical sister and at the same time refuse to go home. Such a scene is never in the play.

How would you call on that improvisation when it came time to do the scene in the play?

You never have to. Once the actors experience what you are talking about, you don't have to even mention it. It's happened to them. It's in them.

You described having gone through improvisations to get the actors up to the quality that they had to bring into a scene. Was there any difference in the way you structured an improvisation to set the given circumstances?

One thing I did a lot was to play imaginary scenes that happened before the action of the play. That helps you explore the narrative both in terms of dealing in the same experience and also as a direct circumstantial preparation for what is going to happen in a scene. I did a lot of improvising before I started *Baby Doll* because there I had three Actors Studio people who were all used to improvising. Karl Malden, Carroll Baker and Eli Wallach. Also, the play was not as brilliant and the actors, while excellent, were not Brando. You don't have to improvise with him. I don't know where he got it, but his experience was so rich that you just had to call his attention to what it was you wanted. He even listened experientially. It's as if you were playing on something. He didn't look at you, and he hardly acknowledged what you were saying. He was tuned in to you without listening to you intellectually or mentally. It was a mysterious process, but I knew him so well in those days that I'd say very little to him, and it would turn on a whole mess of things within him.

What would you do if an actor, say Brando, had a different approach to a scene than what you had in mind? Would he be hard to shake off the choice?

Yes. But Brando never did that, if I told him what I wanted to begin with. He almost always not only gave me what I asked for, but he gave me something different that I was grateful to have. It would always come out in a considerably more interesting way than I had thought of. There was always an element of surprise in what he did. I did tell him what I wanted in Stanley. I'll put it to you plainly. Tennessee Williams equals Blanche. He is Blanche. And Blanche is torn between a desire to preserve her tradition, which is her entity, her being, and her attraction to what is going to destroy her tradition. She is attracted to a murderer, Stanley. So the thing to do with Stanley is not, as Harold Clurman suggested, make him symbolic of the crass new order. Williams didn't think of it that way. He was attracted to things that were replacing him. That's the source of the ambivalence in the play. Blanche wants the very thing that's going to crush her. The only way she can deal with this threatening force is to give herself to it. So she both is frightened of him and attracted to him. He thrills her. And that's the way

Williams was. Like Gide, he was attracted to trash—rough, male homosexuals who were threatening him. A lot of fair homosexuals are attracted to rough trade. Part of the sexuality that Williams wrote into the play is the menace of it. So I had to get that quality from Brando.

Brando's Stanley comes across as a terribly impetuous little boy. When he doesn't get what he wants, he cries, he breaks things, he chews up the scenery. On the other hand, he's sexy as hell, an incredible life force.

And Williams felt that. Williams was not a guy in retreat. He was in the world. That was one of the great things about Tennessee. He was ambivalent himself. And you're right about Brando. He made Stanley petulant. He wants everything his own way. If he doesn't get it, he'll either beat you up or he'll cry. How many times have you seen that in your rough friends? They beat the hell out of their wives, and the next minute they're apologizing. That was the wonderful thing about that character, and that is why I was making the joke about Clurman. Clurman and I had a different approach to directing. He said, "I'm going to direct it correctly, and the first thing you do is to think of every character as symbolic and make them what they are representing." They don't represent any one thing. They are ambivalent. They represent two things at once. That's why Williams was a great author, the best of our dramatists.

In your Notebooks *you've described* Streetcar *as poetry. You said that in order to make it effective you had to find a style for the performance that would equal Williams's poetic vision.*

In *Streetcar* all the externals come from the internals. As I watched the behavior of the actors, I would enlarge upon it a little or guide them a little, but you couldn't superimpose anything. *Streetcar* was the opposite of *Panic in the Streets.* You couldn't horse around—anything that intense is already stylized. You don't need to stylize *Streetcar* any further, you can't. I couldn't do it any differently than I did it. Honestly, *Streetcar* found its own form. I think I directed that play about as well as I've directed anything, but anybody could have made that play feelingful and meaningful.

Vivien Leigh's Blanche keeps floating in and out of reality. Sometimes she seems to be totally occupied with her own fantasies, at other times she snaps back, completely aware of exactly what is going on around her.

Have you ever been with a Southern girl? That's the way they are. For me it was just a matter of finding out how to direct Vivien Leigh. Despite having played Scarlett O'Hara, Vivien wasn't from the American South, and she didn't really know that world. In addition, there is only one way to approach certain English actors. You direct them from moment to moment to moment. I once watched Larry Olivier direct himself. He fooled around over a piece of business for hours, fiddling with an ashtray. I wondered how the hell he stood it.

You did change certain things from the play. For instance, the play started on Stella and Stanley. You started the film on Blanche. You had her coming out of a cloud of steam at the train station.

I stole it from the introduction in *Anna Karenina*—the novel, not the film. I'll tell you a few pictorial ideas I had. I had an image of Blanche being like a moth: she kept flying against a luminous, transparent curtain, trying to get out. The window is closed, but she doesn't know it. You can see through her wings, and you can see through the curtain into the light. She flutters again and again helplessly against the glass and at the last moment falls to the ground and dies. I wanted a lot of white-on-white light—an idea I developed much further in *Baby Doll*, where I actually had a white house and a white dress on the leading lady. It seemed to me to represent a lot about the South, a magnificence and delicacy that is incapable of surviving in the world the way it is now.

I had a lot of images of water in *Streetcar*; but then I use water in a lot of my films. When Stanley rapes Blanche there's a cut to a hydrant washing the street. In *America America* the hero has a fight with his girlfriend and he says, "In America, I will be washed clean." Then I cut to the front of the boat, and the boy was being hit by the spray. I have always had a feeling about water cleaning things. I used to love Keats's poem, "On the Sea," which describes water as "...eternal whisperings around desolate shores...."

How many cameras did you use?

One big, heavy old-fashioned studio camera. It was almost always nailed down. There were a few moves, a few slow dollies, but mainly I shot from eye level with no tricks. I tried to concentrate the viewer's attention on the performances and on the story itself. I made no effort to make a director's statement.

How did you deal with the problem of having already done it all before?

That was the hardest job, but I finally did it. A lot of it had to do with getting to like Vivien as a person. The cast and Vivien didn't like each other at first. She felt Brando was very talented and attractive, but she didn't like Karl Malden and he didn't like her. She didn't like Kim either. It started to feel like the New York gang against the poor English girl, and as I saw her predicament I began to feel for her. And then as I saw her courage and the way she worked, her candor, I began to like her a lot. Then Brando began to like her and Karl began to like her and everybody began to slowly gather around her. Everyone was touched and moved by her will to be good. A will to be good is very infectious and evokes strong feelings of loyalty.

When you say her candor, do you mean as a person or as an actress?

Larry Olivier saw the play, *J.B.*—it was a big success. It won the Pulitzer Prize. I swear I never did a better job of directing in my life. If I never did anything else in my life, I put Archie MacLeish's play over. Larry Olivier saw it one night and came backstage and said to me, "Dear boy, you can't think that's any good. What a simply dreadful play, and your direction is..." He said it straight out, but it had no effect on my friendship for him or his for me. All of us work in a very difficult medium. We can do poor work and fail. In a sense Olivier's honesty was both completely personal and completely impersonal. When he said it, I just adored him. What could be nicer than a fellow artist saying he didn't like what I'd done. Implicit in his criticism was the clear sense that I like you and sympathize with you. The English are like that. When I gave her a direction, Vivien might say "You can't really mean that, can you?"

"Yes, Vivien, I do." And then we'd get into an argument, and something good would come out of it. She was a terrific dame. She won everybody over.

Her relationship to the cast sounds like Blanche's to the characters in the play.

Right. I saw it and I didn't try to smooth it over or make it easier for any of them. It was great with Karl Malden because he was so ill at ease when he was courting her. I certainly didn't patch them up.

Since the action was all blocked and staged, you might have thrown a couple of cameras in and covered it at the same time that you were doing your masters. Why didn't you?

If you light precisely for one camera, you can't light for another from a different angle. If you try to light for both, you won't get either one as good as it should be. Also, I'm a classicist. I made up my mind how a scene should be shot and from where it should be seen and that was it. I was very convinced of the rightness of what I was doing while I was doing it—not always afterwards, however. I covered myself so I could make a cut or two, but often I did not even shoot reverses. I'd been with actors enough and directed enough scenes so that I thought I knew where the values were. That doesn't mean I didn't cover myself at all. But I never shot like some guys did, all the way around the clock, 360 degrees.

Let's go into Zapata. *I'd like to ask you how that approach works out when you're doing big action scenes?*

The big outdoor scenes are different. You have to get a lot of shots there because you have to be able to break up the rhythm. But when it came to just enacted scenes, like in *Streetcar* or *Baby Doll*, I didn't shoot enough coverage even by my own standards. When I got in the cutting room I was stuck with what I had. Later on I shot more.

STEINBECK'S
VIVA ZAPATA!
STARRING
MARLON
BRANDO
20th
CENTURY-FOX
Also Starring JEAN
PETERS
ANTHONY QUINN · JOSEPH WISEMAN · ARNOLD MOSS · ALAN REED · MARGO · HAROLD GORDON · LOU GILBERT
PRODUCED BY DARRYL F. ZANUCK · DIRECTED BY ELIA KAZAN · WRITTEN BY JOHN STEINBECK

VIVA ZAPATA!
(1952)

MEXICO, 1909. Emiliano Zapata (Marlon Brando), a peasant for whom possession of land is all-important, pleas to Díaz, Mexico's dictator, on behalf of his village. Their corn is ready for harvest, but their land has been taken. Zapata is forced into the role of warrior when the Federales attack his village. Hiding in the hills with his brother Eufemio (Anthony Quinn), he is asked by Aguirre (Joseph Wiseman), a cold-blooded, hard-line revolutionary, to fight on behalf of Madero and help return the land to the people. Zapata sends an envoy to speak with Madero, to see if he can be trusted.

In the meantime, he courts Josefa (Jean Peters), the daughter of a rich merchant. He even takes a job as chief horseman for a very rich hidalgo. But his attempt to turn middle class ends when he is arrested and about to be hanged. Eufemio and the peasants set Zapata free. When he orders his brother to cut the telegraph wires he defines himself forever as a revolutionary.

Zapata leads the Army of the South to victory, and now a hero, he weds Josefa. He meets with Madero, now the President, who says that giving the land to the peasants will take time and insists that they disarm first. Zapata will wait, but not for long. General Huerta (Frank Silvera) wants to kill Zapata. But Madero, a decent but ineffectual man, thinks he can do things peacefully.

Zapata's people are stacking their guns when they learn that Huerta's army is on its way to kill them. Huerta assassinates Madero, and war starts again. Aguirre ruthlessly pushes Zapata to execute one of his oldest friends. War is a costly business, but they fight, and they win.

Pancho Villa (Alan Reed) and Zapata meet in the capital and Villa leaves Zapata to be President, much against his will. Peasants from his village complain to Zapata about his brother. When Zapata finds himself reacting exactly as Díaz had earlier, he walks out on the Presidency, grabs his guns and goes home.

Eufemio is killed by a peasant whom Zapata had trained to stand up for himself. Zapata and his guerrillas hide in the hills badly in need of arms and ammunition.

Generals Carranza and Obregón plot to kill Zapata, goaded by a now turncoat Aguirre. They entice Zapata into town for supplies. Despite knowing it is likely to be a trap, Zapata goes and is brutally cut down. But his legend lives on as his horse Blanco is seen, running free, high in the mountains.

How did Viva Zapata! *come to be?*

I always thought Zapata was a fascinating figure because of one act. He got power and walked away from it. The question of political power and personal power has always interested me. I was living next to John Steinbeck, who was a close friend of mine in those years. He was between marriages and had been having a very bad time. Talking to him one day, I said I thought Zapata's story would make a good film. He said he'd been thinking about doing it for years. So John went to Mexico and did a thorough research job. He lived right in Cuernavaca, about twenty miles from where Zapata's capital was. I guess in a way I saved his life. I was on the top of my game at that time—I've been up and down a lot as you gather. I enjoy both places.

Equally?

I really enjoy being in battle. I love fighting out of a hole. It's exhilarating to me. And I like to get people angry because they should be angry. Anyway, I was at the top then. Zanuck would have done anything I asked because of the favor I'd done for him by taking over *Pinky*. So I told him I had an idea for a film about Zapata and the Mexican revolution. He knew none of the history, but there was something about Darryl that was innately rebellious. He got a little intrigued, and when I said that John Steinbeck would write the script, he said he would produce it. That was a blow to me because I wanted to produce it myself. But as things worked out in effect he didn't produce it, and in effect I was at least as much author as John, although I never said it or in any way tried to take credit for it. I was at the typewriter and John was mostly thinking about his next novel, *East of Eden*. He sat there doing leather work. He always had tools. I would write a line or two and say, "How's this?" and he'd give me a line or a way of talking, that sort of semi-classical, rather rigid dialogue. We worked hard at that script, but I don't think we really ever entirely licked it. Zanuck made a few suggestions, one of which was seeing Zapata's white horse in the mountains at the very end. I didn't like it at the time but it certainly worked.

How did you begin preparing the film?

Up until 1941 the Mexican Revolution was the most photographed war in history—not only the battles themselves but also the men behind the battles. There were hundreds of pictures of them—conferring, drinking, embracing, and then going off and shooting at each other. I knew those photographs so well that I knew exactly how I was going to take advantage of the enormous opportunities that the script provided.

Why didn't you shoot the film in Mexico?

John and I wanted to. We went down there and met with a guy named [Gabriel] Figueroa. He was a very well-known cameraman, the darling of Mexican films, but very old-fashioned, always photographing fifty women holding candles and stuff like that. He also happened to be head of the Mexican union of stagehands, a Communist, and very political. After he read the script, he was cordial and sweet, but he said, "No, this must be this way." Whenever I heard the word "must," that was about the end of it. John was even more opposed to what he said than I was.

What was the disagreement about?

The Mexican Communists were using Zapata as a symbol of the struggle for land and bread, a struggle that the revolution has still not achieved. We were going to depict one of their heroes as a wavering man. Figueroa said, "What would you think if a Mexican company went to Illinois and made a picture of the life of Abraham Lincoln with a Mexican playing Abe?" I said, "Why don't you do it?" It was such a silly question. After all, I wasn't a kid. So John went back to New York in disgust. I was determined to make the film and started looking for somewhere on the border to shoot it.

You said that you didn't think you had licked the script. What seemed weak to you?

Nothing was weak. John thought we should have had more narrative in it, but I didn't like that idea. Its virtue was that it covered a lot of ground in very swift, vivid glimpses. The result was that you sometimes didn't know where you were or why. We took jumps and left out a lot of intervening history and some people had trouble following the story. Maybe it couldn't be licked. If I'd solved the problem of historical continuity, the film might have been longer and tamer. One of the things I've learned as I get older is that sometimes flaws cannot be corrected. At any rate, I found a town on the border on the Rio Grande. We used to go to Mexico for lunch. It was 120 degrees, there were rattle snakes all over the place, and Brando was dying from the heat. The heat did something to all the actors' faces. They lost that "actorish" look. I liked the cast and the whole experience very much although I wasn't satisfied with casting Jean Peters as Zapata's wife. I tried to get someone else and couldn't, so I finally gave up.

Who did you want?

Nobody in particular. I tested Julie Harris, but she wasn't right for it. I don't think I looked hard enough. Part of the difficulty was that if I cast a true Latin as Josefa, Brando would have looked like the Indiana boy he was.

What was the picture about for you?

I was trying to create a truthful myth about a hero's life. I was gaining eminence by then. I had received an Academy Award and was very much in demand. I was beginning to feel that I wanted to do my own work. It took me a long time to get to it. As I said, the first thing that attracted me to Zapata was his sense that power was corrupting him. He didn't want it. That's how I felt a lot. The other thing was that John and I were both ex-Communists, and Zapata's story allowed us to show metaphorically what had happened to the Communists in the Soviet Union—how their leaders became reactionary and repressive rather than forward thinking and progressive.

Zapata quit when he found himself doing exactly the same thing as the men he'd thrown out.

Yes, and the ironic thing was that when he walked out, he was defenseless, and they killed him. We dramatized it, but that was essentially what actually happened. He met with Pancho Villa, who was the General of the Army of the North, and they decided on how they were going to run the country. Zapata stayed in Mexico City as an administrator. Suddenly, he found that in order to keep control of the country, he had to become a repressive force, putting down one group or another. No one knows exactly why, but one day he got his best buddies, got on his horse and went back to Morales.

Do you feel that being corrupted by power is unique to Communism or that it's an inherent danger of power in general?

I admired Zapata for doing it, without in any way suggesting that that's a political answer. I still don't know what the political answer is. I guess I like our system best of all.

What was the Joseph Wiseman character, Aguirre, all about?

In another time and another place he would have been a strict Stalinist. He would not, could not, and thought no one should admit of human factors. He was the one who engineered the killing of Zapata in the end.

Aguirre's cold-blooded logic gives the film an anti-intellectual feel.

I've never been anti-intellectual. People have accused me of it, but they're wrong. To me someone with a truly reflective, disturbing, and investigative mind is the greatest fun in the world to be with. But I do feel that a lot of intellectual society people are just cheerleaders. They say things that they know their friends already agree with. Banalities are couched in highfalutin language, and nothing is the result of their own experience. So in that sense I do have an anti-liberal streak in me.

Maybe you're just a tummelor.

What's that? A fighter?

More like a guy who likes to stir it up, get people going.

I'm a gentle soul really. I just can't take much phoniness. I think it's more important for us to ask all the questions than to pretend you've got all the answers.

Let's get back to Zapata. Once you had the script, what did you do?

I have never since and probably will never again work as much with photographs as I did on *Zapata*. The "Casasolo" series was my inspiration for that picture. They gave me a sense of the reality and size of it. Remember the scene where Zapata and Villa were photographed together? That actually happened, and we had a picture of it. I gave that scene to my assistant and the casting director with the photograph and said, "Get types exactly like these people, dress them exactly like these people, and use the same number of extras as there are in this photo. I'll give you a week." I saw what they came up with, and it was perfect. All I did was put in two doors, one on one side for Zapata and his gang and the other on the other side for Villa and his gang. They all marched in and took their seats. The photographer snapped the picture and it was like a freeze frame. It's an exact reproduction of that book. Time after time after time I reproduced the effect of those photographs and in using that technique I found the truth of the period stylization. Later on the Mexican leftwing made a picture about Zapata and it was a disaster even in Mexico. They tried to romanticize the period and make a revolutionary mythic figure out of Zapata, make him a hero who achieved a great deal more than he actually did. He was a great man and a great revolutionary. He did make changes in Mexico. But the truth of my film and not their film is that the Revolution has changed Mexico very little. I know what I'm talking about because not long ago I was in Mexico, and I followed President [Luís Alvarez] Echevería around one day. He had a bunch of rascals walk through the streets with him. I thought, they're not much different than they were in 1910. My first wife was a wonderful woman. She was on location with me for two and a half months. One day Zanuck sent me a telegram saying, "You're murdering me; you're behind schedule." When my wife showed it to me, I let out so many obscenities that she never showed me any of the others that he sent. When we finished shooting the picture she handed me a whole stack of them.

Did you ever read the script from top to bottom with the cast?

No, but I've done it on other pictures. I did that with *On the Waterfront*, *Splendor in the Grass*, and *A Face in the Crowd*, but the problem in *Zapata* couldn't be solved that way.

What did you see as the problem?

To capture the breadth, scope, violence, the misery, pain and idealism in the most physical, classical terms I could. I got a perfect start for that picture. That old Stalinist is on the rocks way down below yelling up to Zapata, and it echoes all across the mountains. That was the right scale, and I set it right off the bat. You can't talk about that picture, it's too much in and of itself. You can hardly analyze it. Also, I cast it well. There are no familiar faces in it. Even Brando at that time wasn't overly familiar. Zanuck kept complaining about Brando, saying, "I can't understand what he's saying." Brando gave a great performance.

He had a unique quality throughout the film, he was always looking out of the corner of his eye.

He was playing a peasant and a peasant does not reveal what he feels. He doesn't show any reaction. He knows that if he does, he'll get killed by the boss. That's what Brando does. He was terrific in that first scene where he protests to Díaz. He showed no emotion whatever.

Did you work with him on that?

Yes, I talked to him a lot. I think I directed him well, but you didn't really work with Brando. You told him what you wanted and tried to describe it in words that had meaning for him. By the time you finished telling him what a scene was about, he'd be way ahead of you. His talent used to fly. I discussed that scene with him in terms of the nature of the peasant, how a peasant thought, how he is almost mask-like, how he is trained not to show emotions, the whole way of coming in silently, not standing out, the humbleness. In the scenes with the men, i.e., where he embraces Gigi through the window, I said to him, "Don't be misled by what is in the script about how Zapata loves his wife. You'd do anything for the comrades that are dying with you, but Zapata has no use for women." I said, "Frankly, in the scene where he's courting, he has middle-class aspirations for a minute and that's okay. But there was a scene afterwards, where he was alone with his wife and I told him not to play it with love. It was not like a modern man's relationship to women at all. Women were just something to be used, knocked up, and left. The men were always leaving them behind for months.

And while they were together they relied on each other. Their safety was in their comradeship. My job was made easier because Brando loved Quinn personally. They were a great combination and had terrific affection for each other. We all used to go swimming in the river at night. It was a marvelous experience. Making films has been the greatest physical adventure of my life. Brando loved it too. I don't know what he's like now, I haven't seen him in years. I have greater admiration for him than any actor I ever knew.

You've described pretty much what happens in the wedding night scene. Zapata is alone with his wife, but he is drawn to the window, to his brother and the activities of his pals outside.

He's not only drawn, he wishes he were there. It is important to understand that with peasants, sexual intercourse isn't a big deal. It's become a big deal with us. Romantic love is a product of the leisure classes. It exists for the leisure classes. By the way, this is the way I would talk to Brando about it. I didn't do that wedding night scene right because they had to wear clothes. She should have had a nightgown on and he should have been naked. That would have been the truth of it. It was romanticized. That's the only scene in the picture I didn't like. But I would say to him simply, "You want to be out with them." I used to tell him that he doubts his capability. He's worried about dealing with the eminence and position he's gotten himself into. If an actor's honest, it's easy to open that door up, and for Brando it was simple.

Another thing Brando understood very readily was looking to another person for help. It was hard for him to do, but for example, once in a while he'd look for help from me. I told him he wanted help from his wife. Zapata was about to meet with politicians, people who had been well educated, and he was an illiterate peasant. He felt totally inadequate. He needed Josefa to teach him to read. Admitting your feelings and reaching out to a woman for help was a very big deal in that culture. But he had to do it. I would try to help Brando by giving him inner actions, what Stanislavsky called objectives.

You say that it was easy for him to open up self-doubt.

That's true for any sensitive person.

On the other hand, what a lot of actors do if they start to doubt themselves is get very tentative, which he doesn't do at all. Was that a result of giving him clear objectives?

No, that was just his talent. He played things full-heartedly.

Would you be so explicit as to say to him something about self-doubt?

Yes, I would talk about that, but I would never talk about his playing it with all his heart—a tummelor, huh?

You don't think so?

I guess I am. I've been in fights all my life. I've always gone my own way.

In your pictures you have a great affection for the tummelor, like Quinn as Eufemio in this picture.

I love Quinn in *Zapata*. One smart thing I did was give Brando and Quinn a way to act out their emotions physically—like embracing a friend between bars or when Brando had to fight with Quinn, I made sure there was a woman lying on the floor at Quinn's feet. I supplied physical elements that were so clear and explicit that it was easier for them to act.

Did you do that consciously?

In *Zapata* I tried to make everything external just as I tried in *Streetcar* to make everything internal.

You mentioned that in Panic in the Streets, *you were careful to not over-psychologize.*

Here it wasn't a matter of under-psychologizing. It was a matter of letting the characters play out their emotions. In *Zapata* if someone felt something about someone, he acted out those feelings. He shot him or embraced him, but he didn't say, "Why did you do that to me?" or "What was the meaning of that?" The emotions were primitive and simple.

When Zapata goes back to Quinn to make him return what he has stolen, the peasants stand and watch. Quinn rages then storms, out taking the woman at his feet, another man's wife, with him.

It's easy to play that. Quinn understood it well. He's half Mexican. And also, as much as Brando and Quinn loved each other, they had a macho competition going, which I didn't discourage.

While Zapata talks to the peasants about the need to do things for themselves, the man who's wife Quinn has taken moves out of frame and we hear shots fired. You cut to the outside and Quinn emerges from a tunnel in a blur. He staggers into the light and into a close shot. He hollers, "Zapata, Zapata," and falls out of frame. Brando is barely visible in the tunnel behind him. He runs out quickly and drops to his knees beside his dead brother. It all happens in the same shot. What did you go for there?

I gave the actors no direction whatsoever. Not one word. By the time we shot that scene they had a good relationship. If you start giving directions to any actor like Brando in a scene like that, you're very liable to hurt yourself. One thing a director has to know is when to keep his mouth shut, to wait and see what the actor does instinctively, personally, without trying to fill any preconceived patterns. That's good director-to-director advice. If I had said something, I would have spoiled it. That's an elemental scene between two people who love each other. Brando fussed with Quinn's dead body, he did something with his face. Then he brought Quinn's dead hands up to his own face. That was all Brando. Only if you're not getting what you want do you start giving directions.

Brando looks at him and look and looks, then finally starts to cry. Almost anyone else would have jumped straight to the emotion.

I could give you a lot of nonsense about what I told him, but the fact is I didn't do anything. I was smart enough not to do anything. Also, the position of their bodies helped a lot, the fact that Quinn was recumbent and Brando was over him. That posture itself was an associative thing. In a situation like that you try to get an original or unexpected reaction. Very often what you will think of will be a cliché of your own, something that you've done before or that you've seen, but not something that you might actually do in that situation. A good actor may do something far more original and uncalculated. Whereas the calculation of a smart director might be subtle but still a cliché.

Did you rehearse that scene?

No, I might have asked Brando to crouch in there for a minute to see if the top frame line was high enough. You frame it full enough anyway so you're not taking any chances. Brando was aware of the technical problem and was attentive to it. As far as rehearsing the emotion, you never do that with any actor in any scene like that. Shoot the rehearsal. The actor is very relieved because he knows you can't get that kind of feeling up often. If you're lucky you can get it once. You stay away from him, don't talk too much, and pray for a miracle.

Aside from the problem with frame lines, isn't it difficult to light when you leave the actor's movements wide open?

In a scene like this, you don't want lighting that's too tricky. You don't want to call attention to anything but what the actor is hopefully going to achieve. It's very important to know when to keep quiet and not be the big chief. It's very important to give the actors the sense that they're more important really than you are.

By contrast what did you do when you had to plan out and set up the big action scenes?

The action scenes were far easier to shoot than I thought they'd be. I had never done a Western on location. I had to be very clear where things came in and where they went out of frame, what screen direction they were moving in, where they passed by the camera and where the camera was going to be, what angle the camera was going to be shooting from. You can pick up coverage by changing your angles a little bit. Frankly, after you've shot horses running across the screen about twenty times, you get better at it.

How much would you map out beforehand?

Remember what I said about *Panic in the Streets* and New Orleans, about how the set is important in terms of giving you ideas? That happened over and over again on *Zapata*. On the other hand, the scene of the peasants coming down the hill and falling in behind *Zapata* when he was under arrest, was an image of my own. It just came to me. I thought of people bleeding down from the mountains. So I looked for a hillside where the bush and the shrubs stopped at a certain point. I chased extras up in there and then had them come down so they suddenly appeared in a clear field, below the brush line. They all gathered behind and around Zapata and finally, they appear in front as well, and bring the procession to a halt.

There's a face-off at the end of that scene which is very interesting. You set it up so the audience expects a huge, explosive confrontation. Instead it's very gentle, very quiet.

The next step to being quiet among these kinds of people is killing. I'd had experience with that. I'd been in a lot of violence, in the war and in the South. Things move very quickly from quiet confrontation to deadly violence. Again I didn't want the peasants to show any feeling. It fit the intention of the scene and their characterization for them to gather around Zapata and his captors as though it was a haphazard, almost accidental, thing.

In most of the action scenes the camera is in a fixed position even if it pans. But on occasion you will cut to a dolly shot.

I think you'll find that dolly shot in the scene we've been talking about is a close-up on Brando.

What informs the decision to go to a tracking shot?

That's just A, B, C. You must always keep in mind the dramatic intention of the scene you're shooting. What was dramatic there was that Zapata apparently doesn't notice or doesn't indicate that he knows that the peasants were marching along with him. He acts as though nothing is happening. We had to go close on that shot and dolly because what I wanted to show was his expression or his lack of expression. We later contrasted that with a similar dolly

shot on the police chief beginning to notice what was happening. The point was to contrast those two attitudes.

Then there's the moment when Zapata declares war. He tells his brother to cut the telegraph wire. Quinn really goes for it.

That was all Tony. He just loved doing that. He reared the horse up on his hind legs and cut the wire.

Did he do all his own riding and stunts?

Oh yeah, he was a terrific rider and he loved it. Brando was a natural athlete and a good rider, but Quinn was brilliant. He dominated the horse like good riders do.

You're very at ease and comfortable in talking about Zapata. *You obviously enjoy acting out primitive emotions.*

You're right. There's a danger though, because after a while you get so you can make anything exciting, you can pep up any scene with violence. You have to be sure that the violence is true and within scale and has some character to it. In *Zapata* the violence was all completely liberating in the first third and in the last third you felt a terrific constriction. Everybody was moving very slowly or just sitting and looking. There were long shots where nothing happened. It was a well-directed picture, better than I knew at the time. I had worked very hard in preparation. John's notes were marvelous, too. That was the first picture I did where I felt, I can really be a good director. Now I'll have made at least one good picture in my life. I really felt proud of that picture when I got it done. I think if it weren't for *Panic in the Streets* I might not have been able to do it. I learned a lot from that movie. I forgave my sins on *The Sea of Grass*.

There's a terrific texture to Zapata.

You know what helped? The fact that they were all perspiring. The actors took their clothes off when they weren't working and then they had to put those hot woolen things back on, and of course there was no makeup allowed.

Brando wasn't made up at all?

He did something with his eyes.

The scene where Brando courts Jean Peters—

Jean's pretty good in those scenes. They're called *dichos*—courtship through proverbs. It's a Mexican tradition. That was John's idea. It was a brilliant one.

They all get so hot. Brando had sweat pouring off him.

It fit well with what the scene was really about. I was trying to say that he was proposing to a woman who was out of his class, that he was suddenly in a society that was stuffy and he felt like he didn't belong. So I accentuated the heat.

There's a lot of ritual in the film.

I'm very aware of ritual in all areas—patterns that are repeated, patterns that are reassuring.

Do you approach ritualistic material in any particular way?

I used to be a dancer. I became aware of the patterns of movement and the fact that the patterns themselves spoke as much as the nature of the movement. I think I have a strong classic feeling and that plays into this thing about ritual.

There is one scene in particular where a classical pattern works itself out. One of Zapata's oldest friends is accused by Aguirre of being a spy. A kangaroo court finds him guilty. Zapata is torn between duty and love when he enters the room where his friend, Pablo, is held captive. Pablo begs Zapata to execute him himself, to not let anyone else do it. You cut to outside and a shot is heard off camera.

You can't go wrong with that because the main thing is the idea for the scene which is that Zapata goes into the room. Once inside the less he responds the better. An important part of directing is having a true idea, an idea that contains a pattern of movement that in and of itself almost tells it all. Then you have Brando as the guy who has to do it. I'm giving credit where it's due. It was my idea, but it's not a particularly original one. That's a characteristic scene in the history of a revolution. A spy is caught, and he has to be killed. Even when you're not sure he is a spy, it's safer to kill him. An often serviceable way to think of a scene like that is to suppose it were silent. That scene was done in purely visual terms. I thought of that whole sequence as a unit. I planned and shot it that way. I wanted the whole film to be pictorially eloquent. I worked harder on that than I did on *On the Waterfront.* The other picture I worked particularly hard on was *America America. America America* is very much like *Zapata* in that it's episodic and full of very vividly pictorialized sequences. There's a great relationship between those two pictures directorally. As far as what the pictures say, the movement of the camera and the movement of the actors, there's nothing accidental in those two pictures. Whatever is wrong is my fault.

Yet, you obviously took great delight in winging it on Panic in the Streets. *You said it was very enriching.*

It freed me from gabbing. I had a personal ritual in *Panic in the Streets,* which was I never carried a script. I just made pictures. After that I hardly ever carried a script around. I may have had somebody check the lines to see if they were saying them more or less right. But my ideal of films is that they are a series of vividly, highly colored moving photographs.

When you said there was nothing accidental, had you worked out your blocking before you went on the set?

I had the general idea. I got on the set and would refine, adapt, or condition any of the moves.

What do you do when in order to get the shot you want, you have to get an actor to be in a place or posture which is physically awkward?

You rely on the placement of objects. You put things where the actor has to go get them. There's often only one place you can put a camera in a realistic location. I've been on locations so goddamn tight that I couldn't get in. There was one in *Panic in the Streets* in the hold of a little motorboat. Nobody got in there. The camera fit but the operator didn't. I don't know how he changed focus. He must have reached in a window or something.

What do you do if in order for it to look right on the screen an actor has to be in a physical position that is not natural for him?

There are a lot of positions in life that are not natural. You make up a reason for it. You're in a natural position now. You're leaning forward because I'm lying down. If I were sitting up, you would be sitting up straight. If there's some distortion necessary, give the distortion a reason. There's nothing better than the fact that the cabin is very low in *Zapata* so they have to bend over. You don't have to look at the actor's face all the time. That's a theater convention. If at a particular moment it's important to see his face clearly, you can cheat the location. All you need is a little piece of a set out of focus anyway. You just move to another set and shoot that part of the scene.

There are a number of places in Zapata *where blocks of scenes seemed to have been visualized as sequences.*

I did that a lot. For example, when they shoot Madero, he loses his glasses. That was an idea that came from my knowledge of gangsters. They shot a guy in Chicago that way, staring at automobile headlights. The film was full of funny things like that. There's a lot of humor in all my films. I'm not witty, but I'm amused at a lot of things in life, and I'm not afraid. Courage has a lot to do with laughter. Courageous people laugh a lot. They're not frightened, not tense, not uptight. I developed a sense of toughness and intelligence. Intelligence and laughter go together. And I'm also candid. I react very well to criticism. Someone can tell me he doesn't like something I did, and it doesn't make any difference. I'll listen. I have some merits, some demerits too.

You said that there was a sense of competition between Brando and Quinn.

Quinn said to me one day, "You son of a bitch, why do you give Brando more direction than you give me? You're always talking to him. You don't talk to me." I said, "Tony, that's not true." He was furious. His face went white, and he wouldn't speak to me for a day because I wouldn't recognize that I talked to Brando more than him. Later he said to me, "He's your favorite." I replied, "He isn't, Tony. I think a lot of you." Then I told Brando that Quinn was suspicious of us, that he felt I was giving him more direction. Do you know what Brando did? He chummed up to Tony, and that was the end of it. Quinn is only half Mexican, but he's typical. The Mexicans I've known are the most suspicious people I ever met in my life, except the Puerto Ricans, who are worse. They're all paranoid. But the competition between Brando and Quinn was wonderfully fruitful and creative. By the way, there's nothing wrong with actors competing, as long as they're competing to be good and not to be stars. In fact, I sometimes try to arouse competition. For example, I often praise an actor openly. That makes every other actor on the set want the same praise. It's nice to tell them they were good when they do something well. It makes them want more. After all, they're hanging on you. They can't see themselves. So when they deserve praise I always articulate it. I don't believe in playing cool. One beautiful thing about actors is that they're so exposed. They're not being criticized only for their behavior, but for their legs and breasts, for their double chin; their whole being is exposed to criticism. How can you not embrace them and how can you feel anything but gratitude toward these people? I like actors and I believe my films show it. You look at them and see that whoever directed them likes actors. And some actors I've really loved. I would do anything for Karl Malden, Lee Remick, Julie Harris, Andy Griffith and lots of others.

After Zapata pays court and gets rejected by the perspective father-in-law, he walks out and gets ambushed. His rescue is elaborately ritualistic. Anthony Quinn picks up two stones and beats them together. A couple of women pick it up, and soon everyone starts beating stones together. A similar action occurs in Waterfront. *When the hoodlums attack the church, they hit the windows with sticks.*

That's not only ritual, it's the way peasants often communicate. They go back to primitive methods. A lot of their communication was under surveillance, under duress and threat so they learned to communicate in ways that unsophisticated people do, with just a look or a gesture or by throwing a rock. They know that if they say the wrong thing they'll get walloped. *Zapata* is full of nonverbal communication, like washing somebody's face when he's dead, like joining in the parade. I searched a lot for true peasant behavior.

You have said that your general approach to material is to look for the moment that is the essence of a scene and build everything towards that. Could you pick a scene from Zapata *and describe exactly what you mean and how you went about getting that moment?*

Take the scene where Quinn and Brando are in their camp and Aguirre comes to convince them to fight for Madero. I could have let Joe Wiseman ride up and say, "I want to meet you. My name is Aguirre." But I wanted to show how far up in the mountains Zapata was, how isolated he was, how everybody was afraid of him, how they were like animals holed up. So I picked the right way of doing it. Wiseman yells across a mountain chasm. You have to investigate the nature of every scene. I always try to investigate scenes on two levels. One is the realistic level, which is that Aguirre comes looking for Zapata. Then there is the poetic level, where you look for overtones. I was influenced in that scene by [Alexander] Dovzhenko. Did you ever see *Aerograd (Air City)*? There's a conversation in the woods between two old men. They are many hundreds of yards apart. They have to yell at each other. I never forgot that. It's one of the great moments in film to me.

When you talk about the realistic and the poetic level, what exactly do you mean?

On the realistic level Jeff Young is sitting here talking to Elia Kazan and asking him questions with a tape recorder between us. On the poetic level a young director is asking questions of an aging director who's been through a lot. Knowledge is possibly being handed down over a chasm of time. So how do you light it? If you're going for the realistic level you can put overhead lights on or do it any other way. But if you light it for the poetic level, Jeff is back lit, there's a breeze coming in, we're both smoking cigars. There's a simple meaning and a real, deep meaning. There's what you see and what you feel out of an event. Suppose you see a fight in the street, that's what you see. But what you feel depends on your mood, above all who's in the fight and the circumstances under which it takes place and that precede your seeing the fight. It's an obvious thing.

Except that you have almost an infinite variety of choices.

Sure, that's why you have to analyze very deeply what everything means to you. Take Brando and Quinn's fight. The only thing that makes a fight mean something is when it's between two people that love each other. That's the hardest kind of fight to have. It's almost unbearable.

Let's see if we can relate that to the last scene in Zapata *where his dead body is dumped on the cistern.*

That's one of my favorite moments in film—directed by me or anybody else. On a realistic level, a body has merely been dumped in the middle of the town square. On a poetic level the body has been dumped on a cistern top which is hollow and makes a heavy thudding sound. You feel the weight of the body from that sound. You know how much life and potency it once had. You don't let the women in the square move right away. They sit there in the shadows and their memories are full of the deaths of heroes. Finally they move, and they wash Zapata's body like they might have washed Christ's body so many centuries before.

You said that you had wanted this film to express the truth of the myth. But doesn't it also support the need for myth itself? At the very end the peasants see Zapata's horse and refuse to believe that he's dead.

That's true, but there's also the feeling, just a very simple notion, that he left something behind, that his life wasn't lived in vain. It meant something to the peasants, especially the peasants who make myths. I think it's a very good thing when the hero accomplishes something that he's unaware of but other people aren't.

MAN ON A TIGHTROPE
(1953)

THE CIRKUS CERNIK, headed by Karel Cernik (Fredric March), a determined though secret anti-Communist, goes from village to village spreading what joy it can in Communist-controlled post–World War II Czechoslovakia. Karel and his circus are being closely watched by the secret police, who suspect him of subversive activities. Karel believes that his daughter (Terry Moore) Tereza's American boyfriend, Joe (Cameron Mitchell), is a spy.

Karel's wife, Zama (Gloria Grahame), makes his life a misery. She constantly belittles him, flirts with the lion tamer, and arouses everyone's anger, especially the dwarf's, one of the clowns, who particularly loves and admires Karel. Krofta (Richard Boone), whom Karel trusts completely, leads the workers, putting up and pulling down the tents and keeping the show running as they move from town to town.

Karel is hauled in by the police for questioning and accused by their chief (Adolphe Menjou) of crimes against the state. He is given 48 hours to conform to the party line or his circus will be taken from him and given to someone more loyal to the party.

Karel decides to take his circus and escape to the West. He's been thinking about it for some time; now, circumstances have forced his hand.

In the meantime, Joe and Tereza go for a swim and she learns

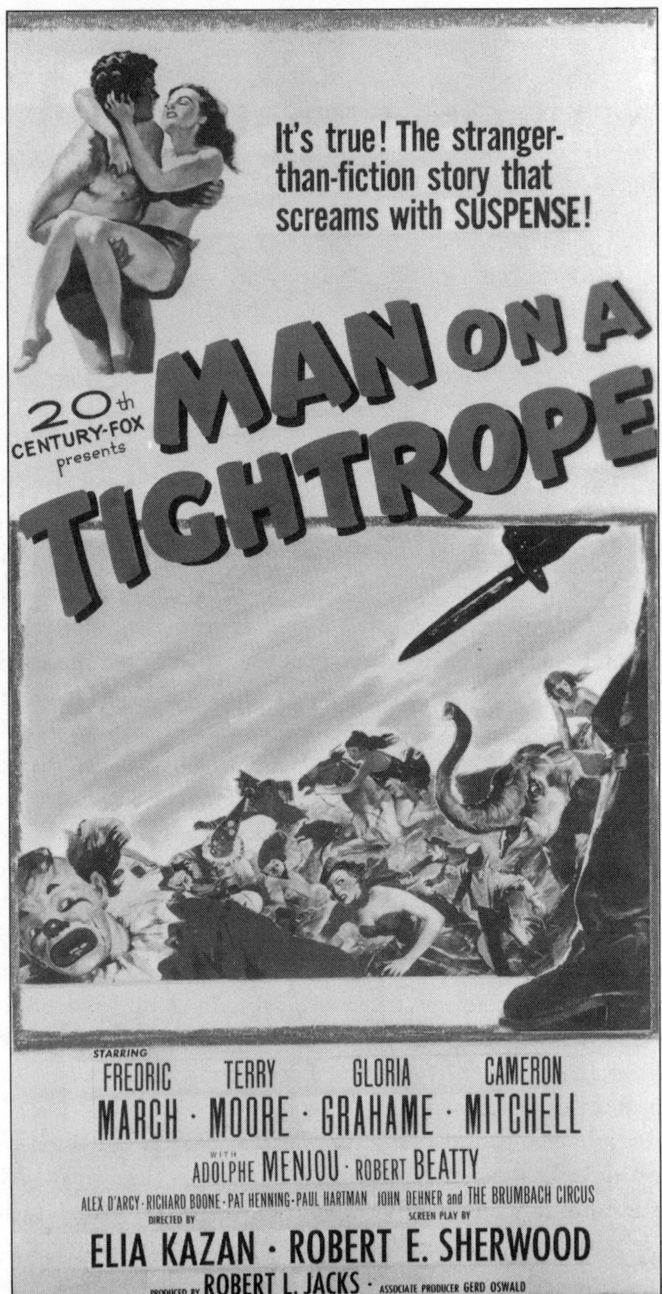
It's true! The stranger-than-fiction story that screams with SUSPENSE!
20th CENTURY-FOX presents
MAN ON A TIGHTROPE
STARRING
FREDRIC MARCH · TERRY MOORE · GLORIA GRAHAME · CAMERON MITCHELL
WITH ADOLPHE MENJOU · ROBERT BEATTY
ALEX D'ARCY · RICHARD BOONE · PAT HENNING · PAUL HARTMAN JOHN DEHNER and THE BRUMBACH CIRCUS
DIRECTED BY ELIA KAZAN · SCREEN PLAY BY ROBERT E. SHERWOOD
PRODUCED BY ROBERT L. JACKS · ASSOCIATE PRODUCER GERD OSWALD

that he is an American soldier. The dwarf, who overhears them, runs off; it looks as if he is the informer.

Karel settles on a plan to make a bold daylight run for the border and swings into action. Zama's love for her husband is renewed, now that he is again the forceful man she once knew.

In an intricate cross-cut action scene full of diversionary tactics, the circus makes it across the border. Karel gets killed by Krofta, who turns out to have been the spy, but he dies a hero, having sacrificed himself for the freedom of all the others.

Man on a Tightrope *is a very simple story about a man's struggle to get out of a repressive state, to be free. How did it all come about?*

I was a Communist once. And despite the fact that I had gone through a violent break with the party, I still found myself thinking like a Communist. *Man on a Tightrope* was based on a wonderful true story, and I thought it was a good yarn, but still, I had great resistance to making it because it was against the Soviet Union. And I discovered that I still unconsciously thought of the Soviet Union as a progressive political phenomenon. I finally said to myself, If you've got the courage, you should make this picture. The script was written by a great and wonderful man at the end of his life, mostly out of a desire to pay his bills. Despite the real inner dignity of Bob Sherwood, he'd written a mediocre script. But I thought if I could get a small circus, the real thing, with real clowns, real freaks, real animals and just do the run for the border, I'd have something worth showing, worth photographing and worth directing.

I fell in love with the Brumbach Circus. When I wasn't shooting interiors in Munich, I practically lived with the troupe. The dwarf used to buy me brandy. "Two friends, two cognacs." That's what he always said to me. Then I got to like the equestrian lady and the old man who ran the circus and the old people around the circus, the trainers and everyone else. It was just great. It's too bad that I couldn't cast the whole movie with real circus people, but that was the Hollywood compromise. I couldn't have gotten the money to make the picture any other way.

I also had a terrific experience working with the Bavarian people. They had just lost the war, and their equipment was very poor. The mud was hub deep, and the trucks, after sitting in it all night, wouldn't start in the morning. The crew was made up of the toughest human beings I ever met. I can't say I liked them all or that I was in any way sympathetic to them, but there was something about their absolute fortitude in the face of continual misery that Americans can never understand or match. We can't even conceive of the hardship these people were living under. The picture was not so hot because the love story was terrible. I wasn't crazy about some of the actors in it. I don't think I directed it very well, but I think that despite all that, what shows through is genuine affection for the circus and for Freddy March, whom I really loved. He was a marvelous, marvelous man. I made a speech for Freddy down at the Players club in New York. That's how much I liked him. It takes me about a week to write a speech. Anyway as a life experience it was great just to know another society. It was an adventure like being on safari and building a building at the same time. And doing both under terrible conditions. It was always foggy in the morning, and it rained at least half the time. We'd hurry up and shoot whenever we had any sunlight. It was wonderful having to rise to the challenge.

Also I partly broke myself of my belief in Soviet Communism. It's hard for anybody who wasn't a Communist to understand how strong a hold those beliefs had on you. Your emotional commitment keeps overriding everything your intellect and common sense tell you. It's akin to a kind of religious faith. After all, Stalin was as bad as Hitler, maybe worse. Hitler killed six million Jews. Stalin killed the same number of people, maybe more. He was a monster, but your mind, once you've been a committed Communist, doesn't want to face that fact. So in a way the film was an important purgative thing for me to do. In another sense, it was a simple play of sweet affectionate people against ritualized violence.

On *Panic in the Streets* I'd hired lots of blacklisted actors like Zero Mostel. Freddy March was blacklisted and I got him the lead in the picture by pulling a lot of strings and throwing my weight around. At the same time, my feeling as a liberal was that I should never work with Adolphe Menjou, who was famous for his right-wing, reactionary politics. But then I thought, he's an actor, not a politician. There's no reason why if I got one side work, I shouldn't get the other side work. A man is an artist first. I've always thought Menjou was a good actor, and he behaved marvelously—professionally and in every other way.

There are several love stories in the film. Which one didn't you like?

The one between Freddy March and Gloria Grahame. She was a fantastic creature, but the love story was ridiculous. The other romance was silly, too—Terry Moore and Cameron Mitchell swimming in the river. That was a lot of corn. They did it. I admired Terry. She had a lot of guts. That water was freezing and moving very fast.

It's a cliché romantic interlude.

The circus though was different. I really enjoyed photographing the elephants and the trainer, Pat Henning. He was a good friend of mine, too. We worked together again in *On the Waterfront.*

I liked the mother.

She was the real thing, and you can tell it immediately. There really isn't much you can say about that picture. It's not very interesting except to me. I had a great time doing it, and I learned even more about how to wing things. I had more adventure off the screen than on. It was fascinating. The Germans either knew how to crawl and be servants or they knew how to be bosses. They were servants around me. The food I got, the attention, the gifts. It was another way of life.

From Zapata *through* Waterfront *there's a political progression and it's coincident with your testimony before the House Un-American Activities Committee and the whole McCarthy era. I don't know how much you're willing to talk about it.*

I don't mind getting into anything with you. I don't have any concern about hiding anything. It just isn't relevant to *Man on a Tightrope*. You should ask me about *On the Waterfront* because that was related to the issue, and it had a parallel plot.

Fine, then. Let's cover the *Waterfront*.

A STREETCAR NAMED DESIRE

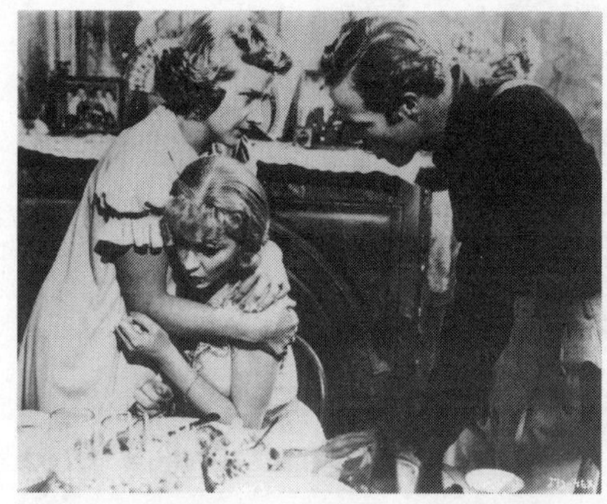

"I did improvisations . . . some had to do with making Kim Hunter (Stella) feel drawn, skewered between loyalty to Jessica Tandy (Blanche in the play) and loyalty to Marlon Brando (Stanley)."

"Tennessee Williams equals Blanche. . . . And Blanche is torn between a desire to preserve her tradition . . . and her attraction to what is going to destroy her tradition. . . . Blanche wants the very thing that's going to crush her."

"Brando . . . made Stanley petulant. He wants everything his own way. If he doesn't get it, he'll either beat you up or he'll cry."

VIVA ZAPATA!

"The first thing that attracted me to Zapata was his sense that power was corrupting him." Zapata (Marlon Brando shown here with Joseph Wiseman as Fernando Aguirre) quit when he found himself repeating the exact same action as his predecessor.

Kazan gave a photo of Pancho Villa and Zapata and their men from the Casasolo series to his assistant and told him to match it. "I saw what they came up with and it was perfect. . . .Time after time after time I reproduced the effect of those photographs. . . ."

Brando was playing a peasant and a peasant does not reveal what he feels. . . . He knows if he does, he'll get killed. . . . He was terrific in the first scene where he protests to Díaz. He showed no emotion whatever."

"Making films has been the greatest physical adventure of my life. Brando loved it too. . . .I have greater admiration for him than any actor I ever knew."

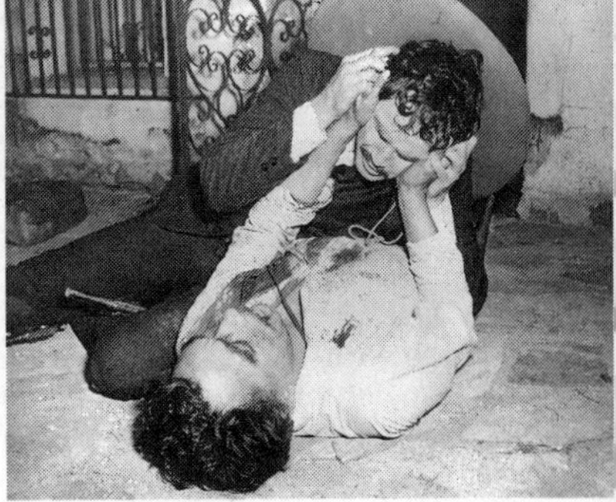

"Another thing Brando understood very well was looking to another person for help. It was hard for him to do, but Zapata needed his wife, Josefa (Jean Peters) to teach him to read."

"That was all Brando. . . . I was smart enough not to do anything. . . . The position of their bodies helped a lot, the fact that his brother, Eufemio (Anthony Quinn), was recumbent and Brando was over him. The posture itself was an associative thing."

An image just came to Kazan. "I thought of people bleeding down from the mountains. . . . I chased a bunch of extras up a hill and had them come down so they suddenly appeared behind and around Zapata."

The dumping of Zapata's dead body is "one of my favorite moments in film—directed by me or anybody else."

MAN ON A TIGHTROPE

"... I thought if I could get a small circus, the real thing ... and just do the run for the border, I'd have something worth filming. ..."

"Freddy March was blacklisted and I got him the lead in the picture by pulling a lot of strings and throwing my weight around."

ON THE WATERFRONT
(1954)

THE WATERFRONT CRIME COMMISSION is investigating mob influence on the docks in Hoboken, New Jersey, and putting pressure on union members to testify against their corrupt leadership. Local boss Johnny Friendly (Lee J. Cobb) is threatened because Joey Doyle has promised to speak out.

Terry Malloy (Marlon Brando), a boxer turned longshoremen, is told to lure Joey up to his tenement roof. He does so, using their shared interest in racing pigeons as a ruse. Doyle is killed. Terry is shaken. He liked Joey. Besides, the bosses had told Terry they only wanted to talk to Joey. Johnny Friendly had always been a pal, and Terry's own brother Charlie the Gent (Rod Steiger) is Friendly's right-hand man. But what they did wasn't right. For the first time something like a conscience stirs in Terry.

His confusion and shame grow as he meets, falls in love with, and courts Joey's sister, Edie (Eva Marie Saint). At the same time, the local priest, Father Barry (Karl Malden), is determined to make the workers stand up for themselves. He tries to persuade them to break the code of silence and talk to the Crime Commission.

Terry is subpoenaed. Because of his awakening conscience and his growing love for Edie, he can no longer remain deaf and dumb. He has to think about right and wrong. Friendly learns of Terry's waffling and orders Charlie to straighten his brother out. If not, Terry will be killed. Charlie leans on Terry, but instead of

COLUMBIA PICTURES presents
MARLON BRANDO
On The Waterfront
AN ELIA KAZAN PRODUCTION
co-starring
KARL MALDEN · LEE J. COBB with ROD STEIGER · PAT HENNING and introducing EVA MARIE SAINT
Produced by SAM SPIEGEL Screen Play by BUDD SCHULBERG Music by LEONARD BERNSTEIN Directed by ELIA KAZAN

being persuaded, Terry realizes that for his whole life he has been sold out by his brother, by Friendly, and even by himself. "I could've been a contender. I could've had class and been somebody..."

Having failed to bring Terry into line, Charlie is murdered. That pushes Terry over the line, and he testifies against Friendly and the mob. His friends, co-workers, and even the local cops turn on him for being a stool pigeon. Everyone except the priest and Edie, who begs him to get away from the people she knows will kill him.

Instead, Terry goes down to the docks to get what he believes is his by right. In front of all the longshoremen, he nearly gets beaten to death by Friendly. But because he has stood up for all of them, Terry emerges as a hero. The men stand behind him against Friendly and follow him in to work.

People who don't like On the Waterfront*—even some who do—see the film as an apologia for a stool pigeon.*

There's a difference. *On the Waterfront* is a story of informing where it seems like the greater good, despite the fact it goes against the code of the community. The script was based on a set of real events which had nothing to do with my involvement with the Communist Party or the information I later gave to the House Un-American Activities Committee. Those fellows in *Waterfront* were criminals. It was based on the life story of a guy named DiVincenzo, who I knew, whose house I ate at. He lived through the same goddamn thing that Terry Malloy goes through in the film. The waterfront was a gangster-dominated, ritualized, Mafia-coded society where no one ever said who was brutalizing them. Even when they knew who killed somebody, nobody ever talked. That was absolutely a valid story of the waterfront. But when people said there are some parallels to what I had done, I couldn't and wouldn't deny it. It does have some parallels. But I wasn't concerned with them nor did I play on them. They were not my reason for making the film. I had wanted to do a picture about the waterfront long before any of the HUAC business came up.

I'm very curious about your version of the McCarthy period and the Hollywood blacklist.

Anybody who informs on other people is doing something disturbing and even disgusting. It doesn't sit well on anyone's conscience. But at that time I felt a certain way, and I think it has to be judged from the perspective of 1952. It all seems like ancient history now, but remember the Korean War was still going on. Russia was a monolithic power. What astonished me is how a lot of lefties went through Czechoslovakia and Poland, then Czechoslovakia the second time and still never said a thing against the Soviet Union. I thought that was a sort of slavery of the mind. I still think so. I used to know a lot about the Communist Party. I used to go downtown to Twelfth Street, where their headquarters were, get orders and go back like a good ritualized lefty and try to carry them out. Our orders were to try to take over the Group Theatre. It was child's play in one sense, but in another sense it wasn't. We were doing something terrible, going into Group Theatre meetings after we had a caucus and exerting pressure and insisting that things should be done a certain way. I thought, nobody knows the truth about any of this. The Party was getting all kinds of money out of Hollywood and out of the theater. Communists were in a lot of organizations—unseen, unrecognized, unbeknownst to anybody. I thought, if I don't talk, nobody will know about it. And although, as I say, it was disturbing to inform on my colleagues, when I thought about what it meant symbolically, about what would have happened if I'd lied and said I had no idea about what was going on, it would have been worse. So I said, I'm not going to do that. But I never told one goddamn lie about it. Also, the guys I named were all known. Everybody knew who they were, so it wasn't a big deal. They, of course, suffered some from it. I also did something else that nobody ever mentions. I told three of them beforehand. I told Clifford Odets. He said he was going to do the same thing. I told Mrs. Strasberg, and I told another guy, who told me to go screw myself. I was open to that extent about it. I didn't duck it. It was a difficult situation, and I felt like I felt. People say I did it for money, but I never did anything for money in my life.

Certainly the accusation about you is that [Spyros] Skouras, who at the time was head of Fox, called you in and said, "Talk or you don't work anymore."

I'm not interested in proving it, but that's an outright lie. He never did that to anybody. He didn't put any pressure on me to do anything. He couldn't have. I wasn't pressurable by those people, and I was certainly not pressurable for the sake of money. Actually, after I testified, they cut my directing salary in half. Skouras never bullied me. Neither did Zanuck. They were not great guys, but they were better guys than that. What I really thought, looking at it in the biggest sense, was that what I did was the better of two mean alternatives. The only other option was to remain silent and pretend I didn't know better when people said there's no Communist conspiracy. Nonsense. There was a conspiracy. I don't know what happened in other unions or what happened in other parts of the country, but I knew what was going on in the film and theater business. I was in it. I was in with V. J. Jerome—the head of our branch of the party—all the time. I was carrying orders to the Group Theatre guys all the time. I was head of their unit. I knew a lot about it. I knew a lot about what their other goals were, the way they operated. I think they were a force in this country. They were in many secret places, including the State Department. People say that was ridiculous. It wasn't ridiculous. At that time the Communist countries were a solid bloc, a single organization until Yugoslavia broke away from them.

Taking all that you say at face value, you still had to live with the fact that you were an ally of Joseph McCarthy.

I hated McCarthy. It was embarrassing to be on the same side as him. But I didn't terrorize people. He did. I didn't lie. He lied. I never said there were so many and so many, holding up a blank piece of paper, claiming it was a list of subversives in the State Department. He did. He lied. I never told a lie in my life about that stuff. It was terrible to be aligned with McCarthy. But as far as doing it for money, it's fantastic, really, because in the first place they didn't threaten me and in the second place they couldn't have and in the third place I didn't need a job in Hollywood. The blacklist did not extend to Broadway and I was at the top of my theater career. All my testifying did was lose me certain things. I knew that I'd lose Arthur Miller's plays. I knew a lot of guys would turn against me, which they did. I've lived through that. In some ways the whole experience made a man out of me because it changed me from being a guy, who was everybody's darling and always living therefore for people's approval, to a fellow who could stand on his own. It toughened me up a lot. I'm not afraid of anybody. People say that too—that I was afraid. I never was in my life. They avoided my eye. I didn't avoid theirs. I have some regrets about the human cost of it. One of the guys that I told on I really liked a lot... well, pretty much. I really thought it was killing him. I thought he had just stopped thinking. He could only see things a certain way. They all went through the Nazi-Soviet pact intact, the whole bunch of them.

As I said, all of my sentiments are diametrically opposed to yours. Nothing you've said changes that.

You know what happened in the twenties and thirties. There was a growth of Fascism in Germany and Italy. At the same time there was a leftist movement here which was very attached to the Soviet Union. I left the party in '35 for reasons that had to do with their program for the Group Theatre which I wouldn't partake in any longer and because of their brainwashing of people like myself. Then the first thing that made me feel that the Party was a menace, not only to the bodies of people but to their minds and souls, was when Stalin signed the nonaggression pact with Hitler. Before that,

American Communists had been saying that America should get into the war and fight the Germans. That Roosevelt was a monster for not fighting the Germans. Then all of a sudden, when Russia and Germany became allies, I watched my old friends turn around and say, "We should not fight in the war." I thought, "What are they for? Not America or Russia." Roosevelt, who had been a villain to the Communists, suddenly in one day changed into a great hero. I had done plays against Roosevelt and against the New Deal before I quit the Party in '35. It was painful to do a play against Roosevelt. He was a hero to me. I felt I was lying against my own experience. I did a play called *The Young Go First,* which showed the inequities in the New Deal. Actually the New Deal was an heroic period and Roosevelt with all his faults did great things. Not only in civilian conservation, but he also set up all kinds of agencies like the Federal Theater. I don't know, it's just too long to go into. The American left condemns me. But the European left, even *Humanité*, the French Communist magazine, doesn't do that at all. They say negative things, but they also mention the positive aspects of what I did. They've had much more experience of that kind of conflict.

Let's go back to On the Waterfront. *I have been told that it was originally written as a screenplay, and it couldn't be financed. So Budd Schulberg rewrote the script into a novel that was published in order to turn it into a property that could get funded.*

That's completely inaccurate. It's amazing what people make up. Schulberg wrote a script that was going to be produced by Darryl Zanuck. We worked on it for five months. When Zanuck read it he dropped it, saying, "Who gives a damn about labor unions?" Somehow, through a series of accidents, we picked up the producer, Sam Spiegel. He had nothing in hand, but he went out to raise the money. He was clever at it, and got $900,000 from Columbia. The picture was criticized by a lot of people—especially the ending. People thought I made the Brando character into a Jesus figure, leading the workers back to work. Lindsay Anderson, the English critic turned director, thought it was a Fascist picture.

Schulberg didn't like my ending either. He thought it would be better if Terry were killed. So he wrote the novel afterward with a different ending. When I started *On the Waterfront*, I was what they call unbankable. Nobody would put up money for me because I had had a series of box office failures. I was also a controversial figure and an embarrassment to Fox. They were glad to get rid of me. It wasn't that I was their hero. I had a hell of a time raising money, but I respond very well to difficulty. If somebody makes trouble for me, I come out flailing around in every direction. One of my happiest moments was when I got the Academy Award for *On the Waterfront*. Schulberg got one, the cameraman, Boris Kaufman, got one, Brando got one, Eva Marie Saint got one, and the film was named Best Picture. It was especially rewarding because we made something out of nothing. Everybody had rejected us. That was a triumphant moment. What happened then? All of a sudden no one cared what my politics were, that I was controversial, or difficult or that people were slamming me all the time. After *On the Waterfront*, I could do anything I wanted. That's Hollywood.

What about the ending? Anderson's criticism of the last scene was actually more that it was over-romanticized than that it was Fascist.

I think it was a bit. I think I should have had that army of stevedores a little more scraggly looking. I knew a lot about the waterfront. I spent a lot of time hanging around down there. I still keep in touch with a lot of the guys I met. There was an election after the picture came out and the reform side—Terry's side—lost, but by a very narrow margin. In other words, a concerted and quite strong opposition to the hoodlum union leaders had developed. The rank and file almost beat the gangsters, who were encouraged by the ship owners and the big stevedores. I don't think our ending was too distant a reflection of that. All Lindsay Anderson knew was what he wanted to believe—that things are corrupt in this country. They are, but what we also have here is constant conflict. Two sides fight like hell, and sometimes things get better and sometimes worse. The country progresses that way, by opposition of forces. That's the nature of democracy. Anderson went on and on about what he would have shown. Look at his pictures. They're full of malice and hate. I think he was a pretty good director, however, despite that terrible dry hatefulness.

What was Waterfront *about for you?*

Sometimes it is the better of two difficult choices to tell that your friends are criminals. It's a hard judgment to make, and you make it against the tide of opinion. That picture is terribly simple. It's all up front. It's mostly about this dumb kid who's unprepared and to whom it's painful to do what he did, who realizes through the girl and through what he knows in his heart and sees with his eyes, that telling on his friends was the better of the two choices facing him. He would have been much more comfortable going along with Johnny Friendly (Lee Cobb). In that sense it's a straightforward action story. What's the hero going to do? But it has a theme which is fundamental and which I agree with. There are circumstances which force you into making difficult choices. People don't realize what difficult means. It means that either way there are penalties, costs you have to pay. You can't win in a difficult situation. That's what I tried to show.

In order to dramatize that Terry Malloy's choice was the better of the difficult options, you're almost forced into romanticizing. Had the picture ended with Terry lying alone, dead behind Johnny Friendly's shack, your point would have gotten lost. He would not have seemed like a martyr, but merely a victim.

Throughout the history of the American labor movement, there were often vital changes that came as the result of the emergence of a martyr figure. Our lives are full of temporary heroes. In the San Francisco general strike, two guys were killed. They laid them out in the middle of the sidewalk. There was a memorial service in the middle of Union Square. After that there was a general strike. Terry does not become a leader until he gets beat up. When the other longshoremen saw him stand up and stagger to work after getting the shit kicked out of him, some irrational, unthoughtful allegiance was born. You can call it anything you want, but things like that have happened. When some of the critics said Terry's battering was Christ-like, they were right in the simple sense that Christ took a beating on all mankind's behalf. That's the way the other workers saw it, "He's taking a beating for all of us," which he was. He was the first one to do what they in their hearts knew they should do but didn't have the guts to do.

Whatever parallels there were between my private life and the film—and there were some, although not as many as anybody said—they got lost when we got down to telling the story. We tried to tell the true story of the waterfront, and it was much bigger than me or my conflict with HUAC. I was in touch with guys whose lives were being threatened at that moment. There were gangsters watching me shoot the picture. One day a guy got me against the wall of a bar. He was going to clobber me. A longshoreman took him out in the alley and walloped him. This wasn't fiction. I was dealing with people's lives. I knew the children who were not getting enough to eat because thugs were taking kickbacks out of their fathers' pay. It was great because they were loading and unloading boats while we were shooting pictures on the same pier. I was photographing life. The issues we were dramatizing were happening right there, all around us. In a way it's my ideal of the way to make pictures. I've done that on several of my films. While we were shooting *Baby Doll*, we were saving blacks all the time and hiding them in our trailers because the whites were chasing them and beating them up. We were right in the middle of a boiling society on those piers. That's why I laughed at Lindsay Anderson's article. *Waterfront* is a hell of a good picture. The photography, the roof, the streets, the props, the faces of the longshoremen, the fighters, the kids in the streets, they're the real thing. That picture is a landmark as far as getting down into reality and showing it. There's no picture been done like that since.

It's a prototypical piece of your work, in the sense that you start with a set of very real characters and circumstances and by the time you've finished dramatizing them, you've created a myth.

Zapata is like that, *America America* too. That's what I think a writer or an artist is—not only a storyteller, but, if he's any good, he's a myth-maker. The goal you should strive for is a mythic goal. You take reality, anchor it in the facts and raise it to the level of myth.

Let's talk about how you did that with Waterfront.

One of the big things was Brando himself because he is a supra-realistic actor. I also tried to give the film a pictorial quality that would make it mythic. The camera work was always poetic. Boris Kaufman was a marvelous director of photography, maybe the best I've ever seen.

How did the script come about?

Just work, work, work, work.

Did you start off with an idea?

No, we started off with a real story. I was going to do a picture about the waterfront called *The Hook* with Arthur Miller. We were way down the line with it, headed for production. I was in a budget meeting over the picture one day, and he called up and said, "I'm not going to make it." I asked why, and he said he couldn't tell me. He never explained it. That made me even more determined—you know how I am when somebody says you can't do something. I called Schulberg and said, "Let's make a picture about the waterfront." He liked the idea. He was trained as a journalist, so he investigated. He spent time on the waterfront. He spent time at St. Xavier's School, where the priests were involved with the longshoremen's families. The beginning of the reform movement on the waterfront both at the Hudson and Hoboken piers was started there. One day, he heard the story of a guy named DiVincenzo, and he met with him. Then he started working on the script. We showed it to Zanuck, and he gave us a lot of criticism. We went back to New York and worked like hell, trying to tighten it up. Then we went back to Zanuck. He was very abrupt. Not interested.

Was the story the same in every version of the script?

Yes, but we never got it well-organized and tight until we got Spiegel. He had a good structural mind and was persistent in those days. He drove Schulberg nuts. We persisted and persisted until we got what I thought was a good script. Even at that I cut out great hunks of it when I shot.

Was the romance between Terry (Brando) and Edie (Eva Marie Saint) part of the real story that Schulberg found in Hoboken?

As far as I know that was a dramatic invention. Schulberg was very affectionate towards women. He talked to them a lot, confided in his wives a lot, a thing which I never did much. I don't confide in anybody. Anyway, it was good. I thought those scenes were marvelous. Her casting was terrific. Her face is terrific.

That's a storytelling device that you've used often—the hero's relationship with a woman dramatizes things about his character in ways that the central action of the narrative doesn't allow for.

That's true but never with this particular type of romanticized, pure, dear conscience holder. That's what Edie is. I don't have that type of woman much, do I? I do in *America America* but he betrays her. That's more my way. It's the same with *A Face in the Crowd.*

The woman isn't always set up as the keeper of the hero's conscience, but a romance is used as the fulcrum for the transition of the hero. For example in Wild River *and again in* East of Eden.

Oh, right, right. I never thought of that. In *East of Eden*, Abra (Julie Harris) is the only one that understands Cal (James Dean). I had that kind of relationship with my first wife. When I was at my orneriest, when I was a young guy and most closed off, Molly helped me a lot. She was very kind to me, patient with me. Yeah, I guess I have that, too. I think that's what love is, not sex or anything like that, but people helping each other, kindness and goodness. I think those virtues, which one usually ascribes to a woman, men sometimes have, too. They're the chief glory of human relations. I love that character in *East of Eden*. Julie Harris was my ideal of that kind of woman. She's strong, tart and tough, and still a most deeply sympathetic person.

Since Waterfront *is such a classic example of your work, I'd like to go into detail with you as to how you approach each directorial choice, from idea to release print. We've already talked about the script, so let's move on to the cast.*

I had a problem right away. The actors had to be in the same league as the scenery. They had to be as real as the Hoboken locations. You rarely get that with actors. I was very close to The Actors Studio then. I not only started it, I was still teaching there. I had guys like Rod Steiger, Eva Marie Saint and a whole bunch of others. They were more people than they were actors. Rod Steiger looked like somebody in a hurry, that's all. After finding leads who would look like they belonged on the New Jersey waterfront, I had to surround them with bit players who would also look real. The problem, of course, was the Screen Actors Guild. That was murder. I don't know what arrangement we finally made with SAG in the end, but there weren't many of their people around. So I was able to use a lot of real longshoremen. The next problem was getting the actors out into the cold, which was not as easy as it sounds. A couple of days I had to go to the hotel and pull Brando out by the hand. It was not only zero degrees on the waterfront, but the north wind was blowing off the Hudson and the actor's faces, therefore, without makeup became like the real thing.

In casting the major roles what were you looking for? What was the essence of Terry Malloy for you?

He wants opposing goals, ambivalence. He was at war within himself. He's the only character that's that way in the whole picture. That was crucial. Brando was that. He had so much shame in him—from God knows what. He had the ability to project the inner struggle of conscience. That's the essence of the story, Terry's inner conflict. It had to genuinely be there in the actor playing the part. Another fellow whom we considered and whom I like and who was ready to accept the part was Frank Sinatra. He would have been brilliant.

Why did you go with Brando?

Partly because I knew him and knew what he could do. I think Frank would have been wonderful, but Brando seemed more vulnerable. There was more self-doubt, more schism, more pain in Brando. With Frank it's in there, but it's deep down and he's been able to cover it up too well.

What do you mean exactly when you say the ability to project the inner conflict?

I shouldn't have said "to project" because I don't believe in that. He has the split in him, he is it. I don't know from what. He has a great range of violently contrasting feelings, and that was the essence of the part. Also I had seen Brando box in the cellar of the Barrymore Theater when we were playing *Streetcar* on Broadway, and I knew he liked fighters and was interested in them. He looked more like a fighter to me than Sinatra. He broke his nose once, right in the middle of the show. Frank had great qualities, too. He was born and brought up in Hoboken. His people were Hoboken people, but Brando had this almost absolute vulnerability. You could almost put your hand inside him when he was tender. He's just so soft; he opens up so much. I really knew he had the love scenes in him. Also, Brando has a great mimetic gift. Almost without knowing it, he imitates people.

Did you always look for the essential quality of the characters in the actors themselves?

Unless the character is somewhere in the actor himself you shouldn't cast him. The person has got to have the essential qualities, the mainstream in him. Otherwise you fake and never get a truly good performance. With the priest played by Karl Malden I was looking for the ability to believe and advocate certain simple, clear values. Karl couldn't stand sophisticated distinctions. I started him off, and I knew him intimately. I still do; he's a close friend of mine. I knew that Karl was that guy. What do priests really know about life? The waterfront priests know more, but they're still dealing in absolute right and absolute wrong. Karl deals that way too. With Rod Steiger you could just smell it. You could look at him and say, "Here is a guy who is going to make it." I just smell the soul and see what the hell is there. Eva Marie Saint was a true-blue girl who didn't think she was pretty, didn't think much of herself. Her role was crucial. If I hadn't found a truly innocent, devoted girl, a girl who had something in her that resembled the simplicity and faith that well-brought-up Catholic girls have, I'd have been in trouble. I'd seen Eva in a play in which I didn't think she was exceptional, but I thought her quality was exactly right for Edie. It turned out I was right. There's always some luck in casting. You make guesses based on your personal, subjective responses to people. Sometimes those guesses turn out good, sometimes they don't. Nevertheless, I think it's crucial to cast people who inside all the fronts and manners and agreeabilities and adaptabilities are like the characters you are casting.

You do the same thing with the smaller roles?

Yes, to whatever degree possible. Like the old actor, John Hamilton, who played Eva Marie Saint's father. I'd known him for a long time from around the street. There was this sense in him of I'm a failure. I'm not going to make it. So much goodness and so much pain.

In all of your pictures you kept turning up new people. Where did you find them?

The Actors Studio helped a lot. There's no mystery about that. Also, I was directing plays on Broadway at the same time so I was "on the street." I was casting all the time.

How do you run your auditions?

I'd usually cast the main parts without a blink. Madeleine Sherwood and Pat Hingle in *Cat on a Hot Tin Roof*, small but very important parts, (snap) just like that. All I had to do was convince the author they were right.

What if you're talking to people you don't know personally and whose work you don't know?

It gets down to the question of genius as far as I'm concerned.

What does the Genius look for?

You've been talking to me for quite a while now. I'm not like what you figured I was at first, right? You frown on certain things about what I'm really like underneath. So if you were to direct me you'd know certain things about my nature, and you'd use them. I do the same thing. I take people for walks. I take them to dinner. I don't do any readings, but I talk to them like I'm talking to you. I veil it. I make it sound like chatter. Everybody will talk to you about their most intimate problems if you give them a chance. They're dying to tell you that they tried to kill their brother once. They're eager to tell you their problems with their father. An actor will tell you anything in five minutes—if you listen. All you have to do is sit down with them, and you'll find out what they're made of.

Say you've got a day where you've scheduled to see somebody every twenty minutes.

I don't do it that way. Well, sometimes I do, if it's just a bit, but then if I'm interested in them, I say, "I'd like to talk to you some more."

What kind of thing would interest you in a preliminary screening?

I'm looking for something—say a guy that really looks mild, but is a murderer in his heart. If I get a glimpse of it I'll say, "Come at the end of the day. We'll have a drink." You put one drink in him and before you know it, he's telling you everything. I'll see if the part's in him or if his anger is a fake. I'm supposed to be so good; sometimes I fail. I miscast a role a little bit or an actor has most of it in him but not all. You get actors to talk about their history and then you bring up subjects. People are eager to unburden themselves. Nowadays what sometimes happens is you sense them wanting to talk about something and you feel, "I just don't want to get in that deep with this person."

You find that approach better than asking an actor to read for you?

Reading usually gets you misinformation. It tells you little except what their voice may be like. It's a trap. Sometimes you do it to see if an actor can concentrate publicly, to gauge the amount of relaxation they have, or their adaptability to direction. You can learn some technical things from reading, but you don't learn anything about your material. Your material comes when they start telling you about their daddy and themselves.

If you have them read, do you let them read something they want to do? Or do you give them a scene from the film or from something else altogether?

No, I say, "You left something in this office when you were here. The secretary's out there. You've come back looking for it and it's gone. You try to find clues in this office as to who may have taken it or where it's gone. And the secretary mustn't know." I sit back here in this corner and I can tell in five minutes what kind of a person they are. "Call your wife, Jeff, and tell her you're going to be a little late tonight." I can tell from the way you speak to your wife what your relationship is to her, how you handle her, your relationship to women generally, etc.

I want to make sure I'm clear about this. Your instinct is to find out all you can about the person more than about their skills as an actor?

What's your material? The material is not an actor's looks, or their voices. Look at the succession of actors who played gangsters. They didn't look like tough guys. Humphrey Bogart looked gentle. George Raft had no violence in him. But you could rely on a sort of an unhealthy whatever-it-was in his nature. That's the real material. One way or another you've got to find that out so you know what you've got. Once you've done that and you start directing, you know what to appeal to. You relate the material to things that you know about them. It's amazing how it works.

You have a lot of confidence that if a person has what you need inside him, you can not only get it out of him, you can make him act. What was your next step after the cast was set?

I had three readings at the Actors Studio with all the actors who had speaking parts. I made all of my basic, general observations to each of the leading players about what their roles were and the problems of their parts and the problems of the production. I warned them that it was going to be rough on location and cold. Mostly I said general things like no makeup, but I also told each of them what to work on in their part. It was valuable. I don't believe in staging things at a reading because, as I said before, a lot of the staging comes from the sets, and at that point I was still finding locations. I think there is a great stimulus to an actor if he comes on the set in the morning and becomes acquainted with it for the first time. There's a tremendous creative lurch that happens when you see where the scene is going to be played. You get totally new ideas. Anything you can do to see to it that there's a stimulus every day that makes the actors play a scene surprisingly and unexpectedly and well is good. I think people who do a lot of staging are essentially people who have never worked in the theater. Staging is second nature to me. It's not the problem. The problem is to get the values right, and to see to it that those values don't get lost or subverted along the way.

Can you tell me more about the process of the reading?

Before each scene I would tell the actors involved the kind of place where I intended to play it, such as a rooftop. Then I would have them read it, just to relate to each other, just to listen to each other. Listening is awfully important in the theater, but it's even more important in films. More often than not you're photographing a person listening. If a scene is good, what little is being said has an effect on the person listening, particularly in *On the Waterfront*, where the whole point of Brando's character was that not only was he inarticulate but that he was only semi-conscious, that he was unaware or only partly aware of the struggle going on inside himself. Listening is more than just hearing the words; it's a total process. You not only listen with your ears but you take in the person's intention. You listen in the deepest sense of the word. It's a total response to the person, not only to what he says, but to what he's trying to do, what he means. I stress that a lot. Very often in my movies you will see people being photographed who are not talking.

When you say you stress it, how exactly do you do that?

I would ask them a lot of questions, but I would also point out what a person wants. "Notice that when he says this to you, he's not telling you the whole truth." I would stimulate them a little bit, begin to make them wonder what was being said. You do that in life. When you listen to a person, you don't just take them on the simple level of what he's saying. You think, "What's he really want?" You become aware of whatever is happening in him that's on the level that produces the speech, that is a deeper level. I would point those things out.

Would you point out to the listener what indeed the speaker wanted?

No, because if you do that you're acting the play out. I would, however, tell the speaker what he wanted. I stress the word "want" a lot when I direct. That's the springboard to action, i.e., the inner action. I try to get the actors off the script and onto the actions, onto the behavior as early and as thoroughly as possible.

How do you do that?

You slight the text yourself, say it doesn't make any difference. I try to get them off just reading the lines because that's a trap. When I first started in the theater I always used to have a script in my hand. It's the least important thing. I tell the actors not to look at it too much. Most of them have read it once or twice to themselves. I don't encourage that too much either. When they read it together for the first time I say, "Now the words will do something to you as you look at them again and they'll also do something to the person you're talking to. Listen and don't study the other guy's words. Listen to what he says to you."

Would you use the reading for anything other than that?

No, you can't do too much in a first reading. If you do too much, you get into a lot of trouble. The rehearsal is not for the director to show off, to give instructions or to give lectures. The rehearsals are specifically for the actors, and you have to push them and lead them a little bit in the right direction. It's a process in which the actors are finding out about the characters for themselves. A lot of directors talk a lot and show off, and then the actors think, "How the hell am I ever going to get that?" You can't unload the whole problem of the part on them. You just get them going right. The reason it's so important to do that in film is that when you get on location, there are so many other problems that it's very hard to say, "Now, let's talk about fundamentals." They're not worried about fundamentals. They're worried about how they're going to play on that set on that day with those weather conditions in that costume. All of which may be new to them. So you've really got to get them going right before all those tertiary, less significant problems come down on them later.

Can you describe the process from one reading to the next?

The second reading had to do more with my introduction to what their main objectives were. I would do just enough to get them going on the right track. You don't tell them each station nor all the curves along the way. You don't tell them the ambiguities or the temporary reversals. But you put them on the right track so they're doing the right thing. I would make the reading start casually and then say, "You see, this is what you want and because" and so on.

Would you fit that into the "spine" for them?

I wouldn't do it up front because that is revealed increasingly as it goes along. There are things each day that reconfirm the original goal, the original objective that I set for them. You must never go faster than they are. You never feed them more than they can eat and digest. You should never talk about the significance of the movie. That is the result of all the other factors being right and has nothing to do with their performances. The significance is a result of their performance. Drawing charts is a dangerous thing. It becomes a lesson in logic, everything must fit into that. It can make a performance very mechanical. But you sure as hell better know where you're going.

In other words, you may do it for yourself whether you do it for the actors or not.

I do do it for myself. I used to take copious notes. But I always acted very offhand about that because what you're trying to do is wake up that element in the actor. You reach into him and find the spine in him and arouse that and get him to enjoy playing that. That's very important—get him to enjoy playing that. But if you say the spine is so and so and this is related, and the actors take notes, watch out. As soon as an actor starts to write a lot, you're in trouble. He shouldn't write, he should just begin to behave the right way, and like behaving that way. For example, when Brando began to enjoy Saint's innocence and find it attractive; instead of putting him off, he began to like it. At the same time it made him feel guilty. His behavior followed automatically without my saying anything. The worst thing you can do is say to an actor, "What you're doing is this and that's right. Now keep doing that." Don't do that. They're doing it already. That's very ticklish. You're dealing with behavior, not cognition. Once you've got it going in the actor it's amazingly solid. They don't lose it. If he or she finds the behavior strain in them awakened, you don't call attention to it. It's very bad to do that. You are careful not to get them to put it into words for themselves. I saw a lot of brilliant guys in the theater when I was a stage manager make great speeches. They should have published the speeches instead of putting the show on. Directors show off a lot, it's a terrible thing. If you could direct a whole movie without a word of direction, you'd be better off because then the actors would be doing it spontaneously. Sometimes, like in the taxi cab scene, which I get so much credit for, I didn't do anything. I read it once, but that scene is so good, the personal intentions in it are so clear, and the actors are so gifted, that I did nothing. The actors knew it all. It's so human and so basic.

Was there any scene you had difficulty with in the reading?

A key scene in which it was essential to get things going right was the one in the pool hall at the beginning. You had to get across the fact that Terry and Johnny Friendly liked each other. It may seem like an insignificant scene, but if you don't get all the relationships going correctly at the outset, the rest of the picture is meaningless. I had to stress over and over again that Johnny likes Terry. He likes his stupidity, he likes the fact that he's agreeable, that he was a fighter. He finds him cute, he likes his inarticulateness. He's physically fond of him, he likes his muscles. That came out very well in the moment when Lee Cobb got a headlock on Brando and horsed around with him. You also have to make it very clear that Terry likes Friendly, too. He's grateful to him. So when the break between them comes, it's a break between two friends.

Do you tell the the actors those things at the reading?

Yes, I would tell them quite a bit, but you don't have to tell them too much because when you say the right things, they are very stimulating to a good actor. When you start talking too much, it's usually because you're floundering around and don't know yourself. The values in *Waterfront* are extremely clear. All I had to do was call these very intelligent men and women's attention to what was already there. In the meantime, I also did another thing. In a hopefully casual way, I took them aside and talked more generally about what the problems were. I did that with Brando, for instance, and he got a tremendous impetus from that.

Did you read the script scene by scene?

I would interrupt at anytime. When I had very experienced actors who'd been trained like these people, I gave them the basic overall objective and then each day reaffirmed it in relation to the scene that was being played that day.

What do you do with actors that are less trained?

You don't tell them so much up front, or you tell them more indirectly. Actors who are less trained—I don't know why—are usually less complicated people and they're closer to the part inside.

What you have to do with them or for them is a process that a trained actor does for himself, which is you have to relate the events in the material to their own life. You're constantly working in indirect ways. In *The Visitors* I told Steve Railsback not to talk to Jim Woods. "When we're having dinner just stay away, stay apart." So there was constantly a sense of "What's he think of me?" Jim Woods got an impression, which I didn't mind at all, that Railsback scorned him, didn't like the way he worked. In other words I worked in the most direct terms, but in an indirect way. You don't have to do that with experienced actors because they do it for themselves. They really relate to the people that they're playing. In *On the Waterfront,* once I had made the basic relationships clear in the reading, they were off in the right direction. They were a very imaginative group of actors.

How do you help the actors shift from the first reading where it's Brando talking to Cobb to Terry Malloy talking to Johnny Friendly?

You mean the emotional life? The values things have to them?

What they mean to them as characters.

You tell them that. If you thoroughly describe what it means to the character and do it with a sense of the history and the human content of the person you're talking to, you can usually relate it to something that means something to them. By examining the basic situation and what's at stake in the scene, you'll find that you've described something that they've known in some other personal context. You try to put little darts into their own histories. I used to know Brando so well that it was a snap. It's very important to work with actors whom you like, whose "human content," as I call it, is rich. In the leading roles it's almost essential. That doesn't mean you approve. The word "approve" doesn't have much to do with art. But guys who you know have been through a lot, whose lives are turbulent in some way. What I like in people is that they are involved in the process of living. That means they have problems and they treat their problems with humor, with passion, with courage, and above all, they are hungry to do something for themselves. It's very important to get actors you like. One of the worst fates that can happen to a director, especially in the movies where you haven't got much time, is to get someone whom in real life you don't like. Again, I'm not talking about approval. He doesn't have to be like me, but he has to have something that you just relish. All of these actors did. I was glad to see them every morning. It was fun. I've had actors I liked less and it makes a terrific difference. Directing is an involved play; you're playing with people, they're playing with you. You're creating something together, and it's very important that you really enjoy each others' being.

Do you ever play the actors off against each other, using the private things you know about them?

I'm very sly about those things. I'm not ducking your question, but I don't really like to talk about that too much. What I do is talk to the actors about each other, not their acting but their personal lives. I'll bring something up before an actor plays a scene, something seemingly off-handed about the other actor in the scene. For instance if I want Brando to do something, I'll say, "Look how thin Eva Marie is." Or I might call attention to her costume. "She looks perfect today; she looks just like a little Catholic schoolgirl." That may wake him up to something about her. A director doesn't have to do much, but you have to do things that go to the core of the actor's problem. Once I called attention to Steiger's camel hair coat—a brilliant touch which, by the way, Steiger thought up.

When you're working with pros like Brando, Steiger, and Cobb, do you ever run into the difficulty of an actor saying, "Oh man, don't give me that director shit?"

They've never said that to me, though I imagine they must have felt it at times. Brando might negate something I suggested, but he would not ignore the basic principle I was aiming at. He might not like my idea, but then he would do something else that was better. A director should never feel that he has to win an argument. Not everything you say is going to be right. But hopefully everything you say is going to be stimulating. And if one thing doesn't work, go right back two minutes later with something else. You don't have to win. You don't have to be the boss man.

Have you ever worked with an actor who resents that kind of manipulation?

They don't because they are so open. One of the beautiful things about actors is that they want to be good and they are eager for any kind of help. I've never had that kind of trouble. Maybe because I quickly admit when I'm wrong, when I've said something which has not done what I hoped it would do.

Do you encourage your actors to spend time alone with each other, to make discoveries about their characters on their own?

I don't go in for that much. Sometimes it works, but I'm not crazy about their rehearsing without me.

I'm not talking about rehearsing. But for instance, two guys have to play brothers. They may want to really get to know each other, hang out together.

Specifically, if they had to play brothers then to a certain extent you may set up a situation where they do things together off the set. But it's better if when they're not working they sleep, to be simple about it. It's better if they don't do too much.

Isn't it kind of inevitable though, especially on location when you're all living together?

It's amazing how much you can control if you're aware of the potential traps. Sometimes it is very valuable, and you do bring them together, I'll say that. But it's better if the actors keep their relationship a relationship on the set. That's partly why I never stop working. There's never a lapse when the actors can just sit around talking to their agent or something. I'm always rehearsing. I stay on them. I don't give them much time off during the day. I'm not even keen on lunch, and I hate it when they have dressing rooms to escape into. I'm not keen on any relationships except the ones in the scenes. I don't even like it when somebody's wife says, "I watched that scene today. You sure were good." Suppose I thought he was lousy? So I try to control everything as much as possible.

Let me go back to the reading. At what point do you stop with a scene?

You should always leave with a sense, I see what the problem is. I see who I am and I see who I'm talking to. I think I know how to go on this scene. You shouldn't rehearse it to that point, which I think some directors do, where the rehearsal takes the place of the performance.

What do you do in the third reading?

I don't do a hell of a lot more. I would encourage the actors to follow their feelings. For instance, a girl may lean over and do something with her dress or a guy may go over and sit next to someone. I encourage them to do whatever the physical result of the action was beginning to be; whatever was beginning to happen out of their own feelings, not out of my saying anything. The only good behavior is the behavior that comes from your objective. That's the only behavior that means a goddamn thing. It's better otherwise if you just stand still. If somebody had a walking scene, I'd let them walk around together. If they got too strained or self-conscious about it, I'd ask them to sit down and say, "I'm not ready for that yet." Also, the third rehearsal was the only one that was sort of for me. I began to watch it and think of how I would stage scenes.

You said that you go into a scene without really scoring the moves throughout, the emotional curves, etc.

Having become acquainted with the actors, knowing the set and studying the scene emotionally for myself, I would have the climaxes, the reversals, and the stages marked in my mind pretty well. Again, I would try to have those come out of causes, out of what happened in the scene, but I would have the beats marked in my mind pretty well.

Can I push your memory and ask you to pick a scene that you recall from On the Waterfront *and describe the process of getting the actors to reach the moments you had worked out on your own?*

There's a scene where Edie comes across the roof looking for Terry. He has a pole with which he's making the pigeons fly in a certain pattern. There's hardly anything in the text at all. She just wants to talk to him. We know that she's come for a purpose. I made her intention clear to Eva. We also know certain constraints Edie has. I made those clear to her as well. Brando's mystic and mysterious personality helps with that because he's not immediately reachable. I counted on that without calling her attention to it. I made clear to Brando how guilty Terry feels in relationship to Edie. I only had to say it once. It's obvious in the script, and he was very aware of it anyway. I tried, then, to give him something to do that would make Terry not immediately accessible to her without him having to "act" it. So he has a pole and he's guiding the pigeons around. When she walks over and wants to talk to him, he sees that she's there to tell him something important but that it is hard for her to speak. He could avoid the confrontation, which he'd rather do, by talking about hawks and playing with pigeons. I didn't have to make explicit to Brando that his dialogue about hawks was like telling Edie, "Don't judge a man by what he does in this terrible city, because it's a question of survival here." Brando knows that and if you make it too clear it becomes obvious and corny. The whole scene works off his avoiding a conversation by playing with the birds. As the scene goes along, they move over to the cage and then I point out to her that as he handles the other birds and offers her an egg, things happen.

Actually there's a little boy in the scene as well.

Yes, Terry's able to avoid her further with the little boy. She finds him charming because of the way he plays around with the kid. And when Terry offers the egg, she can feel the sensitivity, the goodness in him. One thing which is bewildering her, which I pointed out only once, is that on the one hand he's rough, dumb, and crude and on the other hand, he's so gentle withal. Brando has that within himself. Again, you don't have to tell him to be both crude and gentle. You've cast the role right so the guy's got it. You don't have to tell her anything either. I directed the scene by using the business that Budd Schulberg had written, which is the offering of the egg, the way he handles the bird—which Brando liked to do—by his lack of shyness with the boy, which contrasted with his shyness with her, and by giving the boy a tough 10-year-old attitude that girls are somehow inferior, and by accentuating the boy's role in the scene. Actually I directed the boy more than I did either of the leads. You have the scene almost doing it for you by the business you've set up. You know very clearly what values you want but when you don't have to stress them you don't.

In a scene like that how do you define Brando's objectives?

My God, you don't have to define them. They're obvious. His objective is that he wants the girl to like him, and he also feels guilty about her brother. If you talk too much about the guilt, you play that which you don't want to play. That was the damnedest movie because I did a lot of talking for a while at the beginning, but I did very little afterwards because the movie sort of played itself.

But clearly the objective can't be to be guilty.

No, I didn't say that. I said he feels that. You have to distinguish between what a character feels and what he's trying to do. What you stress is that you want to get close to her, get together with her, get her to like you. But you don't even stress that too much because it's all in there, and if you stress it too much you take away from the naturalness that Brando had. Really and truly once I set up the business with the pole and the boy and the egg, the scene played itself. Terry's able to stay with Edie, remain at her side and still avoid the confrontation. That's how you get the ambivalence in the scene played out.

This is the kind of scene you see a lot where someone wants something but can't move towards it directly.

The best kind of scene is where what they want—the object—is present. So it's not just a matter of speech. The object, the girl, is there. He wants a look from her, he wants understanding from her, a certain tone of voice. The way to avoid her is there in business. In other words, where the objects for the actions are there—and they both are there in this case—you've directed the elements of the scene into objects and into objectives. And then it almost plays itself. That's why sometimes in the scenes that are best directed, the actors will say, "You didn't do anything in that scene." But you did. You put the pole there, you chose the roof. You made him put the egg actually in her hand. One of the nice things in the scene is after he gives her the egg and she looks at it. Then I told Eva, "Look at him." I didn't have to tell her what she feels. If I had, she would have tried to show me that he was sweet and you'd get terrible stuff. How can you look at a pigeon's egg and then look at the boy who gave it to you and not play it right? You can't. So you've done the emotional direction by giving the actors physical actions. That's the way I always try to work. I was brought up as an actor in the Stanislavsky Method. That has to do with objectives, with conscious emotions and objects, objects, objects.

In this scene the objectives got deflected onto objects, and the emotions came out that way. But in the scene in the taxicab, which we'll talk about later, there aren't any external objects for Terry and Charlie to work with.

The objects are each other. What's good is that they can't get away from each other. If you can get a no exit sign on a scene, if the characters have to confront each other, you've probably got a good scene.

Did you know what you wanted from them in the cab scene?

What I wanted was to show the moment when a man suddenly thinks of what he could have been, like everybody does at some point in their lives. I wanted Terry to be reproachful, but gentle. If it were just reproach you'd get, "You son of a bitch, I could have been a champ!" But if you say this to your brother, then you do it mournfully, and it's moving. I did have that much in mind. Brando and I thought so much alike in those days. We were so similar in our tastes and feelings that there were a lot of times when he did what I wanted right off the bat, and often he did it better than I thought it could possibly be. He's a genius. He's the only actor I've ever worked with whom I would say that about. And his genius was profound because it had to do with humanity and not mere brilliance.

You described watching Laurence Olivier work. You said he'd sit there and pick up an ashtray and say, "No, that's not right."

Then he'd pick it up with one hand, pick it up with the other, pick it up with both hands...

What is that kind of precise moment-to-moment external, physical work all about?

Brando never did two takes quite the same because he knew he had to be alive on each take. Olivier's system, in those days at least, was exactly the opposite. In a sense he was directing himself. If he did the externals correctly, they would mean what he wanted them to mean. Hopefully, if he did them correctly, he would also feel correctly. There is something to the behaviorist kind of approach. I'm explaining something to you, right? If I do it sitting forward, there is some suggestion that I'm anxious for you to understand. If I do it lying back, there's some suggestion that you can take me in an offhand way and that I'm showing off. Or if I squirm around, it suggests that I want to get this interview over with. Every position means something. Once you start to think that way, there are values in it. My problem, being the kind of director that I am and working with the kind of actors I work with, is to put those things in so they influence the actor without his knowing it. If I were directing myself here, for example, I would somehow get Kazan to sit on the edge of the chair because he's going over things in the past, rediscovering them. They mean something to him. See, I look up now. I don't look down, I'm sort of thoughtful about it. I would tell Kazan, "As you answer this guy's questions, try to rediscover, so that when you direct next time, you know better what work means to you. Try to find yourself again. Try to find who you are in your work." I would try to make the specific nature of the objective clear. I would almost force him to sit properly, but if he didn't I'd say, "Why don't you sit at the end of the chair?" or I'd go up and give him a little push. I would try to work inside out and outside in, but I would not weigh the actor down with the externals. I would somehow impose them on him without his knowing it. For example, it's very important what kind of chair you sit in. I'm sitting in an easy chair now. But suppose I had a tight small armchair, suppose I had a stool. Suppose I was at a table like Mr. Hitchcock was shown with Truffaut. Or suppose I were in an armchair behind the table and there were drinks in front of me. Then you'd be coming in and pleading with me. I set things up. It's my choice of table, my choice of chair, my choice of what you sit on, the pad that you have, whether you wear glasses or not, and so on. I control all the externals, but what I try to do is put equal stress on both. But to the actor I only stress his objective.

My objective right now is to get you to tell me everything you can about directing. If I were setting it up, I might put you in a different kind of chair.

No, not you might, you do. You control the externals, just as much without my knowing it. The externals are essential. In other words, the form means a lot. I'm a formalist as well as I am the other. I think the ideal director uses both. With a guy like Brando it was easy. And you don't just do it with props. You use everything. For example, remember when he comes back from testifying, he walks down a row of extras and they all snub him? I chose extras that he didn't like. So when he walked by them he played it as if, "The hell with them. I'm glad I did it." That's using the externals.

So in summary, you use everything you possibly can to affect the actor.

That's right. You affect him by his own content, the objective you give him, and by reaching in and relating that objective to things in his own life. But you have to do it in a subtle way so he doesn't get self-conscious. When I looked at Larry doing the business with the ashtray, I objected to it because in those days I thought that was all he did. He was a hell of an actor and a wonderful person and artist. That's not all he did, but I think he put too much stress on it. I sympathized with him in that particular instance because the director he was working with was an inarticulate though a very feelingful man.

What if you were working with Olivier?

It would have been an honor to work with a man like that, but I wouldn't have worked with him without knowing him, and then I would have known what to suggest. I would have said the reason he picks up the ashtray that way is because of so and so. I would have found a way to tie that into human values somehow.

You use externals to affect the actor. At the same time you tell him the objective, and at the same time you find something personal to connect it to the actor himself. Is there any particular order in which you do all that?

The thing that holds them all together is the objective. You don't work directly for the emotion, but if you set the values up right, the emotion comes. Emotion comes as a result of the objective either being fulfilled or denied. You don't talk about the way you set the scene up physically, you just do it and you put the person in it. You stress the objective when you direct. The rest all rides on that rail.

Let's go back to the specifics of the film. The first scene is the introduction on the dock. There's a very wide shot, which you hold on for a long time.

The point of the introduction is that the whole waterfront, which is wide and enormous, is in the grip of one fist, one little clique, one little clubhouse. I could have put the entire scene inside the office. But I did it this way because it dramatized what I thought was the situation there. So it wasn't casual. It was a specific choice I made.

In the next scene Terry has to set up Joey Doyle. His objective, I suppose in simplest terms, is to get Joey up on the roof.

No, it's to carry out his boss's orders. Can you see what happens the moment you state it that way—all the feelings that get evoked by your choice of objective? The feeling that he's not himself, a feeling that he belongs to somebody else, a feeling that he wants his boss's approval, a feeling that he's tied up in a situation that he has no choice about. I told Brando the objective, but that alone is not enough. How you dramatize the other elements of the scene is through picturization, and that has to do with the art of cinema rather than the art of directing actors. In the introduction the actors come out of the cabin in single file and walk to a certain point. Terry goes one way and the rest go another. Before they go, Friendly claps Terry on the back. Watch the way Brando walks—he did it himself—in sort of an abashed way, his head down. Next I cut directly to a high-angle shot. Brando is on the ground holding a pigeon and he shouts, "Hey, Joey." The reason I did that was to dramatize that Terry had suddenly made a decision: "I'm going through with it." But I wanted to show that he wasn't comfortable, that he was straining against it. By shooting down on him from a high angle, the point comes across automatically. That's picturization. That's cinema.

I made the mistake of oversimplifying the objective. How do you get beyond the text so that you conceptualize a scene in a richer way?

Part of it is to leave the instinctive part of yourself alive. Behave like an artist, not like a bookkeeper. Don't be a guy that's right. Don't be a professor, be an artist. You get on the set and you see this little boat house and you say, "Yeah, that's it." I don't know why. Maybe later you'll figure out exactly why you responded that way. And above all don't tell anyone.

I wasn't thinking about telling the actors or even about how you shoot it. Rather, I'm talking about the concept—that this is a scene about Brando acting out orders from his boss as opposed to it being about his getting Joey up on the roof. As you said, it evokes all kinds of feelings.

Don't evoke those feelings. Don't go into complications. Not to the other person or yourself. By the way, one good idea is better than two good ideas. As a matter of fact, one good idea is better than three brilliant ideas. Get it down to one good idea. Don't try to play several things in a scene—things in an actor that are ambivalent—get them objects that suggest it. Or make the scene work in a way that reveals it. Don't try to do two things in every moment. If you want ambivalence, do one thing and then later do an opposite thing. Don't complicate it. Make one strong, simple statement. This is the least ambivalent movie I ever did. In other movies I directed how things happen inside a scene much more carefully. But in this movie there were a lot of strong effects which sometimes were contradicted by the next effect.

I'm not sure I agree with you. For instance, the scene in the taxi. You may not have had to articulate the ambivalences as clearly for yourself, but they were all there.

But one way or another everything's played out. Terry says, "What you did to me. What I could have been." He actually says that, I've done other movies where things were not said at all.

The next scene in *Waterfront* is when Terry hears the news that Doyle is dead. It's a terribly important moment. It is the first blow of shame to hit Terry. I started on the sneering faces of Two Ton Tony Galento and Tami Mauriello and panned over to Terry. He just stands there. Brando doesn't have to act much because of the contrast between his face and theirs. Again, you set it up so that the sequence of pictures tells the story. The fact that Brando does act brilliantly is gravy. But if a lug had been in his place, we'd still have made the point through the contrast of images. I'm telling my inner story all the time. I must know that clearly. The extent to which I communicate that to an actor depends on the necessities, as I see things developing on the set everyday.

We keep going past what I really want to get into—the conceptualization of what a scene is about.

But look, Jeff. It isn't a very complex process. What you have to do all the time is tell yourself the story in the simplest emotional terms. Then make sure you tell *that* story and not some other story. The terrific temptation is to be a little lazy and just tell the external facts. Take the first four shots. I could have put them in an office and had them sitting around talking to Brando. I could have shown

Brando just throwing the pigeon up in the air. I could have shot Joey so you'd see his face and think, "Oh, that poor guy." But I told myself the story. It's the story of a growing shame, of an awakening conscience inside the hero that makes him do something that is against the whole code of the waterfront. I tell myself that story every day. You hold onto the simple essence like grim death. Things constantly tug you this way and that. You've got to hold onto what it's all about. That's what you're there to do every day. You're telling *that* story, not *a* story.

That sense of shame goes up a notch in the scene where Terry goes into Friendly's bar. A lot of it is played around a pool table.

The important thing in that scene was the division of the money. I had them lay the money out on the table so we could see there's a lot of cash. They aren't just playing at being hoodlums. The social point is made that they're making a lot of money at the expense of everybody else. You next begin to stress Terry's wishing he hadn't set Joey up. Friendly humors him out of it, and Terry finally accepts it. But we feel that this won't last. I've just told myself what the scene is about. In those few words I've set all the values I mean to get out of that scene.

But in the words that you've used, there is very little definition of Brando's objectives in the scene.

I said that he begins to feel ashamed for the first time. Now that implies an objective which you may have to state to him if he's not doing it right. But he's probably playing the objective if he's a good actor. That's what I mean about it being well-written. Brando sensed Terry's shame right away. You see that he senses it because he behaves in such an abashed way.

Now, there's a perfect instance where the objective and the emotional life of the characters are almost at loggerheads. The implicit objective is to protest, in some way to ease his conscience of what he's just done. The scene would have been a shambles if he came in and just started chewing up the scenery.

Of course. That's a place where Brando's a true actor so he's going to do that within the circumstances of the scene and within the given circumstances of the character's life. The given circumstances being that Friendly is the guy who takes him to ball games and who is his boss and who supports him. If that's not going right then you lecture Brando about it. You also stage it so everybody's laughing at him or hitting him or liking him or treating him like a dunce. You explain just as much as you need to, but what you said is not a problem. The best scenes always have the objective going one way and the emotions or feelings you get out of it going in another.

In the next scene Terry goes up to the roof.

You think that they have humored him out of it. Then he's by himself and whenever there's a lot of open space around a character, it somehow suggests that he is thinking. You begin to feel for him.

It begins on a close-up of the kid who runs over the roofs to visit Terry.

Putting the kid with Brando was another good touch because it points up the fact that Terry is a kid. He plays with the boy on the kid's level throughout.

In Brando's performance in Streetcar *and in this, there's a lot of little boy, a lot of adolescent behavior.*

He had that double quality. He was mature and adolescent at the same time.

Let me get back to the business of setting the objectives and the emotional life at odds. When an actor becomes terribly aware of the objective, there may be a tendency to leap at it.

It's worse than a tendency. There's a danger that he'll play it inhumanly—mechanically. In this scene he is troubled for the first time, and he wants relief. There's no relief like playing with another kid. Again, what are you doing? You're conceptualizing. You're telling the inner story through external things, which is what directing is. *Directing is turning psychology into behavior.* If you don't do that, all you have is people walking around feeling. You have to help that. You have to give them the occasion and the setting for them to feel. You have to make the actors feel and you have to make the audience looking at them feel.

In the scene in the pool hall where Terry comes in to protest...

He doesn't know what he wants to say, that's another thing that's important. Protest is an intellectual word and suggests knowledge. All Terry wants is to be reassured. I wanted to make him not a bright guy. It's very, very important that someone who's not used to thinking is made to think, who's not used to feeling anything like guilt is made to feel something like guilt. That scene is critical. Another thing that is important is that on that level of humanity people do not know their objectives. Most of us don't know what we're doing until after we've done it. Then we may psychoanalyze ourselves. But in life very often we respond angrily or we cajole, we scold, we insist, and it just suddenly comes out of us. Sometimes with actors who are not as good, when they're not giving me what I want, I tell them what it is.

That seems to be a fundamental problem with acting and directing actors. Once actors know what their objectives are, you almost have to make them forget them. You may have to...

Get them to arrive at them unconsciously by themselves, by your saying what the circumstances are and what the relationships are so clearly that they arrive at the objectives without knowing they've arrived at them. You might have to give them a little push, but no more.

But you've said that you stress the question, "What do you want?" And that there are times when you'll tell them the objectives.

I try even then to not say it to them as a sentence. I'll try to "rough it up a little" or just give them the feeling of the objectives. But don't put it in cold words. You're dealing with living, you're not keeping a book. That's why when I see a director's notebook and he's got the whole thing laid out, I just hope for the best. The whole point is to take those ideas and feelings and turn them into behavior which the audience looks at and feels as they do with life—I don't quite understand it, but something's happening. There's another essential element in the Method. The myth, the legend, the story in all its parts, presents a problem for the director and for the actors of justification. In other words, the creatures of the myth do something. You have to set up values, emotions, circumstances that justify that behavior. The script says, "He goes over there and punches this guy in the nose." Then in your own work at home as a director you have to set the circumstances, the past relationships, all those things which justify to the actor what the author makes him do, so you believe it. Everything I've been talking about comes from the desire to make what the script requires the actor to do, the only thing he could do at that moment. All the choices have to do with that.

Let's illustrate what you're saying. When Terry's sent by the hoods to spy on a union meeting in the church basement, the church is attacked. He grabs Edie and rescues her. That begins their courtship. They walk, he sits on a swing in a children's park, and they talk. In terms of your homework, the justifications...

You've done all that by now because you had a scene between them before. The rest of it is done by the fact that the hoods bang on the windows, that Terry sees her, and you tell him to grab her and pull her out.

Terry and Edie met the day after Joey's murder. There's a scene on the docks, the shape-up. Mac, the foreman, starts giving out assignments. At the end he throws the tags in the air. Everyone races to grab one like sharks in a feeding frenzy. Terry and Edie meet over a tag.

It's a big shock to see the sister of someone whose death you've caused. I didn't have to explain that, especially since Brando's other scenes had already been shot. In the scene you're talking about, it's again something that's played out. Edie's in physical danger, and he doesn't want her to suffer. Before the hoodlums showed up, his attitude all through the church scene showed that he wasn't impressed with the union leaders or the priest. You also feel that part of his attitude is an act—not an act exactly—but it's the way that character, Terry, was brought up to think. I had to be careful there, because all you had to do was glare at Brando a few times and he got defensive.

Did the problem ever arise where you had to prevent the actors from playing the end of the scene at the beginning?

Always. You always have to be aware of that danger. There has to be a sense of discovery in a scene. The scene is in the script because the character couldn't get to where he is at the end except for that scene happening. Just the fact that he has to pull her out of physical danger there does a lot. Also, he has to handle that girl, touch her. The whole idea—nothing you have to explain to Brando, although I did—was these girls are either whores or they are virgins. A good girl you don't fool around with and the other girls are bums. That doesn't mean the good girls are angels or anything. But they're virgins when they marry. The guys look up to them for that reason. He relates to her in that way. When he can't stand the sight of that decent girl being subjected to physical danger, he rescues her. But he's also playing out his guilt. It's like he's making up for what he's done to her brother. I don't remember if I explained that to Brando or not, but it's so obvious it doesn't need much explaining. It's not that the script's obvious, but it's played out very carefully in steps.

But in terms of not playing the end of the scene before you get to it—I'll go back to the scene in the taxicab during which Terry clearly makes a discovery.

A lot of that, Jeff, has to do with starting right. Remember I told you about the first couple of readings? You make them listen a lot. I'm looking at you and listening to you. I'm taking you in. I'm not playing my action. I'll take it off you, see what you've got to say. How do you feel about that?

Just fine. My question is, When does Terry discover that Charlie has been using him, wrecking his life? Does it really happen in the scene, or is Terry just facing up to it and talking about it for the first time?

The conversion is awakened by what happens in the scene. But it's not really a discovery in the scene. That would be false. That he's a failure is always in the bottom of Terry's heart and stomach. By the way, all Brando's behavior and disposition in the first part of the film is that of a man who's a failure, who's scornful of himself. There's a conscious sense of guilt not only from the fact that he helped murder somebody but he also feels guilty with respect to his own potential, which he had betrayed all through his life. It makes the conversion much stronger when you stress that.

Let's go back to the opening courtship scene between Terry and Edie.

I think if he hadn't rescued her from that violence, she wouldn't have walked with him. That's what I mean about the script being well-constructed. But then I had to somehow answer the question as to why she stays with him. Edie knows that from the point of view of propriety and public opinion, she shouldn't. Even though she wants to. He wants to keep her with him, but he doesn't want to exert any force. He wants to approach her gently. That was a time when Brando saved me. Eve dropped her glove by accident, and he picked it up and put it on his own hand. I could never have thought of that. When she reached for her glove, he got there first so she had to stay with him. At the same time he could play it cool, as though he didn't know he was keeping her. Also, there are all kinds of sexual overtones implicit in the gesture.

How would you state the objectives in that scene?

You can say that you're trying to get her to like you or you're trying to apologize to her. But there's a case, I think, where you find it exists without articulation, because of the circumstances, because of the past, because of who he is and who she is. If they just sense it, you don't have to say it and it's better not to. I'm very leery of stating objectives.

While you always say as little as necessary to get the scene to play, you have to do your own work before you get there.

I had to find some way to bring them together and hold them

together despite the fact that she would not necessarily like him and would not necessarily like to be seen in his company. I made them walk in a way that reflects that. In the beginning of the scene they're not close to each other. Another thing I did was put it in a playground. The setting returns them to a state of innocence. When the hoods started hitting the windows of the church, it again aroused his shame and guilt. I took them to a place where those kinds of feeling would exist least—in a park, a playground. That's why he sits on the swing.

Would you articulate for yourself what you wanted out of the scene?

Oh absolutely. I talk to myself a great deal. I keep telling myself the story and what I have to get. I get there in the morning and I almost play the scene out in my mind, the delicacies of it—how to get them close believably within that circumstance. I don't talk to them except when I have to, but I do set it up. Why did I put it in the park? It could have been a lot of other places. That's a choice I made after I thought about what the scene should say.

What did you want the scene to say?

That they are brought together overcoming her reluctance and also his. With Edie there as an object, he is able to express, however indirectly, his shame. In a sense, he confesses to her without ever saying a word. His behavior says, "God, I'm sorry about your brother."

Is that something you would ever say to Brando?

I might have told him, "You want her to know that you're not a monster, that you're sorry about her brother." Often as soon as I would do that, he would cut me off. When he heard enough, he'd walk away. I knew he'd gotten it. It was obvious. And he would start to behave naturally.

Was that scene played as written? It feels so real, as if invented on the spot.

There are two things operating. First, I always try to move actors through scenery not in front of it, so they actually touch things.

If they're in front of everything, the scenery might as well be a painted backdrop. And second, Brando does something special. Sometimes it drives you nuts. He never says a line the same way twice. He changes the rhythm so the other person is forced to listen, sometimes frantically, to see what is being said. He is, in a sense, marginally improvising everything. He keeps a certain element—ten percent perhaps—of improvisation in every scene with my encouragement. When he did it too much, as he did in some other people's pictures, he was a pain in the ass. But when we worked together, he kept it within limits and it always gave his scenes a feeling of surprise, of being alive. The other actors felt emboldened to improvise as well. If he said something unusual, they'd answer in kind, and I'd let it go as long as it stayed within the intentions of the scene. All of the scenes are close to "as written" but no scene is exactly as written. What is writing? In movies saying the precise dialogue is usually not that crucial. I try to stick pretty close. I protect everything essential, and usually I protect the text, but if he hit a prop at different times in different takes, I didn't say that on this word you must touch this object.

What do you do about mismatches? The classic example is an actor holding a cigarette in his left hand in one take and his right hand in the next.

If you have a scene you can't play in one shot, it can make you a lot of trouble. It's a gamble. But it's a better kind of trouble, though, than having a dead scene. I hate cigarettes anyway.

Your instincts would always be to sit down, shut up, and let them play the scene?

Especially if I see something live happening. If you see nothing going on, you've got to get the cigarette lit on the same word. But even then you use the word "try." If he's thinking only about touching the swing on a particular word, you're in trouble. Another thing you can do is stay above his hands when you cover. Or you can cut to her as he's doing it, and cut back to him. But in general try to get the life in it. I don't believe in totally improvising scenes, because the author sweated over those words, and they all mean something. If you leave certain words out you sometimes regret it in the cutting room because things don't make sense. However, there should always be some element of improvisation in a scene. The worse an actor is, the more mechanical you have to be with him. That's when you're forced to rely on the business to convey the message, not his behavior.

Do you find that working with neophyte actors or nonprofessionals, which you've done a lot, you have to simplify and give them explicit business?

Business helps them a lot, especially if it's in the frame of reference of their own occupation or profession. Cops are very good nonprofessional actors when they're doing cop roles. It's second nature to them. Or if you have salesmen sell. You do give them more business although there is a limit because they may forget something, and then they blow the scene. I don't know whether you can generalize about it, but if you have somebody who is a nonactor eating something he likes, he's liable to mess it up in a better way than if you don't have him eating something. You constantly gamble that you'll find something expressive, unexpected, lifelike in a scene. What's worse is a mechanical rendition of a dull performance.

Moving on in the film, Edie plays a brief scene with her father then goes back to Terry up on the roof. They do the business that we talked about before with the birds. He invites her for a drink and takes her to a bar. They sit at a table, and he tells her his history. Right in the middle of it he stops and says, "...But what am I runnin' off at the mouth for? What do you care...?"

Brando did that. It was not in the script, and it was not my idea. It's brilliant, a sudden flash of life. He's so in it.

It's a spontaneous articulation of Terry's inner life—the mixed feelings he has and the sense of not being worth much.

Yes, that is it. You hit it on the head. He's full of shame. He's betrayed his whole life.

Why are you smiling?

Because you only got half of it. It's interesting that you got, "What do you care?" There's another part which is...

Of course. He's saying, "Please care."

It's telling that Brando would do that. He was always hoping that people would care about him.

It's the most dead-on kind of flirt.

Yeah, except he did it well and unexpectedly. I don't think even he expected to do it. If a thing like that is planned, it can be terrible. It's very interesting when you reverse your directions in a scene, even for a minute. The whole scene is about his wanting her to care, then he says, "I don't care if you care."

He goes on talking about the dog-eat-dog world, how nobody cares about anybody. They dance, and then a huge guy comes in and tells Brando that Friendly wants him.

What's good about that scene is the end of it when Terry and Edie have to go through a wedding party to get out the door. I don't know why it's good. I don't know why I thought of it. That movie is well-directed. It really is.

We haven't talked about Karl Malden yet. He is, in some ways, a much simpler character than the others.

I believe I got what I wanted. It's been misunderstood a lot. I was born Greek Orthodox, and when we moved to New Rochelle there was no Greek Orthodox church. My father was religious, as some businessmen are. He made me go to Catholic church and catechism school. I hated it. I went to confession once, and I really resented it. I had a lot of dealings with Catholics, and I've always had it in for them a little bit, although I like a lot of Catholic people and have lots of Catholic friends. I thought their religion was simplistic, mechanical, and slightly hypocritical. Anyway, I wanted Father Barry, the priest Malden played, to be a rigidly ethical man who in any circumstance would always tell you what is right. I knew

Malden as well as I knew anybody, and he had that quality. Priests are like that in those working-class communities. I would talk to myself and say, "That's the way the priest should be." When I got Karl, there wasn't much more directing to do.

It's funny because you said before that you hate cigarettes as a prop.

It doesn't tell much. Eating tells more.

Father Barry smokes all the time.

That's to make him a waterfront priest. The man on whom his character is based smoked a lot and drank a lot of beer.

We were at the point just after Edie and Terry left the bar. There is a short scene on the street next. It begins with a very wide shot of Brando walking. A car pulls into the foreground on the lefthand side, makes a U-turn and stops in front of him. Charlie and Friendly pile out. Friendly tells Terry he's screwed up, he's back in the hold and to stop seeing Edie, "Unless you're both tired of living."

That scene was not written the way I directed it. I decided to have them come up in a car at night in order to suggest that they were hunting him down and to propose the greatest brutality I could on Terry. He knew now that his life was in danger. I also wanted an abrupt change in rhythm from the scene in the bar, which was tender and intimate and delicate. Even the noise and the sound contrasted with the other.

Then you move into the scene on the boat where the bad guys drop a sling on Dugan's head and kill him. It begins as a very lighthearted scene, which is interesting because despite the banter, you know something terrible is going to happen. Mac, the foreman, looks down into the hold. Friendly is over on the pier. It's cross-cut, and there are signals between them. Underneath, Dugan clowns around about having finally gotten Irish whiskey to unload, and as he jokes about the advantages of a little man in a big jacket, he stuffs a bottle under his coat. Up at the top Mac screams, "And don't be walkin' off with any of that. You know how the boss feels about individual pilferage." That's a great line! Tell me about the design of that scene.

You analyzed it just right. If it's possible, it's always a good thing to play against what's going to happen. Also, the clowning is part of the innocence of the waterfront. The longshoremen are like kids. They're not very self-conscious or aware. I'll never forget something I saw in the Philippines during the war. Two cocks fighting with long knives on their spurs. One bird dealt the other a fatal blow but the cock that was struck didn't know it. He walked around, picking up grain and eating, and all of a sudden he just keeled over dead. He had returned to the most ordinary things, unaware of the impending doom. We know when a crisis is pressing around us, but innocent, naive or uneducated people do not. They just go on living their normal lives. Of course, I wanted the audience to know what Dugan did not know. Suspense always depends on the audience knowing something the character doesn't. The actor that played Dugan was a former vaudevillian. I got a lot of fighters and vaudevillians in the movie. They are naive and ebullient, and there's always one person in the gang who entertains the others and shows off. Dugan was one of the guys trying to organize the workers, but rather than make him a heavy, ideological leader of the militant group, which the left might have done, I made him just a more innocent person. I think it's truer to the situation.

You did something else in that scene. You put Brando off to the side.

Terry's troubled because he senses something is going to happen. Terry's in the middle all through this, and increasingly I alienate him from both sides. The whole story is about the fact that he's going to lose all of his old friends by testifying, but he's really not with the reformists either. He's mistrusted by all sides. So I moved him away from the center of the action. It was a simple picturization of the emotional relationships in the scene. If you turned the sound track off, the viewer should still be able to understand what the relationships are and what's going on just by the way everyone's positioned—the distance between them or the way they cluster. I had Brando watch from behind bales so that we get the sense that he's on guard and that he unconsciously expects violence to erupt. There's a sense of wariness in him all the time. Animal behavior is terribly eloquent and informative. You should study it. I used something I learned from animal behavior in *Viva Zapata!* At the beginning when the Joe Wiseman character comes to visit, Anthony Quinn watches him from behind spiked cacti, the way animals watch something. I love to watch animals. You can learn a lot about people by watching animals. I put Brando behind the bales in order to show that he's both wary and disassociated. At the Actors Studio these days they say you must feel disassociation, and that is important, but you take that for granted after awhile. You have to show what is being felt through behavior. You can't just talk about it.

Now that you've explained the technique, can you describe how you put it to use?

When I started to direct the scene, I already had a sense of how I wanted it to move so it would tell the inner story. Then I had to direct the actors so they would fit into that scheme and fit into the environment that I had arranged for them. Don't forget, as the director, you also make the set. When you set up the furniture and props, you move or arrange the objects so that the movement of the scene inside the environment will itself tell the story and help the actors do things the way you want them to. What is Brando doing in this scene? He's trying to figure out what to do next. He's aware that the other workers consider Terry a fake, and he's also aware that the guys upstairs, the bosses, have him on trial. He's on the spot with both sides. So I pulled around a lot of crates and got them up to head level so we can see Brando behind them while the rest of the action is happening in the foreground. I photographed Brando's viewpoint, but I also put something in the way of Brando's viewpoint so there was a distance all the time. See it all refers to life. Notice how I keep referring to what happens in life? That is why it's so important to keep watching and studying everything. If you can't make yourself watch or study naturally, start taking notes about everything you see. Put it down, then after a while you don't have to because you're trained. This is a silly illustration, but imagine if an actor were sitting there where you are, he feels free to contest me, to tell me off, to deal with me directly, to be friendly, to make an extra plea or to hang around too long. Whereas if I were behind a desk, he knows I've got the power, and he knows he's a suppliant. When I decided to have an office, I said I wasn't going to have an office that is degrading or humbling or insulting to my visitors. That's my nature. I don't say it's entirely good. It often costs me a lot of time, and I've been insulted on occasion. The point is that if the same scene with the same dialogue were taking place in a different environment, it would result in different behavior and create a different impression.

When you're shooting—whether it be on location or a sound stage—cameras, lights, cables, microphones and crew may be no more than three feet from an actor's face. Experienced film actors learn how to deal with that. How did you help out newcomers like Eva Marie Saint on this picture?

You make sure the actor doesn't feel that he's being judged. You stay on his side of the camera, sometimes physically during rehearsal, but spiritually at all times. You make him feel like a friend who is helping you solve problems, which is in fact what he's doing. That's not the problem. The problem is, Where shall I put this scene, where will this scene be most fruitful and most convey what I have to convey? A good exercise, often given to directing classes, is to take a scene and play it in various places. A corny example is a discussion between a man and a woman about what they are going to do today. If you put it in bed, that gives it one quality. If you put it as he's about to leave to go to work, he may feel irked because she's asked him another one of those questions. Once an actor understands where he is and the circumstances of the scene, you immerse him in the qualities of the environment. If he's in bed, you make the bed warm with blankets. If he's about to go to work, you make him dress all through it. You make him very much involved in the environment so that the environment affects him. Once you get the environment affecting him, he loses a lot of his self-consciousness.

Another thing that is very important is to bring the crew and the actors together. There's usually a terrific barrier between them.

Brando was great with that. He liked the crew better than the producer and the other dignitaries. You get the crew and the actors kidding around at lunch on the first day, and by the second day they're all friends working toward the same goals. The director's personality sets the tone for all that. It's one thing I do well.

One of the difficulties during shooting is that you often have to rush from set to set during the course of the day. There is little time for the environment to affect the actors the way you want it to.

If you feel that way about it, slow things up. Become a nuisance. Go over the budget. Make difficulties for the producer. On the other hand, sometimes there's a terrific stimulus and spontaneity in going to a new environment as I mentioned earlier.

In Waterfront I *have the feeling that maybe even from take to take you would throw a new stimulus into the environment.*

I always did that. But when you're shooting in an environment that's functioning irrespective of you, you cannot control everything. Cars drive by. There are noises all around you. You have to try to make an asset out of everything that could possibly be a difficulty.

We're talking about the scene where the sling drops on Dugan and kills him. At the end of the scene Malden makes his "Christ in the shape-up" speech.

That's the most criticized moment in the picture because the body looks as if it's ascending to heaven under the guidance of an officer of the Catholic Church. It looks like some sort of symbolism, and I suppose inevitably it is. No one believes me, but I had no idea when I shot it, that the scene would look symbolic. I was naive not to think so, but the truth is that's the way you take a dead body out of the hold of a ship. You can't carry it up the narrow steel ladders.

The scene ends with the black guy giving Joey's jacket back to Edie, the one Dugan had been wearing.

Poor working-class people never throw anything away. In cold weather a good warm garment is a valuable thing. And it's a token. He's actually saying, "Here, he'd want you to have this."

That's played in a three-shot; then the black guy walks out, and Terry and Edie stay in the frame. What you are left with most is the confusion and conflict in Terry, though he doesn't seem to be doing anything.

What is so good about that moment is that it makes the audience try to read him just like you're doing now. It's important that the central figures in a drama never be totally clear. You should try to figure them out. When you're casting, talking to an actor and you can't quite figure out what he or she is thinking, it's usually a good sign. It's a quality that all the really good movie actors have. In drama and in life there are many moments when you're bewildered. Bewilderment is a very dramatic thing—you don't know what will come of it, which way it will turn. All Brando had to do was look at Eva, and she brings out his guilt. The guilt is increasing at that point leading up to his coming out and testifying. Usually an actor will show too much. In a scene like that if you are a damn fool, you'll say, "She makes you feel guilty." Then he'll show his guilt. If you under-direct a scene like that, just have him look at her and don't say anything, you'll probably get something wonderful. Especially if Brando is playing the part.

In the next scene Brando is lying on the roof. Edie brings him Joey's coat.

That's terrific. That's a real symbol, Joey's coat.

When Terry kisses Edie you feel the utter desperation of a young man in love. It's like he wants to swallow her.

People like Terry Malloy are by prejudice, by training, and by the brutalized society that they are brought up in taught that sex and love are separate. Making love is something you do to a girl not with a girl. Terry never felt any love for anybody before. He was always on guard, and the macho thing is to put everyone down. What you say is true. Brando's got that quality in him, and also Eva arouses it. She makes you feel tender and concerned about her. You hope she's going to be all right.

Terry is a desperado, a tough. He even says to Father Barry that she's the only good thing that's ever happened to him. She is a repository for his goodness. If she will kiss him, if she will love him, then he must be a good guy.

That's absolutely true. I couldn't say it as well.

That short little scene on the roof is very much a turning point. His alliance is now with her and with what is "the best side of the difficult decision," as you put it. From now on he acts that out.

As I also alluded to earlier, there's one part of the Stanislavsky method that is underrated, but it was very central to his system and is central to all instinctively good actors, i.e. the use of objects. It's very important to think about objects that are redolent of the script or the meaning of the action—symbols yes; the object as symbol. That coat is such an object. It contains the warmth of Joey's life. It's the closest thing you can get to the guy himself. The Stanislavsky method puts a big stress in its classic form on actors dealing with objects so that the feeling and the wish he has is related to an object. To make that object come to life and mean something is part of the system. I always stressed it, and that's why in my films people are always eating or building or playing with pigeons or something.

Aside from the narrative value of those objects, if you give an actor something to do and they're doing it very simply and truthfully, then a kind of unconsciousness is achieved.

Correct.

In the next scene Terry goes to the church to find Father Barry. The priest blows him off, tells him to confess to somebody else. Terry follows him out the door and tells him that he set up Joey. Father Barry advises him to tell Edie.

Originally there was a long scene in the church that I cut. There was also a long scene where Terry tells Edie. I cut that too. In both cases he was not going to say anything that the audience didn't already know. So I cut the scene in the church down to nothing, and in the scene with Edie, I've got a steam whistle going so loudly you can't hear what he's saying. It was also symbolic of what she feels.

A huge jolt occurs because as he starts to tell her, you cut from a very wide shot to a tight close-up. Had you decided to bring that whistle in before you shot the scene?

Yes. I made Brando say the lines, but you should never hear anything for a second time. The only new things were her reaction and his shame.

She runs away and Terry is left all alone. The scene ends with a closeup of Father Barry, who has been watching from a distance, angrily putting a bent cigarette into his mouth.

That was good. Terry being left alone like that, paying his dues. You can't turn around and be accepted. You have got to pay your dues.

Afterwards, he is up on the rooftop with his pigeons. A cop is there as well. Terry spots him and says to the kid, "Jimmy, suppose I knew something, say a mug somebody put on somebody...You think I should turn him in?"

By asking the boy, he's asking himself. That's what he used to be, and no one's more immersed in street ethics than a little boy of the street. You look at his face, and you know that "don't snitch" is the essence of his code. The young actor was a boy from that area, and interestingly enough a few years later he wound up in the jug.

He says, "A cheese-eater! You're kidding!" Then Terry goes over to the cop, and the cop does a beautiful con job on him, working on him to testify before the Crime Commission. He follows Terry to the pigeon coop and sets up the scene in the taxicab. He says, "Didn't I see you fight in the Garden one night... against a fellow called Wilson...?"

That was a beautiful piece of writing. I get a lot of credit for that scene and the one in the cab, and I had nothing to do with either. One thing which I can take some credit for is that you feel that Terry partly knows he's being conned. That's another ambivalence of Brando's. I saw it and encouraged it. Some other actor would have just played Terry as dopey. Brando never made the character dumber than he was, he never condescended or patronized the character. He's a terrific artist.

When the cop gets Terry to talk about how he carried Wilson, you sense that Brando really enjoyed a physical workout.

He was very strong. He used to play football and a lot of other sports.

Then you cut to a scene where Friendly, surrounded by his cronies, puts Charlie on the spot. He says, in effect, "Go handle your brother." When Charlie says he can't, Friendly replies, "You can't have it both ways."

I set the scene up like a kangaroo court—absolute silence—with Friendly and his thugs just waiting to see what Charlie would do.

Much of the effect depends on the background characters. How much attention do you give them?

A lot. I talk to them just as if they were leading men, but I do it in terms of behavior, not psychology. You can screw them up by talking about feelings. I tell them what the scene is about, and then the greatest thing is to put an object in their hands—a cigar they can light or a scratch sheet they can search. Then they don't have to act. Also, I think I'm good at picking background types, because I've traveled around the country a lot. I told you I used a lot of fighters in *Waterfront.* Two Ton Tony Galento hit me once in the belly just playfully and about killed me. I almost threw up. In one scene I just couldn't get Tami Mauriello mad enough. So I told the cameraman to flip the switch, and all of a sudden I hit Mauriello with all my might with an open hand right across the face. He wanted to kill me, but I ducked down out of the way, and there he was on camera with his face livid. Later he forgave me. But I was lucky because he could have instinctively dropped me as my hand was moving.

The next scene is the famous one in the cab, and you've already disclaimed any responsibility for it.

There was no way to ruin that cab scene. All you had to do was get those two guys saying those lines. The only thing that was added was a sound Brando made, something like, "Oh Charlie, oh Charlie." That was really a terrific contribution.

We had a lot of trouble that day because we were supposed to shoot it with rear projection. Sam Spiegel might be good on story construction and script, but as a mechanical producer he was often delinquent. When we got to the set, there was no rear projection equipment. So Boris Kaufman, the cameraman, suggested putting a venetian blind in the back of the cab and shooting straight into the back seat. Then on the sides of the frame, he caught a piece of the windows and had flickering lights going by. Actually it was a blessing because if you had seen the street outside we would have had to have more street noise. But it was a really desperate day. It took most of the morning to solve the goof on the rear projection. Then there was another problem. Brando was being psychoanalyzed while we were shooting the picture. One of our understandings was that I would let him off at four o'clock so he could go to his analyst. So the last shot I did that day was Rod Steiger's close-up and I read Terry's lines to him. Steiger was good enough to do it, but he never forgave me. He thought I treated Brando better than I did him. I sure as hell did! But it didn't hurt. I knew I would only be on him for a few reactions, and I had promised Brando anyway. Sometimes it's important for a director to withdraw himself a little bit. If you've got the characters going good and then you talk about it, they get to thinking about satisfying you instead of playing the scenes. I was smart enough that day or troubled enough by my technical problems not to do anything. Steiger never got enough credit for something he did brilliantly. Throughout the scene you feel an older brother's concern for his younger brother. At the end of it you feel Charlie's sadness because he feels his brother has condemned himself and that he, himself, has been put in an awful spot. Steiger is very touching in that scene. If he has done anything better, I have not seen it.

In a way it's a shame that it all worked so well because it would have been interesting to ask you how you went about getting that scene.

I think it's more interesting to realize that I didn't do anything. That it was set in motion long before. That they were aware of the elements in the scene, which were that you have to make your brother do something that he doesn't want to do and your brother is in danger. Steiger knew all that without my telling him. And Brando knew everything. How Brando understood that emotion—having to do with his dignity, the fact that he could have been something—I don't know. When he said, "Oh Charlie," the melancholy and depth of pain were just terrific.

Part of that feeds off the fact that Charlie has pulled a gun. Terry puts his hand on it.

He did it so gently. It looked like he was putting his hand on his brother's arm. That was beautiful. I could never have told him to do something as good as that. They were both tremendously talented.

Considering all you've said about the importance of the environment, why had you planned to shoot that scene on a stage with rear screen, as opposed to doing it in a real cab on a real street?

I did it because of the intimacy and delicacy of the scene. If I had used a hand-held camera or even a fixed camera in the front of the cab, photographing while riding through the streets, the technical problems, the jiggling, the wires and all that would have taken on too much importance and have been too much of a distraction. By the way, that's the only set in the picture except the scene we added.

What was the scene you added?

The cutaway to the "big" boss looking at the televised hearings of the crime commission. Budd and I felt there was something missing, which is: Who is Johnny Friendly's Johnny Friendly? Adding that scene was an effort to show that there were higher-ups, men who never came near the waterfront but who were making fortunes off of the corruption there. We thought we were letting the system off a little lightly if we didn't show that the corruption went way up. If we didn't say that explicitly, then it is easy for the audience to think that *Waterfront* was a film about a couple of gangsters. The viewer could dismiss them without understanding that it was a pervasive evil. That the evil went throughout society and they themselves were part of it.

When the scene in the cab ends, Terry gets out and walks away. Then you cut back to the interior of the cab, and Charlie says, "Take me to the Garden." He slides over to the right, and as he does so, the cab driver slides over to the left in the foreground, blocking Steiger's face.

Real melodrama! My Warner Brother days coming back.

The driver makes an abrupt turn into a garage and on a level above, you see Johnny Friendly in an office.

That was an instance where I found an environment to tell my story without saying a word. Charlie went down a hole, and on top of the hole sits the predator.

In the following scene Terry breaks into Edie's apartment. She's cowering on the bed dressed in a white slip.

My wife used to hate those slips. She said, "You keep putting women in white slips. What have you got about white slips?"... Actually I always did like white slips.

Terry slams through the door, and she says, "Get away from me." He says, "Edie, I need you to love me. Tell me you love me." She replies, "I didn't say that I didn't love you. I said stay away from me." He kisses her, and while they embrace, there's a call from off screen.

It's the same call he made to Joey at the beginning of the film.

It's chilling because you know what's going to happen to Terry. Still, he runs out, and she follows him. They discover Charlie's body hanging on a hook.

I wanted to get across the brutalization—he's just meat.

Was it written that way?

No, that was my idea. There was a hook in the wall there. That was some night. The crew was going to leave Spiegel. They called him a Jew bastard to his face. They were a largely Catholic crew, and they couldn't stand Spiegel's chiseling pettiness. They were going to kill him. If it wasn't for me, they were all going to go home. Also, it started to snow, and we hadn't shot the first part of the sequence in snow so we had to run around throwing green dust on top of it.

Was it particularly difficult to work when everyone around you is ready to kill?

No, they were a nice bunch of guys. Also, I felt the same way about Spiegel. That side of him was intolerable. It was a tough picture to do, though, and I don't blame Spiegel as much in retrospect as I did then. After seven or eight weeks of that cold, everybody's nerves were on edge.

A number of things are striking in that scene. First, you show Charlie hanging on that hook in an enormous wide shot. He's in the corner of the frame, and as a truck pulls by, the headlights reveal him. You look and think, "Is that what I thought it was?" Secondly, what Terry does when he sees Charlie hanging there is amazing. He barely touches him. He puts his hands on the wall on either side of him and leans toward him but doesn't look at him.

The idea of not taking him down, the fact that there's nothing you could do, really gives you the sense that it's all over.

When Terry lifts him off the hook, he drapes Charlie's hands around his own neck. It's like an embrace.

All that stuff is Brando. He's so full of feeling.

In a sense the score has been evened, brother for brother. It's a kind of symmetry that gives a mythic feeling to the picture. Were you consciously trying for that?

No, not consciously. We were just trying to make an absolutely characteristic, typical story about that area, that mood and that time. I suppose we were dealing with universals, but I wasn't aware of it. Part of that mythic size comes from the fact that it was well-done by the actors, and the actors were themselves of a certain size. Also the script was sparely constructed. It went from event to event to event. If you look at the old narrative poems like *The Iliad* or *The Odyssey*, you'll see that they leap from event to event to event also. You're able to read into these events whatever you feel. In a lot of modern writing the author is always nudging you saying, "This is what you should feel, here's what this means."

Another thing that happens is that the characters, while remaining very particularized individuals, also become forces in opposition.

That was intended. The events on that waterfront were of that size. It was a clear and elemental struggle. It didn't have overtones and shades. It dealt with fundamental issues in an arena where no small talk was possible. You either grabbed your count or you didn't. You got picked or you didn't. Someone kills you or he doesn't. It has the same qualities as a Western. A lot of Westerns become mythic because they deal with fundamental movements and basic events.

Of all of your films the ones I liked most have certain elements in common. The narratives are straightforward and the issues clear. Then you add texture and ambivalence and depth through the particularization of the characters.

I believe that the central characters are only interesting when they have an inner conflict, i.e. the events happen outside, but the events also happen inside. The event inside is the war between two sides of the guy. That's in all my films. And I suppose I have been that way a lot of my life too.

By the way, it's not only that the score has been evened—brother for brother. That's true, but Edie loves Terry now and is concerned about what's going to happen to him next.

She says, "...let's get away from here, first Joey then Dugan, now Charlie—and any minute...I'm frightened—I'm frightened." Terry clenches his fists and says, "I'll take it out of their skulls." He pulls a gun out of his back pocket, the gun Charlie gave him in the cab, and repeats to his dead brother, "I'll take it out of their skulls." He rises to his feet, and to me it's the most heartbreaking moment in the film. He says to Edie, "Go get the priest and get back here. For God sakes don't leave him alone for long."

You asked me how it gets the universal, classic quality. When you get down to elemental things, a dead brother, you don't leave him alone. You stay with the body. That's like Greek tragedy. That film is underrated now. People say it's just a melodrama. But actually it's a very deep film. The British and the French put that film down, can you imagine that? I think it has something to do with a feeling that there's something politically rightist about the film. So what? I have a right to say anything I want. I don't care if you agree with me or not. I think they ought to look at it like a work of art. Say, "That guy out of a pain which was caused by a deed we totally disapprove of, but out of his very genuine self-defense and genuine emotion did this film." The right question is, "Is the film good?" I don't ask my best friends to agree with me.

By the way, you left out the scene where Terry and Edie run down the alley and a truck almost hits them. It's how they discover Charlie—lit up by the headlights.

You call it a scene. I looked at it more as a transition.

I call it a scene because it wasn't in the script and I added it. It got you to the body in a shocking way. Directorially we were going from a still scene in the apartment to a very still scene with Charlie's body. The effect of the latter scene depended strongly on how it was set up.

Terry wants revenge. He goes into Friendly's bar with the pistol. Nobody's there.

The very emptiness of that bar was threatening.

He walks all the way through the bar to the back room. There's a closed door, and he makes an interesting choice. You expect him to blast the door open. Instead he gently nudges it with his foot. Then he crosses back to the bar and demands a drink, the pistol resting on his bloody arm. Father Barry walks in, and there's a barrage of overlapping dialogue. "What do you want from me, Father?" "Your gun." "...go chase yourself." "Give me that gun." "You go to hell." "What did you say?" "You go to..." Father Barry flattens him with a right before he can finish the sentence. As Terry goes down, two guys scurry out the door. Terry gets up off the deck, and the priest lays out the morality of it. "Don't fight like a hoodlum down here in the jungle...Fight him tomorrow in the courtroom..." All through Father Barry's impassioned plea Terry screams, "It's none of your business." Was that written to be overlapped?

No, that's direction. Both of their emotions were uncontrollable and riding very high. The punch released that. You couldn't do it otherwise. You couldn't have had Terry listening, it would have been false and killed the scene. Another thing that helped was the two guys scurrying out. There's a lot of rhythm in directing. You don't take a step up here, you do it in stages. And again, the fact that I had worked with these guys and that they knew each other made it simple.

Actors are often hesitant about jumping somebody else's lines. They're very courteous.

That is very easy to take care of by making it your responsibility, not theirs. You tell them, "I want you to talk while he's talking." Once you directorially sanction it, it's okay. We do it all the time in life.

The end of that scene illustrates a weakness in the film—the ways in which you tried to humanize the priest, make him one of the boys. It seemed to me they were superficial—the cigarettes and the way he orders a beer.

Actually he's all stirred and hot, and he wants a cool drink. But I know what you mean. That's a tough part. There are so many traps in playing a priest. It's tough to avoid clichés.

The button on the scene is when Terry throws his gun at a photograph of Friendly and a politician.

That's the way he makes up his mind to go to court. Then it picks up in court.

When Terry takes the oath. He makes it his own by saying "right" instead of "I do."

"I'm going to testify, I'm going to testify." That's where his concentration is.

At the end of the scene, as Terry walks out, he passes Friendly, and a brawl almost breaks out. Friendly wants to kill him with his bare hands.

That's right. There was going to be a price to pay for testifying, and it starts here.

It continues into the next scene. He walks into Edie's apartment house. There are a couple of cops with him, and even they needle him for having broken the code of silence. He says hello to a guy he passes on the steps, and the guy totally snubs him.

A lot of that kind of thing happened to me after I testified before HUAC. I was snubbed. People I knew well would look at me, but not talk. People looked down on me. They couldn't accept the fact that correctly or incorrectly it was something I did out of principle. Maybe nobody agreed with me, but I thought that was the right thing to do. Maybe I did wrong, probably did. But I really didn't do it for any reason other than that I thought it was right. But that reaction was also completely true of the waterfront environment. The best part of it was the way Brando responded to it. It was a fantastic adjustment, one I couldn't have anticipated. There was something wry about it. It was as if it gave him courage. It stiffened him in his resolve. All his behavior was as if he felt, "I'll be goddamned. Screw you." It made a man out of him.

That's what you said happened to you.

It was painful but yes, in some ways it made a man of me. Until then I had been very hung-up on the approval of my peers. I got rid of that need during that period.

Terry goes up on the roof, and a dead pigeon is thrown at him. The tough little boy we saw earlier, now with tears in his eyes, screams, "A pigeon for a pigeon." You say he was a street kid. How did you get him to do that?

Just genius, that's all!

Right, but what did that genius do? Or what would the genius do if he had to do it tomorrow?

I don't know, man. It was hard work and it took a long time. I really just kept after him. I remember that. I didn't quit on it, it's very important not to. And I remember that I was never quite satisfied. Making him actually throw a pigeon was helpful. It would have been very difficult for him if I had him just yelling "pigeon" and crying. When you do it in a piece of business with a symbolically resonant prop, it isn't so important that he feel it. That's the whole theory right there in a nutshell.

Then Terry goes into the coop. Edie comes up from behind. It's a very wide shot, and when she calls to him all you see is his hand waving her off. It's very moving.

That's good direction. I think I had seen a gesture like that in some painting or maybe in life. I watch people in grief a lot. I go to funerals. In moments of stress people's gestures are inevitably eloquent. What he's saying is, "Stay away, just stay away," and that gives more of a sense that there's something horrible in the coop, than if I'd shown it.

Then you cut to him with the dead birds, seen through the screen door.

If you shoot through screens or curtains, you see shadowy figures, which gives the audience a chance to imagine or feel along with you. You get much more emotion that way than if you thrust it at them. That's something I have to watch all the time, because my tendency is to be explicit, to be too clear.

Edie pleads with him to get out of town, go inland, get a job on a farm or something. He won't go. "You always said I was a bum. Well, not anymore. Don't worry. I'm not going to shoot anybody. I'm just going to get my rights." All through the picture she'd begged Terry to do the right thing. Now that she's in love with him and he's determined to do what is right, she switches over and tells him to watch his own ass, to be expedient.

That was part of the intention. She's concerned about him now so she wants to save him. Remember, Edie was born and raised on the waterfront. She knows he's going to get it. But the more significant part of it is how he changes. What he's done has made a man out of him.

There's one thing that I stress a lot that many authors and directors disagree with me about. They may be right. I may be wrong, and I say that truthfully. I put a great stress on the idea that in a good film or play the protagonist changes. He's not the same at the end as he was at the beginning. Tennessee Williams disagreed strongly. He said it was the "drama" that I'd learned in my lefty days. That it's an emotional correlative of the political notion that, "Now I see." But I do believe that events cause people to change, that heroes are made by events as much as events by heroes, and that in difficulty a person gets stronger, harder and more resolute. I myself have only learned from pain. I never learned anything any other way. So the significant thing to me was that Terry said, "No, I'm going down and get what's coming to me."

That, I think, is a very romantic notion.

Maybe, but I have seen it time and again in real life. The most obvious example is FDR, who was a good-looking playboy until his disability made a man out of him. The same thing happened to Bobby Kennedy, who was just a kid until some rough things happened to him and he became a tough guy. I value that quality in life, and I feel it's dramatic too. I feel it's hardening. I feel the human race progresses that way. What I feel about democratic peoples is that they progress not in great overturns, which is what I used to think in the '30s, but through resolution of dissension. When a problem is resolved, there's a tiny step forward. I think we progress that way, perhaps through learning as a people. The revolution I did see in my life was in Roosevelt's time. The idea that government owes a job to every one of its citizens was something that Henry Wallace and Roosevelt advocated. They won out, and we made a small step forward at that time.

I believe that if a leading character in a play or film or book is worth anything, he changes. The events change him. In life a hero arises or in art he is created to fit a certain set of circumstances. All of my movies have that in them. The change is not necessarily always for the better. In *A Face in the Crowd* the hero is affected by events and becomes worse. But there is always a change. In *Waterfront* it is for the better. It is romantic, but so is hope. It is also dialectic in the sense that at a critical moment in Terry Malloy's life a little change in quantity brings about a change in quality. I believe in that. I also believe that people are created by the pressures they are under. It's very much a part of my life experience.

From the time I was a kid, I have always felt I was up against it. I had to survive through persistence and continued courage, partly because I was an immigrant, partly because people told me I couldn't do this or that or I wasn't equipped for this or for that. I didn't do well at first, but I persisted until I did. I see in myself growth through overcoming difficulty. I learned most of what I know that's of any value that way. I've experienced a lot of rejection of all kinds. I guess everyone has. But I'm very persistent for whatever reason. I had to be. There's no choice when you're an immigrant, except to be swamped. I never learned a taste for that. One of the bad things about this country is that we're so anxious for the approval of our peers. The old inner-directed thing doesn't exist anymore. We're outer-directed, especially in the theater and film, where an actor's whole life is devoted to pleasing the director, and the director's whole life is devoted to pleasing the playwright, and the playwright's whole life is devoted to pleasing an audience. We should be pleasing ourselves like any decent man does. When Terry Malloy walked into the showdown with Johnny Friendly, he was inner-directed. He was like a different person, he even walked differently. His ordeal had made a man of him. He no longer does things in order to gain other people's approval. That's crucially important. In life we are all unconsciously doing a lot of things to please others. That's why directing, or writing even more so, is a very selfish business. You are cutting yourself off from people. You are saying things about people that are painful to them and to yourself, and you have to persist despite that. You ignore your wife and family. You make a choice. It's a painful business. The whole life of an artist is that way. We are selfish people. If you examine the life of any artist, you'll see that none of them are nice guys. They're not particularly kind or sweet. I'm very tough. You don't survive any other way. There are all kinds of things pulling at you. For example, the crew gets tired around four o'clock. That's when you've got to be at your strongest because you need to finish the scene you're shooting without settling for less than the best. You want another take so you've got to be tough. It's even harder when you write, because to write is to reveal oneself, and revealing things is painful. But you've still got to persist. People turn you down and make fun of you in the *New York Times*, and you say, "I'm going to write another book." You have to get to the point where you don't even care if the audience applauds you or not. We're so hooked on being liked that it's very painful to not be liked. Sometimes the most you can ask of yourself is just to sit in the same spot and take the same beating, but not to back off. I've seen that in the ring. I've seen guys that catch everything the other guy throws for five rounds and then they come on.

This takes us to the last scene in the picture. Terry bellows at Friendly, "I'm glad what I done...I was rattin' on myself all them years and didn't know it, helpin' punks like you against people like Pop and Dugan..."

That's where the parallel people have tried to draw between my HUAC testimony and Terry's falls short. I never felt that. I always felt my situation had values on both sides. I was always wavery about it—informing on your peers is not an easy thing to do. In making *Waterfront* I drew from what I had been through in my life. It's what any artist does. But I never meant any parallel between Terry and me because the issue in the film is terribly clear. The corrupt union bosses were brutalizing and exploiting their fellows. It wasn't even another class. And they knew they could count on the code of silence to protect them. Terry was right to smash it.

You have mentioned a number of times how much you love Brando as a man and an actor, how his sensibility was so much like yours. He seemed like a perfect extension of you. That scene could have been terribly melodramatic. What makes it work is all the physical and emotional pain revealed by Brando's performance. Despite the fact that the issues are simple, he pays very dearly, and we feel for him.

That's right. I believe in courageous acts, but when you perform courageous acts, you often get the stuffing kicked out of you, and you've got to be ready to take it. You may not come out of the beating the same man. When he yells, "I'm glad what I done" to Friendly. That was an important choice. It made it into a real political act. I made him proclaim it to the world. That was the way I felt.

You had Friendly and his cronies on the same little houseboat where the picture started. Terry's on the gang plank between that house and the pier. Behind him the rest of the workers start to assemble, watching.

In a sense the fate of the waterfront is being decided. By doing it that way Friendly can't back off.

Friendly goads Terry to get him onto his turf, and finally he charges. He and Friendly fight. When Terry starts to win, Friendly calls for his gorillas, and they stomp the hell out of him. You did most of that action off camera around the corner of the house.

You gather that's important, don't you? Not only because it suggests more than showing the violence, but it's shot from the point of view of the jury. The other workers are more than an audience. They're going to make a choice. The victor is going to be the leader of the union.

It's interesting that they don't do anything but watch. They do not go down and help Terry even though they know he is being ganged up on.

Oh no. They wouldn't do that. That's against the code. A lot of people resented that they didn't come to his aid. But they wouldn't. That's the fact of it.

Edie and Father Barry show up with a couple of longshoremen. Terry's lying there, semi-conscious in a pool of his own blood. Father Barry gives him a snow job, and we watch as Terry makes his decision. He says, "Get me on my feet." His physical acting is superb.

Sensational. He must remember getting knocked out on the football field.

Then there's the dramatic last beat in which Terry staggers into work, and the rest of the longshoremen follow him past the bellowing Johnny Friendly who screams, "I'll be back! I'll be back! And I'll remember every last one of ya!" But the stevedores keep moving toward the warehouse. The gate comes down and that's it.

What I was trying to do was accurately portray the situation and not pretend the gangsters were overthrown. Friendly yells, "I'll be back." He's still there. He's still the head of the union.

I'd like to go back and ask you some technical questions. The photography, for example. Boris Kaufman shot it. He was a great cameraman. You stopped using him after Splendor in the Grass. *Why?*

He was terrific on *On the Waterfront* and *Baby Doll.* But on *Splendor in the Grass*, I told him, "Boris, I don't want the concentration of the scenes to be your lighting. Get it down and give it to me." He was never fast. I'd buy that, but he kept sending a gaffer in-between takes. The minute the take was over this little guy would dart in and start moving the cutters. The actors never did the scene exactly the same way twice so the correction didn't matter. I said, "Don't get too fussy with me." But he got more and more that way, and everything got to be a hassle. But he did a good job on *Splendor in the Grass.* Some of it was beautiful, excellent. Some of it was not. I never really liked the color of anything I did. In addition I found that too much of the time was spent lighting a master. I got more aware of the importance of cutting as I went along, and if you are going to make a lot of cuts, you have to have a lot of shots, and I was not getting them. I was getting a well-lit master of which I used very little. I was going home time after time feeling I didn't get enough coverage. I still admired Boris enormously, though. I loved the way he worked. I've liked every cameraman I ever had, but Boris was the most artistic. When we were filming *Waterfront*, one premise I set with him right away was that I didn't want to make the skyline of New York picturesque. Don't stress it. He gave me some real beauty, the kind of beauty that we like. He had a lot of guts, in the cold with a rebellious crew. He did a terrific job, and I admire him.

Can you describe how you worked with your D.P.'s [directors of photography]?

I always told them what I wanted in a scene, but I also tell them that I'm open. I show them a rehearsal and say, "Give me your suggestions." And very often I'd take their suggestions or part of their suggestions. As I got older though I began to get a clearer and clearer idea of what I wanted from the camera and the way I wanted a scene to be shot. I respect those guys, and I always listen to them. But I never waiver from my basic intention. The nicer they are, the more dangerous they are. The sweeter they are, the more agreeable, the greater the menace. You have to be tough, but you must listen to them because they are artists. Also, as time passed, I wanted broad strokes. I didn't want half-tones anymore. I went to Paris and saw [Raoul] Coutard shooting a film for [Jean-Luc] Godard. All he had was a big baffle and nine photo floods up on a stand coming down somewhat at an angle. Godard was free to do anything he wanted. That's what I did on my last picture. Just lit it generally and went around and got what I could. A whole thing had been built up out of a tradition which was based on how to photograph aging female stars so they still looked desirable and how to make old men look like they're still heroes.

Tell me about the music.

Once we had completed the picture, Spiegel showed it to Leonard Bernstein. Spiegel kept apologizing for the film. That was one of his tricks—to seem slightly above everything. I had a terrible scene in the cutting room with Spiegel. I yelled at him, "It's a great picture. Don't talk that way about it." Anyway, Bernstein liked it, and I think he liked my enthusiasm about it too. I didn't like the opening piece of music. It says, "These are the heavies." It sets a tone of highfalutin melodrama that's more befitting *Aida* than *Waterfront*. The rest of the music, though, is excellent.

After you showed him the picture, what happened?

Then we talked about every sequence. The first thing you talk about is where there should be music, where it will help, and what kind of music it should be. Then you determine just where it comes in and cuts out. Then you determine what the music should do to the scene, augment it, modify it, or add a new color. Sometimes they'll play stuff for you on the piano while the picture is running to give you an idea of how it will go. That's very helpful. Music is terribly important to me. I like native sources—the blues, jazz, folk, rock. There was less of that with Lennie. He was the most highly regarded man in the field of American music. So he went off and did a score by himself. I don't know if I even said much of anything to him because I was so glad to have him.

The music is mostly used in the old-fashioned tradition of underscoring, telling the audience what they should be feeling. How do you decide to underscore a scene?

Sometimes you plan a scene with music. Generally I try to make music force its way in. I try not to use it except where I've got to have it, where it's going to help or mean something special. Sometimes silence or the real sounds are better. There's a very great danger with music, which is that you beg for sympathy with it. And also, it gets predictable. "Here's the love scene music."

Although the music is often used in the way in which you just described, it is not necessary. The emotion is already there.

I try not to bring another personality into the picture through the music. But there was no way to avoid that with Lennie. So you're aware of the music. It put the picture on the level of almost operatic melodrama here and there. That's the only thing I object to.

How do you describe the kind of music you want?

I told him what I wanted the music to say that was not already being said by each scene. It might be that the music should be indicating what a character feels, the one you see reacting all the time for instance.

How specific do you get?

I don't whistle! But I do occasionally refer to analogies.

The other general question is how did you work with your editor?

I was right on top of that guy. I like to go in every day and see what's been roughed out. I tell them what I want a scene to say. If they're good, they ask me that. I discuss it as though they were co-directors, which they are. I place the highest value on their contributions. It's critical. It's really a third of the filmmaking process. You can very easily be deceived or misled by good editing. At the beginning of a project, I write a notebook about what I'm trying to get out of the whole picture, what the picture means, and what each scene contributes to that. I try to write it down. I don't look at it again while I'm working except when I'm desperate. But I do look at it again when I'm editing because it takes me back to my original intention. You can make a thing go along smoothly story-wise and still not make the right point. You have to have something to go back to, to remember.

How directly do you work with them?

I'm right next to them on the machine. I've gotten so I don't do any editing while I'm shooting, but I used to see all the rushes every day and say, "Here's how I want it to go together." I told them exactly how I saw it, where I wanted each close-up to be, how I thought a scene should start, what its climax should be and which takes I liked best. I'd lay out the whole cutting, and then I'd say in my generous manner, "Now you're free to do it the way you think. What are your suggestions?" But I lay down the law exactly. I'm not vague about that. It's my picture. As soon as they have a scene roughed together, I come back, see what they have and make corrections. When it's all strung together, you see the rough cut. It's always disastrous, and you have to remind yourself that it is. Then you begin to work on it, you take out the redundancies and overstatements. You begin to get it down so it joins as a story. You do all that work right with them. I'm there all the time, a little less so with Dede Allen.

Why less with her?

Partly because I was still in Europe while she was roughing *America America* together, but also because conceptually she's very able. She's got a good head and thinks like a good director. I would discuss my intentions just as much, but I would give her more freedom than I have given other people. She is a terrific editor. She contributes, and she helped me particularly on my weak points—overstatement and redundancy. When I look at a lot of the pictures I made, I wish they were shorter. More and more now I do my own editing, and I know when I shoot a scene just the way I want it to go.

Do you prefer to be in there on your own rather than using someone who's as good as Dede?

No, I'd rather have someone to balance me. I often feel like what I want is some sort of deputy producer, somebody to fight with me. It's stimulating to have somebody to argue with me, to put me down. I'd resent it and retain the right to fire them, but I think it's good for me to have somebody who understands what I'm trying to do but who gives me the audience viewpoint on it. I had a lot of fights with Spiegel, but he helped a lot in *On the Waterfront*.

You talked about going back to your notes to check what you have against your original intentions.

It's very dangerous not to. You can waver off them a little bit without realizing it. I'm a great believer in unity, though I haven't always had it. Each scene has a relationship to the climax of the work and should point ahead to that climax. It should only do that and not wobble off.

Have you ever found yourself having moved off the original intentions for a scene, and what did you do in that case?

You correct it by cutting or maybe by reshooting. You can do an awful lot, as you know, in cutting. Another thing I realized as I got older is how little you need to say to get your point across, particularly nowadays when people have been trained by television.

Do you find that if your intentions change or a scene doesn't fulfill your original intentions, you begin to say, "What else can I do with this material? How can I make this material play?"

You have to watch that because you can make a scene effective ten different ways. The thing to do is make it effective the way you want it to be effective. That's a bad, bad phrase—"making it play." If you get in trouble, you have to remind yourself of what your original intention was and somehow or other you get it, even if it means reshooting. That's why putting it down early on before you get bogged down in the complexities and disturbing things in the material and personalities is important. Just write yourself instructions as to what you are supposed to get out of every scene.

What do you do when you find redundancies or overstatements, where, for argument's sake, you've got a series of scenes which escalate to a certain point and you find that you may have overshot the mark in an early scene?

Cut, cut, cut, cut, cut and cut. I overstate a lot. I think all directors do. Very often you'll find a scene that's logy in the middle. If you take out a previous scene, the scene that was previously logy suddenly works.

Have you ever lopped out a whole scene?

Oh yes. But it never works as well as you hope. Unfortunately, there's always some little piece of information missing.

Was there any dubbing in Waterfront*?*

There was some, but not a lot. There's a lot in *America America* because we were shooting a lot in the midst of hostile crowds, and the street noises couldn't be stopped. Also, the lead actor was just learning English as we shot the picture.

How do you work in the dubbing studio?

I'm on top of that. I don't do it mechanically. Just psychologically speaking I say to myself, "Here's another chance. You can improve the scene." But I prefer not to dub at all. I really don't like it. I've never been satisfied with a dubbed scene. Another important thing you have to remember when you are shooting is to keep getting background tracks. If you hear any interesting off-camera sound in the distance, shut everybody up and get a track of it. Get all the sounds you can so that when you do dub you've got the room sounds and whatever sounds were outside. Prepare yourself in each scene for the possibility of dubbing.

In the studio you've got to redirect in a sense.

I get both actors at the mike, the one that's speaking and the other one looking at him. As near as I can, I try to make them recreate the scene they were playing. We also hear the way they did it originally, which helps. Sometimes, however, I change interpretations.

How do you deal with the technical problems of matching voice to picture at the same time you're trying to get a natural performance?

Persist. It's very easy to get licked by it, but I'm very tenacious.

Have you learned any way to cool a guy off when he gets tense?

One good thing is to stay in the room with them—at the beginning anyway. Keep going in there and giving them food or kidding around with them. They seem to get over it. What's deadly is if you sit behind that cold plate glass and say, "Now give it to me." Just be human. They are your helpers, you're not testing them. You must make the actors feel that you're attempting something together. They never get tense when you do that. It's an essential part of your job, and there is no way to get around it.

At what point do you address yourself to the sound of the picture?

Basically not until I'm putting it together. I'm aware of sound much more than I used to be. I never had much of a trained ear, but now I'm slowly paying more attention to music and especially to background sounds. Often while I'm shooting I give the script girl whatever ideas occur to me. "Steam drill very, very far off coming in here and here and here and here—four times." That way I'm very aware of the totality of what I'm trying to get over.

To what extent do you turn your editor and sound cutter loose to make suggestions?

A lot. As long as they know my basic intention. Otherwise, they can bore you and take up your time with irrelevancies. I usually tell people twenty times anyway. My tendency is to say it again and again as though I've just discovered it. I do praise them very highly for the first suggestion they make that I like. There's no stimulus like praise, and they've often had some wonderful suggestions. You have to get people to work with, whatever their proficiencies are, that are to some degree artists, who are trying to express something. It may cost you a little more time, but they may give you the one thing that you value most. You create an artistic atmosphere. That way it's fun. You are no doubt the center and head of it, and you've got to keep them cooking. You never know where you're going to get a good idea. The doorman may give it to you on your way to work. I listen to everybody.

Tell me about the mix or, as it is called in Hollywood, the dub.

The only thing I don't like about mixing is that it usually goes too fast. It's a very creative process, but you never have time to experiment with it because it's so expensive. One very simple thing I do is try to make the dialogue loud enough so that when it's informing you, it's central.

How do you work with the mixers?

I go through a scene once or twice and hear it with them, tell them what I have in mind, what my concerns are, and then I go away, usually for two or three hours, and then I come back, and we really start to work.

Why do you go away?

They have a lot of tedious technical work to do first. They have to equalize all the dialogue tracks. In putting a scene together, you're always using takes that were shot at different times. Not only do the background noises vary, but the ratio between the dialogue and the background noise varies as well. All of that has to be carefully balanced, or else there is a jolt every time you make a cut. It's all mechanical and takes quite a while to get right. If you stay for all of it, you find yourself concentrating on details that are not important. You have to try to retain some objectivity. In the editing I do the same thing. I'll be on top of it, but I won't be there during the mechanics. I come in when it's been done and give notes. When I've got it rough, I let it go and do the next scene.

Are there any particular problems you've found arising in the mix?

The worst problem is when you realize that despite all the care you've taken and all the work of everybody, a scene still doesn't come off. Sometimes when you see it all together with the music and everything, you discover that your point is made more quickly than you thought. If the audience is way out ahead of you and calling your shots for you, you're in trouble. In almost every picture I've said, "Let's take that hunk out." I do it by asking the dumbest question, "Does it mess you up a lot, fellows, to take that little piece out there?" They want to kill me. But it has to be done. You have to leave room in every process for change, keeping yourself alert, not mixing in and getting too friendly with everybody, not talking too much, not getting too involved in the details. Just be the boss, a nice guy seemingly, but basically a mean guy that's got his eye on the main chance. You try to make each step a creative process in which you more and more tell what you have in mind.

Do you get involved in approving prints from the lab?

Yes I do, but I'm not too good at that. I wish I were better at it.

I never got a color print yet that I really liked 100 percent. Nearest thing to it was *East of Eden*. I don't know, it must have been an accident. And I've had terrific cameramen. I always make the same speech about wanting things grey, but I know the damn brown mare will come out golden brown, like the color of a beautiful sable coat, gleaming and shining—just awful!

Have you ever been in a position where you were told that the changes you wanted to make in the closing phases didn't justify the expense?

No producer ever dared tell me that. They just won't give me money anymore until I've proven myself financially viable again. That's happened before, but it doesn't bother me.

It doesn't bother you at all?

If you write a good script, they'll be fighting each other to get it. If they don't want to finance a film, I'll get it published as a book. That's the great independence that an artist has. If you try to please yourself basically, what in the world can anybody do to you? If worse comes to worse, I'll borrow money from the bank. I've always done what I wanted in one way or another. I've had three box office disasters in a row. Two of them lost millions, *America America* and *The Arrangement*. And *The Visitors* lost its negative cost, and I lost some money on it besides. So I've got to prove again that I can earn people I don't care about, money that they don't care about. So what can they do to me? I live just as well as I want to. I eat what I want, wear what I want, go where I want when I want.

You produced a lot of your own films. Did you get involved in the advertising?

Always. But I'm not very good at it. I was great once with *Baby Doll*. I had Carroll Baker 300 feet long, lying in a crib sucking her thumb. It was a great ad. Of course, the picture didn't do much business anyway.

You won an Oscar for Waterfront. *What was the effect on you personally of the public and critical response?*

It was pleasant. I was very low before that, like I am now, and not a desirable commercial director. It's great to turn the tables on people. It vindicates you in a sense. It's also important that people are aware of you. We're in the communications business and people are listening to you. They haven't been able to turn you off or knock you down or silence you. Silencing an artist is like killing him.

Did you ever go through any kind of personal crisis as a result of a public failure?

Sure. I directed four plays that were failures, and I just kept going. You're insane to expect success. I've always taken the hardest possible route. I've always tried to make a statement about what I individually feel about our times. I'm not in anyone's stream. I really don't like any sort of establishment, right, left or whatever, where you are to think what people expect you to think. I don't exactly like to be with other people. I'm not against anyone, I just like to go my own way, and that's a hard route if you're trying to make a statement in a film.

What did you do when your work wasn't accepted?

Where's the next hill? That's all you can do. Hell, I'm proud of myself. Who can actually hurt you? Not at my age.

I'm not talking about you at your age.

I was made tough pretty early on. I can't be put down. I've never stopped working, and I like my work. The only thing that could hurt me is if I weren't able to write or make films. I did *The Visitors* for nothing. No one can really hurt you unless you're self-doubting.

And there was never a point in your life where there was doubt?

Plenty about my talent. The main problem an artist has is with his own limitations. When you come up against a brick wall and say, "That's as far as I can go," that hurts. You do have bad times that way. I've made a lot of mistakes. After I finish every movie or book, I always write a criticism of it, whether it is successful or unsuccessful. I always start a new project while something is being finished. I always have a program of work I'm going to do. I really don't have a lot of respect for the establishment critics. They don't tell the truth, and they're not really trying to do the same thing I'm doing. It's as if you're a sprinter and you're being judged as a mile runner. They're judging me from another point of view. *Time* magazine said I'd had a bad five years. I'd had the best five years of my life because I was writing books about what I cared about. Once you know some of the critics, nothing they say can bother you. They're all entertainers essentially. They're all trying to make a living and be colorful. So God bless them.

What about the public?

I like it when audiences like what I do. I felt hurt by *The Visitors* because very few people got a chance to see it. I thought it had worth. I think with every work of art, the more difficult the thing it tries to do, the more flaws it has. In my opinion, *Panic in the Streets* was the only perfect film I ever made. It's easy, it didn't try to do much. If you're going to do something difficult you are going to have faults. Every great book I know has faults. Dostoyevsky has chapters that are unreadable in my opinion, and Tolstoy gets very tedious at times. They're the guys I admire most. I try to do difficult things, and I don't entirely succeed. I've always put myself on the line. Sometimes publicity and public attention embarrass me. It gets too much. But I've always done it. If I believe in something, it's not hard to sell it. I used to be an actor. I'm relaxed as hell on the air because I'm confident about what I mean to say. I believe that if you write something and spend a year and three months on it, you ought to get up and tell people about it and say, "You ought to read it. Even if you don't like it, you should read it."

Was there ever a time earlier on when it was desperately hard for you to get financing?

The hardest time I ever had was just prior to *On the Waterfront*, which every studio in California turned down. The public attention

I got by the HUAC testimony not only put me on the left blacklist, the right and center turned against me as well. As far as they were concerned I had been a Communist and therefore tainted. I was also an embarrassment because all the publicity had made me a controversial and unsavory figure by their lights. Also, my latest pictures had lost money.

What were your feelings in the face of all that?

Struggle. What does an animal do when he's cornered? What do you do? What choice have you? You keep on. I have a dumb, stupid persistence. I'm not so bright, but as I say, I put my head down and keep pushing against the wall. I'll find some place that gives. Maybe I won't this time. I can keep writing. A friend once said to me, "Your favorite stance is to fight out of a hole, and if there's no hole there, you'll dig one." It's true. For example, right at this very moment in my life another director might worry and say, "I've had three flops in a row. Nobody will back this picture I want to make. What am I going to do? I'm in terrible shape." I don't feel that way. I've kept my standard of living at a level where I can control my life. If I respected the critics, then I would think, "There must be something wrong with me. They won't accept me anymore." But I don't respect them. I really just enjoy life. I wish I could live my whole life over or live again as long as I've lived. I learned in psychoanalysis that you should enjoy just being by yourself, enjoy your own observations, your own thoughts.

There was never really a point in your life when you were scared?

I've had plenty of bad times in my life, but they were always personal.

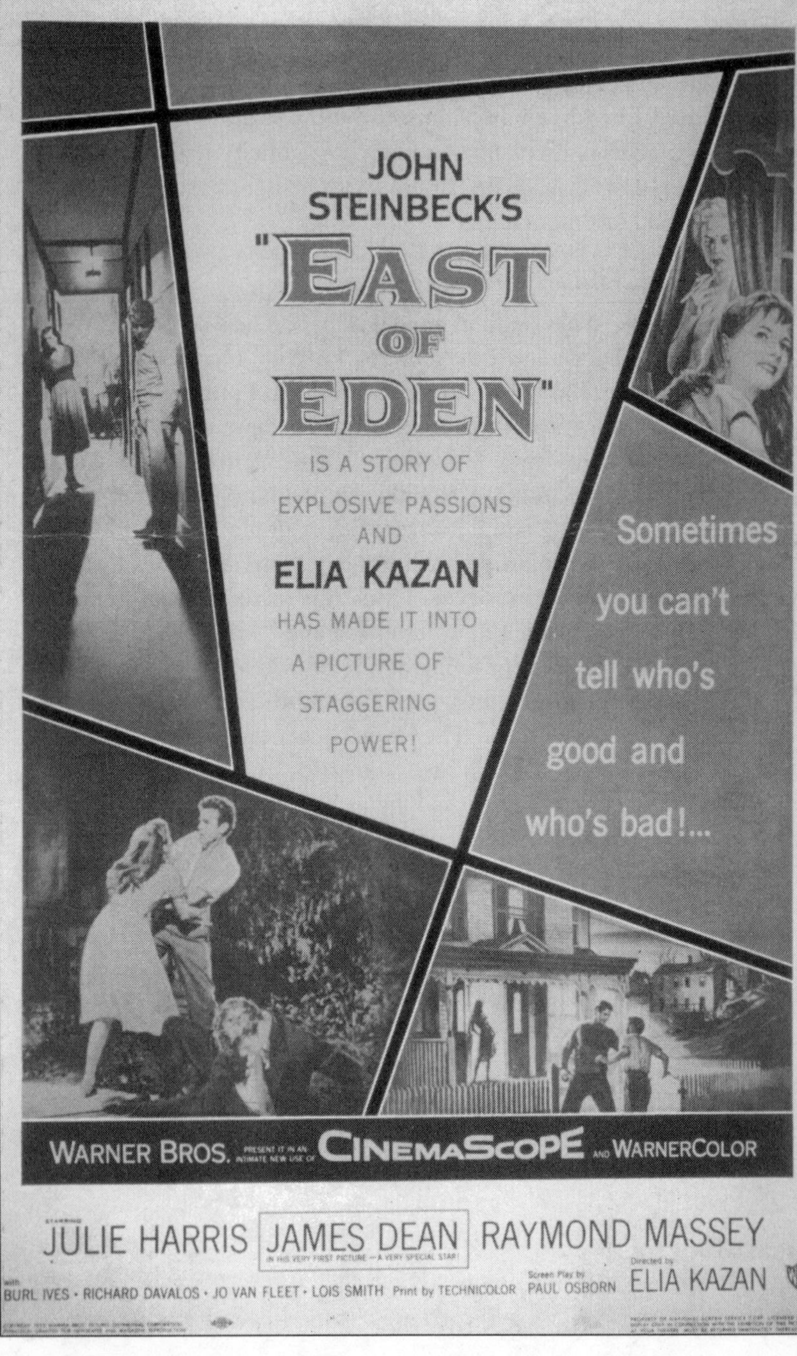
JOHN
STEINBECK'S
"EAST
OF
EDEN"
IS A STORY OF
EXPLOSIVE PASSIONS
AND
ELIA KAZAN
HAS MADE IT INTO
A PICTURE OF
STAGGERING
POWER!
Sometimes
you can't
tell who's
good and
who's bad!...
WARNER BROS. PRESENT IT IN AN INTIMATE NEW USE OF CINEMASCOPE AND WARNERCOLOR
STARRING
JULIE HARRIS
JAMES DEAN
IN HIS VERY FIRST PICTURE — A VERY SPECIAL STAR!
RAYMOND MASSEY
with
BURL IVES · RICHARD DAVALOS · JO VAN FLEET · LOIS SMITH
Print by TECHNICOLOR
Screen Play by
PAUL OSBORN
Directed by
ELIA KAZAN

EAST OF EDEN
(1955)

NORTHERN CALIFORNIA, before the First World War. Cal Trask (James Dean) is desperate to win the love of his father, Adam (Raymond Massey). As the film opens Cal follows an older woman named Madam Kate (Jo Van Fleet) to her front door in Monterey. She has her bouncer (Timothy Carey) run him off.

Back home in Salinas, he meets up with his brother, Aron (Richard Davalos) and Aron's fiancée, Abra (Julie Harris). Just as Cal can do no right where his father is concerned, Aron can do no wrong. Aron relates his father's idea for preserving and shipping lettuce. Later at the ice house, Cal and his father spar.

Cal hides in the ice house, spying on Aron and Abra as they plan their marriage. Abra admits that Cal scares her. Cal, upset and frustrated, shoves block after block of ice down the chute, ruining them. When his father demands an explanation, Cal only responds that he wanted to.

It gets worse when Cal remains unrepentant during a bible reading. His father bellows and Cal goes back to Monterey and learns the truth: that Madam Kate is his mother. He and Aron had always been told that their mother was dead. Cal lands in jail, where the sheriff (Burl Ives) explains his parents' troubled past. Cal warms to his father. After he returns to Salinas, he helps Adam with the lettuce and wins a begrudging smile from the old man, who likes his ideas if not his tactics.

Cal starts to accept himself through the affection and attention shown him by Abra. And when his father's scheme fails, Cal decides to rescue him. He buys beans, persuading his mother to lend him the seed money.

At a local carnival Cal and Abra grow closer when they get trapped on a ferris wheel. They look down and see Aron trying to break up a crowd that is baiting a local farmer of German birth. Cal joins in to help his brother, and it becomes a donnybrook. After the sheriff breaks up the melee, Abra goes off with Cal rather than Aron.

At his father's birthday party, Cal presents him with five thousand dollars. Instead of gratitude he is given a stern lecture about war profiteering. Cal runs off, Abra goes after him. Then Cal drags Aron to meet his mother. The shock is too much. Aron, a confirmed pacifist, gets drunk and joins the army. The shock of that causes his father to have a stroke.

In the end Abra smooths the way for a reconciliation between father and son. Cal glows when his father asks him to nurse him. At last he feels loved and needed.

East of Eden *is a very long novel. Why did you choose to make the film out of only the last section?*

I didn't like the first part of the book much. Around that time I was thinking about the importance of unity in a work of art. John Howard Lawson said in his book on screenwriting that unity comes from the climax. That is a very fertile thought. Every element in your story should lead up to the climax. Using that idea as sort of an aesthetic guide, I thought that a good film could be made out of the last part of Steinbeck's book. John had a tough front, but he was an extremely vulnerable man. He was hurt badly by criticism. So I asked him as gently and tactfully as I could if I could fool around with it. I had to tread softly because I wanted to use Paul Osborn to write it instead of working on it with John himself. John agreed, and Paul Osborn and I decided to write a script in which we just followed Cal, the main character. The image of the boy was very clear to me. I knew a boy that was like that, in other words, myself. Every day I got a couple of pages from Paul, and we went over it. Cal was in virtually every scene so the script became a test of that unity theory. I thought it was a good picture, though not my favorite. I meant it to be an attack on the puritanical point of view. I wanted to show that a boy whom people thought was bad was really good, and a boy whom people thought was good was actually quite bad and destructive. I've dealt with a lot of puritans in my life. So this was really a very personal film, one of the most personal I ever made, much more so than *On the Waterfront*. I was very like Cal, so *East of Eden* was for me a kind of self-defense. It was about people not understanding me. It was about my relationship with my father, how he disapproved of me all the time, how he didn't think I should be doing what I was doing. It also proved to be prophetic because a few years later, shortly before my father died, for the first time in my life, I got friendly with him, just as Cal gets friendly with his father as Adam is dying.

So your real attraction, aside from wanting to test Lawson's unity theory, was a very strong personal reference?

Testing the theory was not per se an attraction, it was just technically speaking the task I set for myself in that film. I try to set a problem in every film I do. Before I start a film I write extensive notes. I set out what I'm trying to achieve, what I'm trying to say, what the theme is, and how it's going to be dramatized. I learned a lot about unity from Sam Spiegel. The way he worked on the script of *Waterfront* made quite an impression on me. On everything I worked on after that, I said to myself, I've got to be able to do what Spiegel did. I've got to be as tough on a writer or myself as Spiegel was.

Do you get a stimulus from setting yourself an aesthetic problem in addition to the problems inherent in the material?

Yes I do. As I say, you have to set certain goals for yourself, mostly because you may have to refer back to them later. Sometimes when things are going wrong, it's very stimulating to open up a book and say, "Now why did I start this picture? Oh yeah, that's what I was trying to say here." If you go back to your original goals, you can say, "My real problem in this scene is to communicate X." The other things that are troubling you don't matter so much.

What was the spine of Cal, the central character?

Hatred/love. Not mildness. Vicious hatred and anger because of love frustrated. James Dean had them both. It was the most apt piece of casting I've ever done in my life. But it was accidental. I didn't search around a lot. Paul Osborn had seen him in a play and told me I ought to take a look at this kid doing a bit at the Royale Theater. So I met with Dean. I talked to him about ten minutes and called Paul up and said, "This kid is it." I knew right off the bat. You could just see it. You know how a dog will be mean and snarl at you—then you pat him, and he's all over you with affection? That's the way Dean was.

It has been rumored that you didn't like Dean.

That's not true. He was a very, very neurotic kid. You can't not like a guy with that much pain in him. Later, however, when he got a taste of power, he enjoyed it and became abusive. A lot of insecure people behave that way. They yell at their dresser, who can't afford to answer back. Dean got spoiled very quickly, and he was impossible with Nick Ray in *Rebel Without a Cause*, and George Stevens had to yell at him and threaten on *Giant*. He never got along with any of them. He was good with me right up until the end, but I could just see it happening. He had a terrible time with Pier Angeli. She's dead now so I can say it. She found somebody else, and that aroused all of Dean's sexual insecurity. There was only one actor I disliked in my whole life really, Tallulah Bankhead. She was very witty, a good storyteller, very strong, brave, ballsy and contentious. I sort of even liked her. We worked together when I was just starting out. It was the first good play I had, and she tried to get me fired twice. But Dean was a sick kid. If it hadn't been for Julie Harris I don't think he would have gotten through the picture. We were both good with him. I left the place where I was staying and moved into one of those star dressing rooms on the Warner lot and put Dean into the one next door. I made sure that I would be with him night and day and take care of him. You don't do that with everybody. I had no life at all. Fortunately, I had a lot of good help on that picture. I had a wonderful girl in wardrobe, my favorite, Anna Hill Johnstone. If you ever are lucky enough to get her on a film, you are just blessed by God. I told her I wanted a peace march. She did a lot of research. I picked about ten elements and then said, "Okay, you can hire the extras, you can put the costumes on them, arrange the floats, etc. You can do the peace parade." She did it all, and I think it was terrific.

What about Abra, Julie Harris?

Julie Harris is one of the most beautiful people I've known in my life. We had worked together on stage so I knew her—her friendliness and warmth. She was both a girl and a woman, an extraordinary person. Her soul is beautiful. It comes out of her eyes and her voice, the way she touches things. At the same time she has a plain look. She was just exactly right. She has a wonderful combination of purity and sexual awareness. When you go with that kind of woman it's very intense. You think they've got it, but only for you.

What about the father, Raymond Massey?

I didn't do justice to the father because Raymond Massey had only one color. He was just the way you think of somebody when you're angry with him. I don't think I would have wanted anything different, but I think the part might have been cast a little better.

My hunch is that what's wrong with Massey in that role is that you personally didn't like him. If you cast someone that you liked, it might have had the other colors as well.

But he might not have been as good in the role. Do you recall the way he said, "I was presumptuous to think I could do it," in the scene where Adam learns that all the lettuce has been ruined? That was a line by Paul Osborn, whose own father had been a minister. His choice of words was brilliant; I could never have written that. Steinbeck kept talking about a Biblical quality. The characters were all meant to be extreme. Madam Kate was extreme, especially the way Jo Van Fleet played her. Now, there was a good actress.

This was your first film in color and CinemaScope. Did that present any problems?

Yes it did. Like every hotshot director I said to myself, "I'm going to be the first one who does color right." So I got a color consultant and talked with him. I also had good luck with the cameraman, Ted McCord. I really loved him. I told him I wanted grey—that I wanted the color to help tell the story. He looked at me, but at first he couldn't hear it. Finally, we did achieve some dramatic effects through color, I thought. We emphasized green throughout. For instance, the room at the end in which the father dies, was painted a particular shade.

CinemaScope was new in 1955. I got instructions from the camera department at Warner Brothers. I must have the camera at least six feet from the actors. It really got my back up. So Ted and I made some tests and pushed in closer to see what would happen. There was some distortion; it was curved at the sides. But sometimes I moved the camera very close and used the distortion to help the drama. Another thing I did with CinemaScope was put objects in the foreground so I constantly changed the frame. First

I would block off a third of the frame on one side and then in the next shot do the same on the other side. Otherwise you had this great big screen, and it goes against cutting. You can't suddenly cut to a shot with just one face in it. It looks silly with all that room on the side no matter what you do with proportion. So I would always put somebody's shoulder in the foreground or a door or pillar. That technique was often copied by other directors. I did break a little ground.

Then Ted said, "If we're going to go that route and distort, then let's start tipping the camera." Nobody had ever done that.

East of Eden *is not a picture whose content lends itself logically to CinemaScope. It's a very intimate personal story. Not one with vast landscapes.*

That's true. But that was the rule in those days. Nearly all the big pictures had to be shot in CinemaScope.

Were you aware of the problems before you started to work?

Oh sure. George Stevens said about CinemaScope, "They finally found a way to photograph a snake." So we all knew the problems. But I'll never forget the day I kept pushing the camera in. All the departments are your enemies. They're all nice guys, but they all want their work to be up to a certain standard of their kind of technical perfection. When I brought Dean on the set to do the first wardrobe test, the crew thought he was the stand-in. They couldn't believe he was the leading character. I've chased hairdressers off sets a lot. I tell them right off the bat, "All you're going to do this whole picture is sit here." The union insists on it. "Entertain yourself, but don't touch the leading lady."

Let's talk about the film in terms of the unity concept.

I think I achieved that. The film is well-constructed, mostly because of Paul. He taught me a lot. "Follow your nose," he used to say. "You know where you're going to end up, but leave yourself free while you're getting there."

What was the climax for you?

The climax is when Cal gives his father money and his father refuses it. To win his father's love, is the spine of the film. He wins it at the end, when his father is dying. I think the film is pictorially good. The best shot in the film is where the train goes away with the lettuce. There's a big crowd on the left, and you pan right with a train. When you come to the railroad station, the train disappears from sight. There's all sorts of hullabaloo as you come past the station, and there's the little train going off in the distance. The shot was carefully calculated. It's a perfect shot because it shows that their hope is going off. It's sentimental and still emotional. I like another shot where Cal and Abra are under a willow tree. You only see their feet.

The picture opens with Cal chasing after his mother, a successful madame, played by Jo Van Fleet. He follows her through the town to her "house." She sends a bouncer out to get rid of him. He says, "Will she talk to me?"

Cal's trying to find out what's messed up his life, why he's a bad person. He is obsessed with the fact that his father doesn't like him and prefers his brother. He's trying to find out why. I'm not like my father. I must be my mother's son. So he finds out who his mother is.

He hops on top of a train to ride back to Salinas. You have him curl up into almost a fetal position.

He's cold and lonely, a parentless child. He looked like an orphan. That's unity, right? The emphasis was on his loneliness, not on the fact that he's riding on top of a train.

Then there's the transition to the rest of the picture. Abra and Aron, his brother, are in the foreground, and behind them there is a hedge. Cal darts in and out of the trees, but you kept him outside, behind them.

He is excluded, rejected—a "bad" person trying to find love.

You immediately set the relationship between him and his father. Aron says, "Dad's worried about you." "Yeah, I bet."

Plus his hostility toward Aron. He's jealous of Aron with a girl. Aron has all the good things given to him. He doesn't get any of them. How can he get his father's love and get the good things Aron has?

At the ice house you meet his father for the first time. He says that he wants to do something for the good of mankind.

That's puritanism for you.

When his father asks him what he's got to say for himself, he replies, "I think if war's declared, there's going to be money in beans."

He pretends that his father's response doesn't mean anything to him, but, of course, it does.

Geographically, you did an interesting thing. Abra and Aron come into the middle of that wide CinemaScope frame, and you left Cal off in the corner.

You'll find that I often put Cal in the corners of the frame. He's always off in the back except when he's alone with Abra. His father is big, dressed in black, wears a big hat. All of his friends are larger than he is. I kept accentuating that Cal is a kid.

The next scene is in the ice house. Cal hides behind big blocks of ice and remains silent throughout. Aron and Abra talk about how much they love each other. But the focus of their conversation turns to Cal, and Abra says, "He scares me. He's like an animal."

Sex. She had spirit, she found Aron dull, but also as far as she knew, Cal was like an animal, and she was scared.

Even in this early scene, you sense that she's more attracted to Cal than she is to her fiancé.

She doesn't know it yet though, Jeff. She only gets sympathetic later on when she gets to know what he's like. She's not aware and you should not make her aware that she's sexually attracted to him. She's not that complex a person. None of the characters are that complex except Cal. Cal is not that complex except that he has a schism, a complete division. I didn't have to say to her,

"You're really attracted to him." The fact that she talks about Cal already raises that in the audience's mind.

What did you give her to do?

Just to try to get Aron to help her understand his brother. And he's there. Don't they know it?

Not at the beginning. About two-thirds of the way through the scene, he gets up and heaves a few blocks of ice down the chute.

That's right. That's like a kid.

It's characteristic of the men in your films to have a kind of charm, a kind of purity, an innocence—"a little-boy quality." Brando has it in Streetcar *and* Waterfront. *We'll see it again in Andy Griffith in* A Face in the Crowd. *But there's always a "spoiled" quality mixed in, too.*

My dear Jeff, our puritanical business-oriented civilization has defined adulthood and manliness as the absence of playfulness. But playfulness exists despite that. It is a sign of life in a person. It's creativity. Playing is a product of your imagination. I find that charming in the men I know, and in my dealings with so-called adults I always try to get out of them moods and aspects of playfulness and fantasy and kidding around. It's lovable when you see it. I try to get people off their high horses. I feel people choke down the best of themselves when they deny their creative fantasy life. Formalism is used as a protective shield where the person in effect is saying, "I'm dignified, and I want to be taken as a dignified adult." Dignity really comes from much deeper and more worthwhile things.

But what I was getting at was there's an impetuosity, a kind of "aginner" quality.

I admire that quality. I've noticed it in the best men that I've known, like Winston Churchill. He always had a playful side. He was always sassing and horsing around and kidding himself and being self-deprecatory. I wish just for one minute in *East of Eden*, I had had Massey do a dance by himself. If he had just broken down, you could have seen the humanity in Adam that he had suppressed.

But there's more to it than playfulness. There's also a quality of being a spoiled child.

Spoiled? By what standards?

Take, for instance, Cal Trask or Stanley Kowalski or Lonesome Rhodes. Their attitude is, "I want what I want and I will take everything apart to get it."

What's wrong with that? That's not being spoiled. That's a natural drive, though it may be concealed in the character's cunning. It's a way of taking the cover off hypocrisy and saying, "Now, come on. You're not that dignified." But you're right. I do always have that quality in my pictures. I admire it. I see it suppressed in people, and I try to reveal it.

The Bible reading eventually turns into a big scream, out between Cal and his father. You tilted the camera there. Why?

To show the strain of that kind of social activity. To show that Cal was always under pressure to conform, which he resisted.

I found the device distracting. It called attention to itself and took me out of the scene. Were you really satisfied with that as a solution?

No, not particularly, but it was an attempt to solve it. It does give you a sense that even Cal's meals were pressurized. It was intended to quickly convey the story of Cal's life—to show what he's up against and his rebellion against it. It's supposed to show quickly the relationship between Cal and his father, Cal and his brother, Cal's father and the brother. Before you know it, you've got this simple, schematic setup. One of my problems was to have Aron be glad that his father prefers him but also to try to understand Cal and have some love for him.

Cal goes back to the whorehouse to try and talk to his mother, and there's a wonderful scene in the bar between him and a young waitress played by Lois Smith.

Cal finds somebody who's in the same condition that he's in, another emotional cripple. Her whole body was that way. Waif meets waif, and therefore feels less alone.

He so desperately needs to talk to his mother, he does a macho number. "I'm not afraid of them throwing me out of here. Let them try it."

He's defending his exposed, rejected self by being brazen. It's classical and so simple. You know it by now so you're sympathetic. Also, the element of sexual jealousy is introduced, the fact that he's excluded and not found desirable by the opposite sex.

Then he freaks and breaks into his mother's office.

She has Timothy Carey, the bouncer, throw him out and beat him up a little bit. An important moment to me is the way Cal holds onto his mother's door. That's one place I used the CinemaScope distortion. His hands seem extra big because they're in the foreground.

When Cal winds up in jail, Burl Ives appears as the sheriff. By the way he tells Cal about his father and mother, he's used to humanize Adam.

That's exactly right. At that point in the story I could not humanize the father directly. It's a terribly important scene because it brings the boy into an effort to win his father.

In a scene like that there isn't any conflict between the characters. One character asks questions, and the other simply answers them. What do you give the actors to do so that it doesn't boil down to boring exposition?

What's important in that scene is the awakening of understanding in Cal in relation to his father. So I played it not on the sheriff, but on Cal so that we could see the result of what the sheriff says. You are recording a change in Cal by getting inside him with the camera. You see an awakening of some appreciation in Cal that his father wasn't always just a harsh authoritarian—that there is something human, warmer and bigger in his father. So the scene isn't really expositional. It's about the beginning of Cal's movement away from pure resentment to his father and towards allowing the feeling of love to put down fragile roots.

You gave him that to do?

I made sure he did it, whether I said it in so many words or not. I was going for the look in Cal's eyes. As I said, it was all there in Dean because his own father had rejected him. He was full of love and full of the need for somebody to love him. I had a good relationship with Jimmy. All I had to do was touch him sometimes.

What did you do with Burl Ives, the one who's answering the questions?

Nothing. It's all in the casting. All I said to him was, "He's an ornery kid but you sort of like him." You can confuse someone like Burl by telling him too much. He was never trained as an actor. I made an actor of him on stage in *Cat on a Hot Tin Roof.* The whole second act was the aria of Burl Ives. That's what his part was, and it was something he was familiar with, standing down center talking to an audience.

Another interesting thing about that scene was the staging. Ives was on the driver's side behind the wheel. Often, Cal was almost hanging from the top of the car. It was such a pained desperate kind of gesture.

Jimmy was always getting himself contorted. There was always some awkwardness, some tension in his body. He couldn't sit still. His tension always came out physically. His body was very eloquent in that way. That posture was his contribution. I saw it, liked it, and let it go. It came out of an excess of shyness. It was so excessive in Dean's case that it was almost psychotic. He was exactly like the people you see in insane asylums.

There's a nice little transition that follows. Cal is on the porch, and inside you see his father playing with lettuce. It sets up the whole next section of the film.

That was very cleverly directed. I wanted to make his father appear sympathetically to Cal. So I showed him alone in his house at night with a head of lettuce, trying to figure something out. Any man alone, womanless and familyless in his house, is sympathetic. If you watch through a window, it's even more touching. I tried to make the audience feel the first glimmering of sympathy. Then they intuitively know that Cal is beginning to feel the same way.

Next comes the whole episode with the lettuce. Cal works energetically. He steals a coal chute, and they load the lettuce. It starts with his father praising him but ends with his father finding out that he's stolen the coal chute. While continuing to praise him, he chews him out. In the beginning when he is being praised, Cal faces camera. But later when he's being worked over, his back is all that we see. Why?

His body told it best. I probably shot it on his face too. But in the cutting room it was obvious which way was more moving. An actor is already a formed instrument, not an abstract being. His body is already an expression of his life. His face is a piece of sculpture, so is his body. If you watch people in movement, you see how they sit, how they stand, how they walk. You can learn a lot about them. Also, you can see what expressive means they have available to them. Dean's body was eloquent.

In between there's a scene of Cal and Abra. He flirts a little bit, and she tells him a story about how alone she felt when her father remarried and how she took a $3,000 ring and threw it in the river and everybody was very angry but she forgave them.

It was a meeting of souls. She's saying, "I understand you," and she's also saying, "Forgive them." He's being warmed to humanity as expressed by her. We all have anger in us. You have to forgive people who make you angry.

What did you give her to do?

Oh, not much. She's naturally that character. I did divide that up for her a little bit in sections. That's important to do with a long speech. But she's a very thoughtful woman. All you have to do is read that speech with her voice. She has the most beautiful voice of any actress I ever worked with. It's all soul. She'll say, "Hello, I'm glad to see you," and you melt.

One of the things Dean does best is listen.

He wasn't capable of listening completely, but then neither is that character. Cal's always turning over all kinds of thoughts and suspicions. Why is she telling me that? What does she want of me? He's thinking all the time. In that sense he listened great. But he listened to people that way in life, too. So there again you note it, and instead of saying to Dean, "Now listen to her," I would only say, "That's good." When you cast right, so that the character is inside the person, you're getting a bonus all along the way. They play the scene in a field of mustard flowers. That was Ted's idea, and it was a good one because it brought them closer together despite what they're doing.

There are moments when her openness and tenderness are apparently a threat, and he starts to back off.

That's true. I don't know if you know people like that. You're probably very unlike that, but I was very like Cal in that way. When someone moves you, you are suddenly more vulnerable—without your usual, experienced defenses, the defenses that have worked in the past, and you suddenly feel, "Oh my God, I have to be careful because if I expose myself she'll get the advantage of me." That was the way I used to be. I know that well. Dean was very like that, too.

The next scene is where the train pulls out, and off go their hopes in the distance. Then there's a scene in front of a garage. His father's bought a car, and he's learning how to drive. Cal gets a real kick out of watching his father enjoy himself.

Cal feels, "Oh, the old man is getting human. He's going to like me." It's all centered on Cal's coming out in the world. They say you can't like other people if you don't like yourself. Cal's beginning to like what he did. That whole scene with the car is a love scene between Cal and his father. Dean's laughter was so tense. Neurotics can't laugh. You can always tell a lot about a person by their laugh.

The scene ends with the information that there was a snowslide and the train got blocked. The ice all melted, and the whole frozen lettuce scheme was ruined.

I did that well because I had Burl Ives come up, somebody whispers to him, and then he whispers to somebody. The audience guesses before they know. It builds up a sense of apprehension and concern. "Oh, don't tell me."

The father reveals no emotion. He utters the line you talked about.

But by now you've gotten them close enough so that Cal is able to hear his father be pompous and think, I've got to save him. Then you're in the gym, right?

Cal's rhythms in the locker room were intriguing. Will Hamilton, a businessman and friend of Adam's, offers to cut Cal in on his bean deal. "You'll need $5,000," he says. "What are you going to do, borrow it?" There's an enormous long pause before Cal says, "Yes."

That pause gives Cal—and the audience—a chance to wonder how he's going to get the money. You shoot it that way with a proviso in the back of your head that if it doesn't work, you can cut right to the mother. "How you going to get $5,000?" Wham, close-up, Jo Van Fleet. That's a bore. The point here is not to shove the plot along faster but to reveal more about Cal's insides. That's really unity. During the pause the viewer will hopefully think like Cal does. I've got to get that money from her.

Then you cut to Cal and Kate, walking in the street. I wondered how you handled all the misinformation in that scene. She claims not to even know Cal's name, but she couldn't have disappeared before her own child was born. She says things that are an impossible cheat.

But doesn't their scene make you feel how completely his father threw her out of his life, how rigid, cruel and inhuman puritanism is? And she has her own kind of absolutism. She's the kind of girl that says, "All right, then, I didn't have any kids. You take them."

There's an interesting beat when Cal says to her, "I'm just like you, I'm bad."

He flirts with her, and she likes it. The scene's about her getting to like Cal, Cal getting to like her. It's a love scene. It's amazing how helpful that way of thinking is. For instance, you can have a business conference where two guys are antagonistic to each other and never get together on a deal, but by the end of the scene you feel they both think, "Well, he's a shrewd son of a bitch." There can even be love scenes between a man and an object, like a man with a racing car, a man with a horse or building a house. If you just say he's building the house, it's one thing; but if you say he's loving the house and doing something that he likes to it, you're dealing in emotion right away. It's good to think of a scene in terms of the emotion that rides through the apparent abstractness or the apparent impersonality of it. Arthur Penn had a gorgeous scene in *Bonnie and Clyde* where they had a picnic with Bonnie's family. It had very little relationship to the story. You just got to like them as people and it was very important because it was a love scene between you and these people. It's really one of the best scenes I've seen in modern film. He staged it so truthfully. You should always deal in the emotion if you can, rather than the fact.

Almost every scene has both informational and emotional content. It's always best, it seems to me, to play them, if not at odds with each other, in some way so that there is texture. That is the problem in the next scene where she gives him the money. He asks her a lot of questions about who he is, who his father is and who she is. It all feeds back on, "Who am I? Why am I the way I am?" She describes how moralistic and suffocating her husband was.

She's defending herself. "That's why I abandoned you. He would have killed me if I stayed with you." But she's also trying to win Cal away from his father.

It played to me like a pure self-defense, which was exactly what the words told me. I didn't get the other color.

That's what I tried to do. She liked him, and he woke up something in her that she thought that she had killed.

How did you go about trying to get her to do that?

I told her. Jo Van Fleet is a brilliant actress. She can take intellectual direction or analysis and turn it into completely spontaneous emotional behavior.

Do you like to work with someone like that?

Oh, actors are all different, but I've always liked her. She really has greatness in her, and a lot of pain. I thought she gave one of the best performances I ever saw in *Wild River*.

She does a scene in Wild River *that is similar to this one in that it is essentially a monologue. In* Wild River *it worked beautifully, and here it didn't.*

I don't agree with you. Kate's guard is up. It's been up so long, and she is so encrusted with barnacles of hate and mistrust that she can't show much. But there's one moment at the end where she reveals the crack.

Yeah, there is, but the beats were totally separated. It seemed to me it would have been richer if there had been more of the impulse to crack throughout, even if she fought it.

Maybe. I can't say. The way I planned the scene was that Kate would defend herself and defend herself; then suddenly she'd let go. She changed her mind about lending him the money. I think all through the scene you feel she isn't going to give him anything and all of a sudden she gives in.

What do you do when you prepare a scene that's burdened with so much information? How do you keep the actor from getting drowned by the text in a way that stops their behavior?

One thing I always do in scenes like that, and with an actress like Jo Van Fleet, is plot out the scene in stages or beats. I try to do it a few days before so she studies it that way. I also have her fuss—eat or dress or undress. You have to use whatever chance you can to tell the environmental, cultural aspects of the scene. In life we don't have scenes. Something else is always going on around us. If you choose the external things correctly, they become emblematic and the rhythm of the scene changes. The actor is affected by what's happening outside, so you can further demonstrate or reveal what's happening inside. It's very important to get something happening in every scene so you don't just have two people jawing at each other. The trouble with the playwright, Paul Osborn, which most screenwriters avoid, is that he'd write long speeches. In the scene in the mustard flowers I had Cal and Abra eating lunch. In this scene Kate is always moving around the office. Cal tries to see her hands, and she notices it. She did great things with her hands. She's the only actor I've ever known who spent a lot of time making up her hands. In *Wild River* she used to get up at 3:30 a.m. to make up. Her face alone took several hours, but she spent an extra hour putting liver spots on her hands despite the fact that the viewer isn't even aware of them.

What do you do when you've got a scene in which the emotional qualities that the actors bring into the scene because of what has happened off camera have nothing to do with the scene they are about to play?

It should never happen. The objectives, what they're trying to do, should always be tied in with the emotion. The failure to get the objective should increase the emotion.

Yes, but let me give you an example. For argument's sake, assume that I was incredibly angry about something when I came up here today and that something was bothering you and you're distracted. My objective is to get you to tell me as much as you possibly can. What I came in here feeling isn't even related to my objective.

The director's got to take me in a corner before the scene and get me on a phone and have me play a scene with my accountant where I suddenly find out I've got to pay a large tax. I start the scene not listening to Jeff. "The hell with him and his goddamn book. What am I going to do about this tax?" At the beginning of it I'm distracted. Then the director should get you to read part of the book before you come into the scene. "This might be a pretty good book. It sounds interesting. I've got to ask Kazan some more personal questions, don't let him off the hook easily, bedevil him a little bit. If he gets sick of me, he can throw me out, but I'll come back the next day." Then we meet, and neither of us is neutral. I used to have Dean run around the set before he came on. That's another theory in the Stanislavsky system.

You mean setting the given circumstances?

That's what it's called. It's basic. The important thing is you don't talk about it. You do it to the actor. And a good actor does it to himself. You've got to make sure it's conditioned, that they're not faking. You can give them circumstances that are not exactly the given circumstances of the scene, but they're not as good because you're not building the part. What you should do is give them circumstances that are about that character and generally about that moment in the piece. You can add elements that are not in the script, but they should be about the character.

Do you always do that? For instance, you've repeated again and again and again the need to know that person, to know that material.

Tie it to their lives.

But you do it within the character?

Yes, you say to Dean that your father did something that Cal's father did to him. It's out of the script. When I took Dean out to California, instead of riding first class and putting him on another plane third class, I went with him, got in a car, stopped to see his father on the way into town. I watched Dean and his father. That's golden. I could have been doing something more interesting, I suppose, but not if I was concerned about making a good movie.

In addition to setting given circumstances that are both related to the script and to their lives, you said you often play the actors off against one another as people.

You use absolutely everything. For example, you say to the actor, "Jeff's pretty nervous today. He's got a pimple on his forehead today. That shows he's not a composed, controlled guy." Everything is useable. You're not playing to an abstract. You're playing to Julie Harris. You're playing to James Dean. You're talking to a face. People's faces have different qualities. You say to someone, "Did you ever notice how his eyes are? Notice his eyes when you play the scene." You awaken the actor's relatedness to one another. They're both the character and themselves.

The next section is the peace parade. Aron says that he's against the war.

That was during my more affectionate period. I have a different sense of that war now.

A series of transitions follow. Cal is alone in a field where the beans have been planted. Then there's a bit with his father and Albrecht, a citizen of the town but of German birth. The father says, "City life stinks. I'd like to go back to the country, back to the ranch." Cal laughs affectionately at every word. Then there's a cut back to the beans as they've started to grow. Cal does a wild, excited dance around the field.

I could have just cut to a close-up of the beans so that you see that they're sprouting and a close-up of Cal's face being happy. But Dean said, "Suppose I run through them?" I kissed him that day. Brando would never do that. He couldn't. He was much more contained. But Dean was actually like a kid. That dance was one of the greatest contributions he made to that performance. He never could have done it if his father or his brother were there. It was what Lee Strasberg called a private moment.

The next scene is the carnival and the beginnings of a romance between Cal and Abra. The meat of the scene is played with Cal and Abra locked in together on the ferris wheel. She says, "Aron thinks I'm all good like the mother you never had. Not that I'm bad, but I'm not all good... Does Aron really like me?... Tell me what other girls are like? You go out with them. Are you bad?"

He's aroused something in her, and she's coming on to him like a nice girl would. Julie understood that very well. Didn't we cut to Aron down below looking for her?

Right. He gets caught up in the middle of everybody going off to stomp the local German, Albrecht. Aron tries to break it up. Cal sees what's going on and jumps off the ferris wheel. While Aron tries to reason with the local citizens, Cal crashes into the group and starts a brawl. Ives finally comes and sends everybody away. Then Aron accuses Cal of jumping into it just to show off.

The way Ives stops the fight is a specific culturally acted out piece of rural American behavior. He doesn't touch anybody. He just says, "What are you doing, Jack? What are you doing, Bill?" There's a long pause and they all stand around. They're all neighbors. It's not just the cops. Everybody knows him. He says, "Why don't you folks go home now." They go home and that's all there is to it. Small town America. That was a good choice.

After the confrontation with his brother, he runs off and Abra, rather than staying with Aron, runs after him. Cal sits in a bar. His hands keep twisting as he toys with a glass.

That's not direction, that's him. He was full of psychological gestures like that.

He says, "I was just trying to help him. Who am I kidding? I wanted to kill him." It's a desperate appeal to her.

That's right, and he's trying to figure it out too. Psychologically it's a big step forward for him, trying to accept his own being. What's wonderful about Paul's script is that all through the film you see this kid wrestling with his self-knowledge. It's very touching.

You also bring the father into that scene. At some point Cal says, "One of these days he'll know who his real son is."

Cain and Abel. That's Biblical. I was trying to keep it on a certain elemental level.

He sells his beans then climbs up on the roof of Abra's house, wakes her up and tells her about his father's birthday.

That's the scene he couldn't get. That's when I got him drunk. Something must have been wrong in his personal life. Normally I would expect him to have no trouble with that scene, the fact that Cal's all worked up and hysterically hopeful and aroused should have been easy for him. But he never could get it.

The next scene is the birthday party. It starts with great excitement but ends in total despair when Adam rejects the money Cal got from war profiteering. Cal puts his head straight down on the table, defeated.

And he drops the money all around on the floor. Then he runs out crying.

She runs after him, and they play a scene under a tree. You can't see them, but you know that she's making a commitment to him. Aron freaks. Why did you play it so we couldn't see their faces?

Their bodies, their position told it better. By the way the next scene, when Cal takes Aron to see their mother, is the biggest lie in the film. How do they get from there way over to Monterey all in one move, and how does Cal get Aron to go? I never believed Aron would go, but there's a basic truth about scenes like that. If an audience wants to see something, they'll forgive you a lot, but that was a false thing.

Did you know it when you did it?

Sure, that's why I got past it as fast as I could. There was no way to make it real. You had the emotion going, so you take advantage of it. It was better to be false that way than to put in filler.

When Cal barges in and throws Aron right on top of Kate, telling him that she's their mother, Jo Van Fleet is lying on a couch, and there's a horrified look on her face. What were you going for with that?

The physical equivalent of shock and an expression of Cal's vengefulness. That scene's a good example of what you might call exaggerated direction. It's not quite real. Dean might have done something like that in his life, but it's close to crossing the line. I've been criticized for being excessive for that kind of scene. But personally I like it. I'd rather have that than, this is your son, close-up, close-up, out.

If you were to do it again, would you do it the same way?

I don't know. I'm not the same person. When I see it, I still rather enjoy it. It makes me feel like what the scene is like—shocked. The whole sequence is unrealistic. How do they get there? What happened on the way? It skips all the realism.

There is another part of you that is very realistic.

I try to base things in realism and take off from there. I don't think of myself as a realist. I think of myself as a poetic realist or "essentialist," as I call it. That may be just a big rationalization for my lacking.

The next scene is the confrontation between Cal and his father. Cal rocks on a swing. He says, "I'm not mad about the money. You keep on forgiving just like you did with Mom, but you never loved me and you never loved her. You never loved anybody."

That's real growth when he's able to say that to the man. I love the way he acted that scene.

Did you give him anything to do?

I told him he had grown up and that he's just stating facts. The defiance is all contained, not in the acting, but in the fact that he swings back and forth. Sometimes if you get a good physical equivalent it's better than acting. That's a good one because it's childlike. It contains all the nose thumbing, and at the same time it makes it possible for Dean not to have to do it all by acting, which would be pretty rough going. The script often reads like a psychological analysis. "I always wanted your love. I took Aron to see mother because I was jealous, and so on." So I think there's a place where that kind of direction helped. I tried to heighten it to an area of poetic essentialization. I don't consider the end of *On the Waterfront* or the last half of *A Face in the Crowd* or *America America* realistic. It's essentialization. That's what art is to me. But still, I admire [Yasujiro] Ozu's *Tokyo Story*. Everything is exactly the way it would have happened. It's very deep. But I wouldn't do it that way. I'm unable to.

Even though he confronts his father like an adult, the rest of the film reveals that Cal still needs and wants his father's love. They both race to the train station, where Aron, drunk and hysterical, has gone and enlisted. Adam has a stroke. The scene ends with him lying cradled in Cal's arms.

It was planned that way, considered that way, and that's exactly what we tried to do. That's what happens in life. Both emotions exist. That's what ambivalence is. Feelings are aroused by conflicting impulses that you can't resolve. I love you and I hate you. That's something with which I deal all the time. The ambivalence of emotion. That's my specialty because that's what my life experience has been. I very rarely have a pure emotion. Even my feelings about America are ambivalent. In all my films I knock it, and tear it down. I'm highly critical. I love Southerners, whom I criticize more than anyone else. I'm very traditional and reactionary in certain ways. I think there are things about the oldest customs and standards that are terribly good and terribly important. And even after all I have said about Puritanism, in many ways I'm puritanical. I believe in work, in service to my fellow man. I believe in leaving something behind. At the same time I detest puritanism for all the reasons I've stated. I think it's absolute and rigid. I like marriage, and yet, I'm against it. I believe in closeness between people although I've never been able to achieve it as a permanent state. I'm that way about everything. The only thing I'm absolutely pure about is my love for my mother and my children. That was hard won too in terms of their returning it. I have great doubts about myself and still I'm proud of myself. I believe that that's the truth in life. So I try to deal with that ambivalence.

At the same time that Cal's telling his father that he never loved him, he's loving him by saying that. He's able to hold him that way because his father is helpless, which is a terrible thing. That's the way life is. You say that you should be able to love somebody anyway, but you don't. Every work of art that is deep and true is a result of one's experience. A good artist permits himself to show the reprehensible, embarrassing, undignified aspects of his own life. That is the gift that a good artist makes to you. When a writer dries up, it means he no longer looks frankly at his life.

At the end of the picture where his father is dying, where do you see the ambivalence there?

There's the Freudian thesis that the son has to kill the father, that he becomes a man by killing his father. Cal sits in that room, and as he waits there's a feeling of terrible pain and tragedy and regret and still a sort of silent triumph. He sits there watching his father's last moments, full of love for him but also waiting for him to die so that he can be set free. The scene has a grandeur when you think of it that way. He sat there, and he wouldn't leave the room. Julie Harris just killed me in that scene. I cry now when I see it.

She tells Adam, "I love Cal, but he'll never be a man unless you forgive him, unless you accept him. He'll walk around guilty. He'll never be a person and only you can do it."

Once again that was Osborn's script. His father was like Adam Trask. She knits them together. She makes the old man's death easy.

You end the film by craning way back and we see the bedside group—Adam, Abra, and Cal.

That was to show they were now, truly, a little family.

Were you satisfied with the final cut of the film?

Yes. But the studio insisted on a preview. I honestly don't know how but word had gotten around, and the theater was full of kids. The moment Dean appeared on the screen they went crazy. A star had been born. It was one of those occasions when you don't know what hit. I thought, "Geeze, is he that good?" Then I realized that even though the picture was set during World War I, Jimmy had caught something precise about that very moment in the Eisenhower era. It was the way the kids felt towards their fathers at that time.

Have you ever changed a picture based on previews?

If I have control, I don't have any previews. You never change a damn thing. It's insulting.

East of Eden *is the first picture you produced as well as directed. Did that make any difference? in the work?*

Less tension, that's all.

ELIA KAZAN'S PRODUCTION OF
TENNESSEE WILLIAMS' BOLDEST STORY!

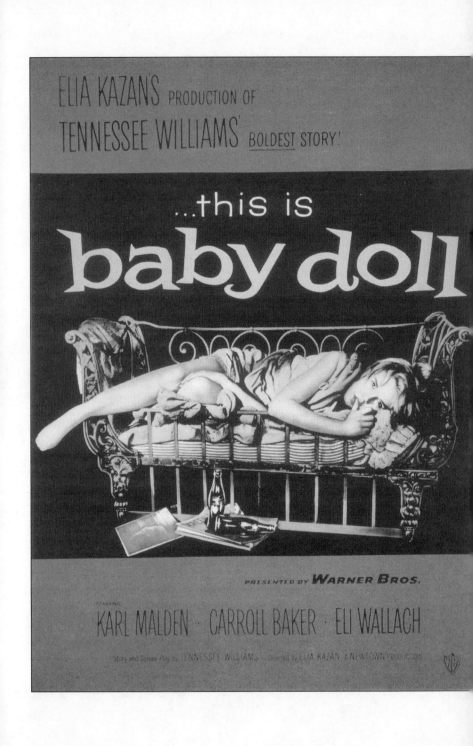

...this is
baby doll

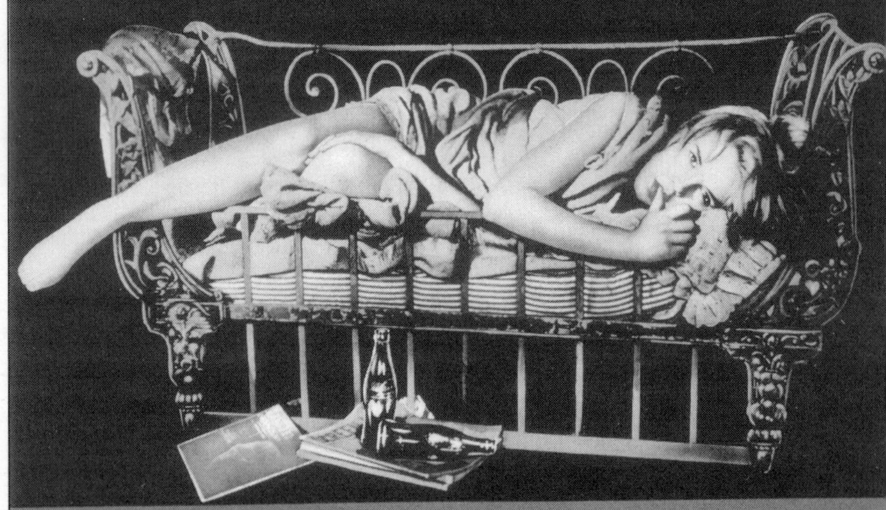

PRESENTED BY WARNER BROS.

STARRING
KARL MALDEN · CARROLL BAKER · ELI WALLACH

Story and Screen Play by TENNESSEE WILLIAMS · Directed by ELIA KAZAN · A NEWTOWN PRODUCTION

BABY DOLL
(1956)

ARCHIE LEE MEIGHAN (Karl Malden), a middle-aged bully, married Baby Doll (Carroll Baker) when she was eighteen, and promised not to consummate the marriage until she turned twenty. That birthday is only a few days away. She is so delectable and he so horny that he peeps at her as she sleeps in a crib, sucking her thumb. Because she knows that Archie Lee can't wait to get at her, she constantly makes fun of him.

In fact, she hates just about everything about her husband. Instead of looking after her as he promised, Archie Lee has allowed his business and his home to deteriorate badly. This is mostly due to competition from the new Syndicate Cotton Gin, run by the latter-day carpet-bagger, Silva Vacarro (Eli Wallach). In a fit of rage and desperation, Archie Lee burns down Syndicate's gin.

Silva swears to get biblical justice. After sending all his business to Archie Lee, which guarantees that he will be away from home, Silva sets out to get proof from Baby Doll that Archie Lee set the fire. Through a series of ploys, Silva seduces and manipulates Baby Doll until she signs an affidavit proving Archie Lee's guilt. During the course of this business/revenge-motivated seduction, Silva grows fond of Baby Doll and her maiden aunt, Rose Comfort (Mildred Dunnock), who lives with her.

Archie Lee comes home and leaps to the conclusion that Vacarro has slept with his wife—exactly as Silva hoped and planned that he would. Archie Lee gets hysterical, eventually going for his shotgun. Baby Doll calls the sheriff; Silva hides in a tree. The officers arrive and take Archie Lee away. Silva leaves, and Baby Doll and Aunt Rose are left waiting until tomorrow.

What the hell is this picture all about?

Baby Doll is a black comedy. It has no meaning. It's chaos; it's a microcosm of the changing South as I know it and like it. It expresses my affection for people coping with the stress of change with a sense of humor and fun. Archie Lee is the old, landed aristocracy. The new uneducated drive forward and the fulfillment of self is Baby Doll. And the catalyst between the two is Silva, the hot-shot industrialist whom Tennessee Williams caught in the form of a little cocky sparrow. It's the story of the South at that time played by small little insects. I like everything in the South except its ideas, standards and beliefs. But the way the people are has always impressed me. It's part of my own maverick anarchism. I find them very funny and cute and human, very Chekhovian.

Why then isn't Archie Lee treated with more affection?

Everybody says that, but I don't agree at all. I think the way Karl Malden plays Archie Lee is darling. His foolishness is so attractive to me. He's so human. I can't even answer that question. Well, that's me. That's my personality. I do like that character, I like them all. I think Eli as Silva is absolutely foolish, too. He's as ridiculous as a rooster because you know tomorrow morning somebody's going out there with an axe and cut his head off, and still the whole thing is poetic.

I don't see any dignity or sense of struggle for it in Archie Lee.

He had none. Don't you know any middle-aged cuckolds? They're pathetic, funny, amusing, tragic. There's nothing dignified about them. At that point in my career I had lost all interest in doing another "sympathy" picture. *Baby Doll* is where I felt it most strongly. In *On the Waterfront* you sympathize with Brando. Injustices and abuse are heaped on him, and then you watch him come through it all with courage. It's a sophisticated and honest version of the hero who is put upon and who triumphs in the end. Act One: get your hero up the tree. Act Two: throw rocks at him. Act Three: get him down. That's the corniest statement of the corniest theatrical philosophy possible, but *On the Waterfront* falls into that tradition. In *East of Eden* I tried to turn the sympathy around. Aron, the person whom the other characters in the film sympathize with—the puritans—is not that damn good. By the end they all—and the audience—sympathize with Cal. By the time I got to *Baby Doll*, I was determined to make a picture with no sympathy and no heroes. I don't believe in that anymore. A picture that has no heroes is appealing. *Bonnie and Clyde* has no heroes. I like that about that picture. All the great novels are that way. It's just the theater which has this corny tradition that you should root for somebody.

My point is everyone—and I think you did it intentionally—is laughing at Archie Lee.

Don't you think I'm laughing at Silva, too, with his pomposity? When I directed Eli, I told him, "You're like Vittorio De Sica; you come in here and give these Italian gestures and laugh at Carroll Baker"—I thought I was directing with affection. But my friends tell me that I was sneering at everybody, putting them down, which I didn't feel. I know a lot of girls who are like Baby Doll. You say to yourself, "She's such a bore." Fifteen minutes later you're going to bed with her. "God, she's a good kid. Oh boy, she's a cute little animal." And you like her. You think, "What's the difference what her ideas are?" That's life to me.

I felt compassion for the other characters even though they made fools of themselves. But Archie Lee is a bully who reveals no real human pain or remorse or understanding. Even at the end of the picture he's still bellowing, "I got friends...I have power here." You know he'll throw his weight around and hurt others as soon as he has the chance. What's worse, he's not even interesting.

You're being too serious. I was forty-four years old when I made that picture. Up until then I was like you. But as I got older I was able to feel the charm and the attraction of foolishness under tension, which is by the way what you usually find. The picture expresses the affection I have for the foolish of the world. I mean you can't take *Baby Doll* seriously. It's like a fairy tale. It's ridiculous, improbable, unrealistic. Sometimes people draw that way, like Chagall, who paints guys flying around the roof.

Fairy tale or not, Silva seduces Baby Doll in order to prove her husband's guilt. The Legion of Decency went berserk.

If you actually watch *Baby Doll* carefully, I never even show Silva put his hand on her. He threatens it, but the act is entirely in the minds of the Catholic priests and bishops and cardinals. The fact that she sucks her thumb doesn't means she wants a penis in her mouth. All babies suck their thumbs. Cardinal Spellman had the filthiest mind of anybody. He made a dirty picture out of it. There's no indication of actual sex. All that Silva does is lay in her crib and take a nap. Latin men often stop suddenly after they've exerted themselves and take a nap. She thinks it's cute. And by now, when he's quiet and not bothering her, she rather likes him. She comes on to him; he doesn't come on to her. The cliché of clichés in American films is that everything leads up to sex. It doesn't in life. Silva probably has three or four girls in that community. He's getting laid whenever he feels like it, but sex isn't the most important thing in his life. Only in American movies and in the American middle class is sex the most important thing. It's adolescent. To a man the most important thing is his business or his career or for an artist his work. All too often the American aesthetic in films still hinges on whether Clark Gable gets Claudette Colbert into bed or not. Who cares? Sex doesn't solve anything. Every Latin knows it. Sex can be one of the most casual acts in the world.

Archie Lee comes home and finds his wife, dressed only in a white slip. Then Silva comes down from upstairs where the bedrooms are. You can't exactly blame Archie Lee or even Cardinal Spellman for jumping to conclusions.

She has invited Wallach to dinner, that's all.

Yeah, right...You have a real thing about putting women in white.

That's what my first wife used to say. I had Barbara Loden in white in *Splendor in the Grass.*

You had Dorothy McGuire in white, Lee Remick in white, Caroll Baker in white, Vivien Leigh in white, Eva Marie Saint in white and Patricia Neal in white, Julie Harris always looks like she's in white. That's just for starters.

Innocence aroused is erotic to me. But there are personal reasons for that.

The whole picture is loaded with sensual images. You've got Carroll Baker licking an ice cream cone.

I meant all that. A girl like that, although she is stupid, is awakening.

The picture begins on the outside of Malden's dilapidated plantation. It's a very stark, beautiful opening image. Then you go right inside and the exposition takes place. Baby Doll is in her crib sucking her thumb. Archie Lee goes into the next room, punches a hole in the wall with a knife and peaks in at his own wife. The knife going through the wall and Baby Doll sucking her thumb is very sexy stuff. Later, she's in the bathtub and Malden's outside the door. Again, it's very erotic. What would you have done if you hadn't had the censorship restrictions to contend with?

I probably would have messed it up somehow. Although I've always believed in suggestion. I've never been explicit. What is erotic about sex to me is the seduction, not the act. The most erotic thing in the whole sexual relationship between men and women is that little moment when the girl stops resisting you and you know it's there. She starts to come after you. When will that happen? That's what interests me. The scene on the swings in *Baby Doll* is my exact idea of what eroticism in films should be. I don't give a damn about the rest of it.

Carroll Baker has never, as far as I know, done anything to compare with her performance in Baby Doll.

There aren't many great roles. She really had a terrific role in *Baby Doll*, and it was very close to her life.

Let's talk about the scene on the swing. Silva moves in on Baby Doll. He seduces and pumps her for information. You shot the scene very tightly.

In order to get into her experience. The camera is like a microscope. It's not simply a recording device. It can be a penetrating device when you want to use it that way. I wanted the audience to really feel her arousal so I had to get very close. The interesting thing about some young women is that if you scare them, as Silva does in this scene, they get turned on. They want you to comfort them. They get aroused at the same time they get frightened.

Later she runs to Archie Lee at the gin, and he belts her. Silva comes in and sends Archie Lee off to get a new part for his gin.

Then Silva and Baby Doll have the most touching scene in the picture where he dries her eyes by the pigpen and the pigs keep grunting right through it all. That scene reflects the whole tone of the picture: ignoble, ridiculous, pathetic. It's hard to discuss *Baby Doll* by standard values. It's so funny. It makes its own laws.

Did you approach it differently?

Absolutely. I used to tell Wallach, "Come on Eli, it's not realistic." I tried to get Brando to play that part. He's a good comedian but I would have directed the whole picture differently, much more realistically. I love actors who have the ability to play comedy. It means they're smart. A person who plays comedy sees the turns, the surprises. Eli, Karl and Carroll are all smart. Millie Dunnock was very hip too.

You cast a lot of locals in the picture. How did you get them to act?

It's very simple. If what they have to do is something they do in life, then all you have to do is tell them what you want. They'll direct you. "No, I wouldn't do that. What I would do is..." "Never mind, don't tell me, just do it." I set up the camera loose enough and told the cameramen to be alert to their spontaneous moves.

Do you deal with them differently than pros?

Oh sure. They're only playing small parts—bits usually. You can't do more with them than that. You can't build a performance. You can't talk about contradictions or feeling two things at once. If something is very difficult I'll have three or four people just sitting around while a guy says his lines. It keeps him off the spot. If you can get it in the range of their knowledge and again stay on their side of the camera both physically and spiritually it helps. After all, they're doing you a favor. They don't have to do it. They've got a job. They're beautiful. It sounds like the corniest thing in the world, but they are. It's very important to have affection for them, touch them a little bit. You talk to them, and you'll see they are bigger than you are. In addition, it wasn't hard to play a scene with Eli Wallach or Karl Malden because they're so nice themselves. They are human beings. Brando was the same way. When the longshoremen had to play a scene with Brando in *On the Waterfront* they had no problem because Brando was like another longshoreman.

At the end of a long game/chase in which Baby Doll signs an affidavit, she puts Silva to bed in her crib. After a rather lunatic dinner cum shouting match, the Sheriff takes Archie Lee away.

The sheriff's his friend. It's a friend taking him away.

Then the last piece is with Aunt Rose and Baby Doll on the porch. Baby Doll says, "There's nothing to do but wait for tomorrow and see if we're remembered or forgotten."

I love that line. That's on a par with "I have always depended on the kindness of strangers," from *Streetcar*. A guy who can write lines like that has to have a beautiful soul and Tennessee does.

In many ways Baby Doll *seemed less you than your other films, especially coming right after* East of Eden *and* On the Waterfront *and just before* A Face in the Crowd.

Baby Doll is part of me, too. But as I said before, the main thing I was trying to do was to break down the convention of having someone sympathetic to root for. Here you root for nobody. So it was an important departure for me. I don't think it was entirely successful, but I'm very fond of that movie. I had a great time making it. I had a great crew. The food was great, and I went fishing a lot. We even saved a black man from being lynched. We hid him in a trailer. Also, *Baby Doll* is photographed better than any of my pictures. I told Boris Kaufman that everything should look bled out. Karl Malden is bled out. Carroll Baker wears no makeup. The house hadn't had a coat of paint for a long, long time. To me the movie is hilarious. But it was not particularly loved by anybody, even my best friends. Even the French don't like it!

I don't think I've ever done anything yet that really represents exactly my point of view. If I can portray a sense of "humanness," that's all I want. That's why I admire [Jean] Renoir so much. Everybody in his pictures, representing all points of view, is sympathetic. It comes from the soul of the man. And I've got it in me. I don't think I've ever quite done it.

For me the feelings that you are describing are closest to being captured in A Face in the Crowd.

ON THE WATERFRONT

"I directed the scene by using the business that Budd Schulberg had written, which is the offering of the egg, the way he handles the bird . . . by his lack of shyness with the boy which contrasted with his shyness with her. . . . "

"The point of the introduction is that the whole waterfront which is wide and enormous is in the grip of one fist, one little clique, one little clubhouse."

"The important thing in that scene was the division of the money . . . that they're making a lot of money at the expense of everybody else."

"There has to be a sense of discovery in a scene. . . . Just the fact that he has to pull her out of physical danger there does a lot."

Eva Marie Saint dropping her glove by accident which gave Edie a reason to stay and walk with Terry even though "Edie knows that from the point of view of propriety and public opinion, she shouldn't."

"Brando was always hoping that people would care about him."

"That's the most criticized moment in the picture because the body looks as if it's ascending to heaven under the guidance of an officer of the Catholic Church . . . but the truth is that's the way you take a body out of the hold of a ship."

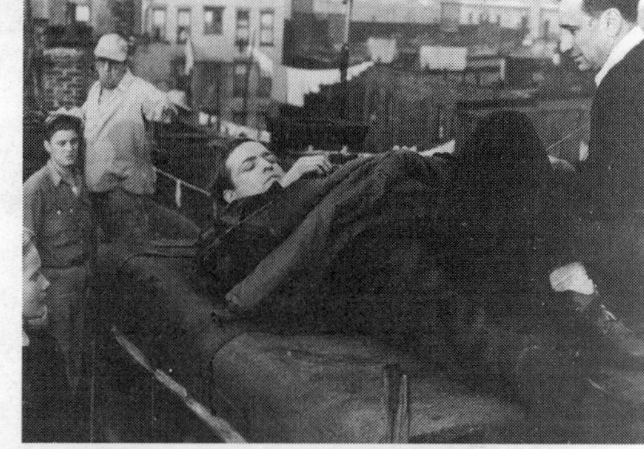

"That's terrific. That's a real symbol, Joey's coat."

"There was no way to ruin that cab scene. All you had to do was get those two guys saying those lines."

"I wanted to get across the brutalization—he's just meat."

"The scene where Terry and Edie run down the alley and a truck almost hits them . . . wasn't in the script. I added it. It got you to the body in a shocking way."

"If you shoot through screens or curtains, you see shadowy figures which gives the audience a chance to imagine or feel along with you."

"When he yells, 'I'm glad what I done' to Friendly, that was an important choice. It made it into a real political act."

"The other workers . . . are going to make a choice. The victor is going to be the leader of the union. . . . A lot of people resented that they didn't come to his aid. But they wouldn't."

Father Barry about to give Terry a real snow job.

EAST OF EDEN

"Cal (James Dean) flirts with Madam Kate, his mother (Jo Van Fleet), and she likes it. It's a love scene. It's amazing how helpful that way of thinking is."

"The birthday party ends in despair when Adam, Cal's father (Raymond Massey), rejects Cal's gift."

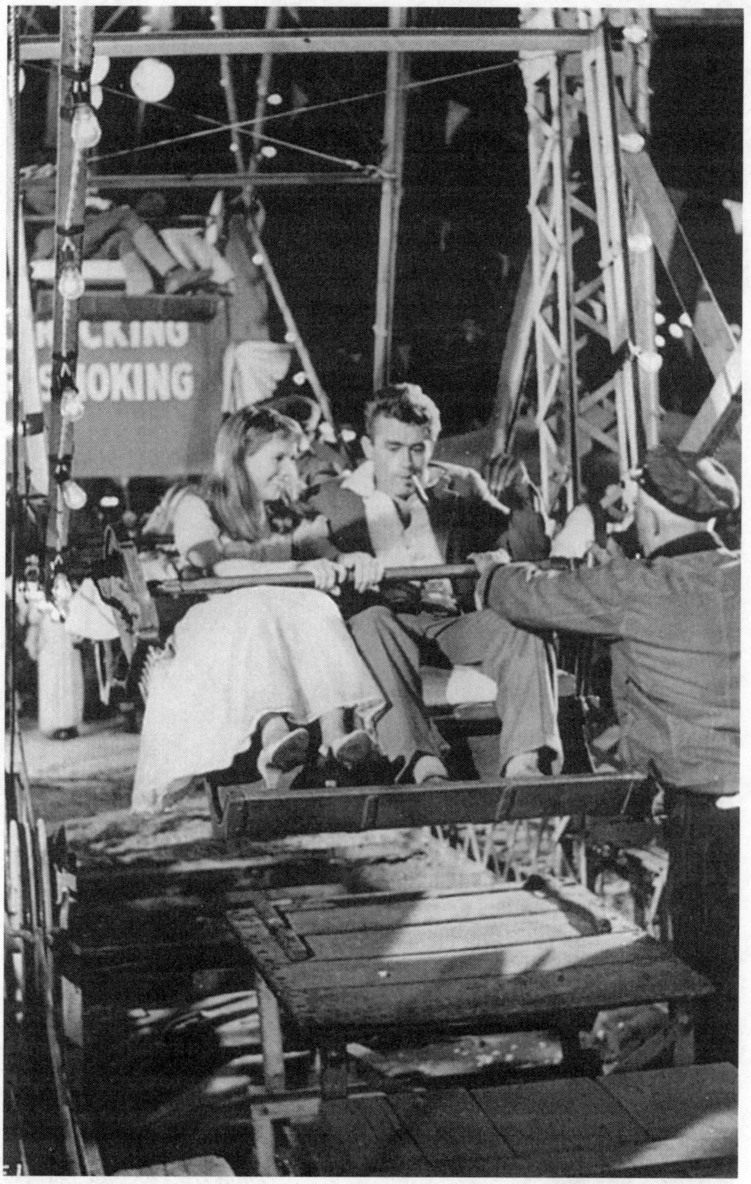

"Cal aroused something in Abra (Julie Harris) and she's coming on to him like a nice girl would."

BABY DOLL

"The fact that Baby Doll (Carroll Baker) sucks her thumb doesn't mean she wants a penis in her mouth. All babies suck their thumbs."

"... then Silva (Eli Wallach) comes down from upstairs where the bedrooms are. You can't exactly blame Archie Lee, her husband (Karl Malden), or even Cardinal Spellman for jumping to conclusions."

"What is erotic about sex to me is the seduction, not the act. ... The scene on the swings (Eli Wallach and Carroll Baker) in *Baby Doll* is my exact idea of what eroticism in films should be."

A FACE IN THE CROWD
(1957)

MARCIA JEFFRIES (Patricia Neal) takes her radio show, "A Face in the Crowd," to the local jail in Piggot, Arkansas, where she comes upon a natural-born storyteller, jokester, and singer whom she dubs "Lonesome" Rhodes (Andy Griffith). She recruits him as a permanent part of her show. Instantly his success and power grow. So do their feelings for each other.

Rhodes is signed up for a Nashville TV show, and he takes Marcia with him. Again, he is an immediate sensation. His popularity increases as he is seen to be a truthteller in a world of sham and lies. The public loves him for making fun of his sponsor. The sponsor does not and fires him. But by then Joey de Palma (Anthony Franciosa) has moved in and gotten him an audition with a national sponsor and a network in New York. He goes to say his goodbyes to Marcia. Instead they become lovers, and the threesome head for the big city, accompanied by Mel Miller (Walter Matthau), one of Lonesome's writers, whom he scorns for being overeducated.

By now, Rhodes knows his own strengths. He wins over the sponsors and gets his own show. He sticks to his guns when it comes to telling the truth where others lie or sugarcoat, and soon the entire country falls under his spell. But throughout his rise he becomes increasingly aware of his power, comes to enjoy wielding it and gets corrupted by it. He throws his money and his weight

AN ELIA KAZAN PRODUCTION
BUDD SCHULBERG'S a Face in the Crowd
ANDY GRIFFITH PATRICIA NEAL A NEWTOWN PRODUCTION
4
57

WARNER BROS.

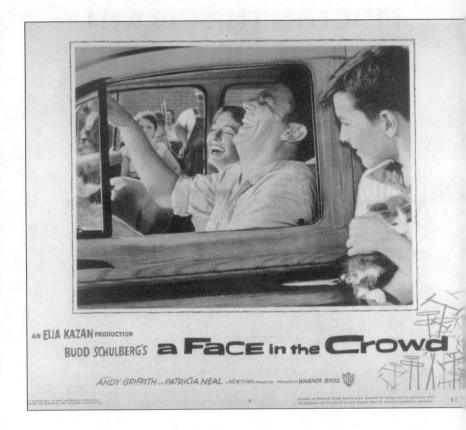

around, womanizes, drinks too much, and becomes an almost grotesque version of his former self.

Marcia, despite knowing his faults and suffering from his betrayals, is hopelessly in love with him. He, in turn, remains dependent on her despite—or perhaps because of—his incredible success. He promises to marry her; instead, he runs off with Betty Lou, a seventeen-year-old baton twirler (Lee Remick).

Lonesome's influence on public opinion and his salesmanship have become such a force that he is asked to guide a staunch, right-wing senator's campaign for the Presidency. His power to move an audience has evolved into the power to manipulate them. His love for his audience turns into contempt. He becomes a brutal, dangerous demagogue.

Marcia can no longer stand by and do nothing. Despite still loving him, she reveals his true nature by turning on a microphone in the TV studio's control booth. Lonesome's nastiest, most abusive remarks about his supposedly beloved audience are broadcast coast to coast. The outraged public immediately drops him, his power evaporates, and he is left alone to bellow into the night.

All of the characters in A Face in the Crowd *aroused ambivalent feelings. In spite of their failings, it was impossible to overlook the humanity in any of them. Tell me, first of all, what you wanted to make the picture about?*

I was trying to make a political picture, a warning about television and television personalities. "Listen to what he says. Think about it. Don't be taken in by what he is, or appears to be." Budd Schulberg and I were very close in our views of everything. We were both aware that television could be what it has, in fact, turned out to be, an almost hypnotic terrible force. We knew television was selling "personality" because we had Eisenhower up there on

TV all the time. You looked at him, and there was Grandpappy. And everyone wants to be nice to Grandpappy. But if you listened to him he was saying nothing. In the character of Lonesome Rhodes I wanted to show the ambivalence in someone who was almost evil, but who said and believed many things that were right at the same time. I wanted him to be seductive and say out loud things that other people didn't. For example, I think in his time George Wallace in some ways reflected the truth of what a lot of people were feeling. When he talked about tax loopholes for the rich, I didn't assume he was cynical. I took it that like a lot of poor white kids he was aware that there was an Eastern establishment of industrial-military forces that got vast privileges, though he didn't put it in those words. There was something about that little guy that everybody despised that I liked. I felt the same way about Huey Long. His roots were in Populism, the concerns of the common man. Budd and I wanted our hero to seduce his audience so that they would think, "Yes, I can see why he's got that power." Then gradually show that power corrupts and he becomes corrupted, but that he's in part aware of what he's becoming. There is a dualism about television. On the one hand, it can be very beguiling and can turn a man into a hell of a salesman. On the other hand, if you get very close and expose a man enough, sooner or later he's going to reveal who he really is. McCarthy, in my opinion, was hurt more by one incident than anything else. He was seen on television whispering smugly behind his hand to Roy Cohn during the Army hearings. That image was repeated time after time on the nightly news. We made up the plot of *A Face in the Crowd* out of those dual or dialectic realizations. On the one hand our hero seduced the American public. On the other hand he exposed himself so much to the American public that his real nature came through.

Was there any source material for all that?

Budd and I had such a good time doing *On the Waterfront* I said, "Let's do another picture together." He knew the kind of thing I was thinking about so he suggested a short story he had written called *Your Arkansas Traveller*. I read it and liked it and that was it. Then we spent literally months doing research. We went to Young and Rubicam product meetings and talked to advertising people. We went to Nashville a lot and got into the Nashville sound and the Grand Ole Opry. I hung around with a camera. We met a lot of stand-up comics, some of whom are in the picture. Every aspect of the film was carefully researched. It was about a phenomenon that was happening in America at that time. We were always talking about and looking out for native, grass-roots fascism. One thing that a lot of people overlooked is that Fascism always had attractive elements of populism in it. Hitler's followers initially, the members of the National Socialist Party, were guys who were on the outs, who had no power or even jobs. Mussolini's party was made up of "the regular guys."

What was the aesthetic problem you set for yourself?

To be seductive and yet funny. I wanted to have an amusing picture and still have a lot of "warning" in it. I don't think I blended the styles quite right, I mean the satiric and the tragic. That's a very hard blend to achieve. I think I came close, but I don't think I achieved it.

Where do you think you failed?

I don't really know. I thought there would be more sympathy for Rhodes than there turned out to be. I saw the film again a year and a half ago. The house was full of kids, and they were stamping their feet. Maybe it was ahead of its time. You see there again, like in *East of Eden* and *Baby Doll*, I was trying to create a figure who was both attractive and a menace.

This was Andy Griffith's first film. Where did you find him?

He was a stand-up comic. He had no training or experience as a professional actor. But Budd and I heard his record, something about football, and when we talked to him, we both liked him a lot.

Given his inexperience, how did you work with him?

I showed him what I wanted a lot. Take for example the early scene in jail when the sheriff wakes Lonesome. I knew from my own experience that a lot of animals fight on their backs. It's their favorite position because they fight with their claws. I also knew that good street fighters always use their feet and legs. So in the scene I made Andy throw out a foot, and that gives him time to pull himself together. I illustrated that to him and he imitated me. It affected his voice and everything else and made him fierce. He understood it too. He's not a brawler, but every country boy has seen fights.

You actually acted it out for him?

I did it more and more though certain scenes I didn't have to illustrate. Nobody could beat him in front of a microphone. I did all kinds of things. In the big scene at the end of the film when he's up on the balcony, I got him drunk for two days. Somebody wrote an interview attacking me, saying that I got him drunk against his will. An absolute falsehood. Andy will tell you he wanted to be good and couldn't do it. When he got drunk, it was easier so he got drunk. I called it the Jack Daniels school of acting.

Did acting it out for Griffith embarrass him in front of the others?

No, they all liked Andy. And I'd made a big favorite of him. He didn't take it as an insult. He didn't know anything about directing, so he took it as if it were the normal way to work. I did have a talk with Walter Matthau, because I wanted him just as simple as he could be, to just walk through playing Mel Miller. Pat Neal I had to keep ambivalent. I had her keep her mind on the fact that Marcia loved Lonesome but was fighting it off.

Once again you use a relationship with a woman to reveal the central male character.

A man, in every phase of his life, is moved by the same things. You watch a man playing tennis and you see the way he's going to be in his work, how he treats his children, how he is in bed. You watch the way a man walks and you see where his tension is. It's all one piece. What he does on the social and political level, he's also going to do on the personal level. What's touching about Marcia is that she sees the good in Lonesome and thinks she can change him. She fights for the good in him and waits for the good in him to dominate. She's in a sense like a mother who keeps thinking, he's all right—in his heart I know he's okay. And in Lonesome's heart he was "okay," but too little and too late. Early on the viewer sniffs out that he is a rascal—a lovable one, but still a seducer. But Marcia contests your suspicions. The fact that she believes in him does two things. It keeps the ambivalence going. The audience thinks maybe she is right. Maybe the good will win out over the bad. They also watch the woman being fooled and fooling herself and are very touched by it, because she gives her whole life to him.

Did you set for yourself any kind of pictorial style?

I wanted it photographed very plainly. There were great technical difficulties. I had to open up the f-stop on the camera enough so that I could photograph what was happening on the TV monitor screens and still photograph people and get some sort of exposure on their faces. If you opened up too much, there would be too much light and all of their features would wash out. That was a very hard thing to balance. I also wanted a lot of cuts, which meant shooting more set-ups. I had worked with Harry Stradling on *Streetcar* and adored him. He was temperamentally a model to me of what a cameraman should be. He was always cheerful, nothing was too difficult for him. You could say to him at ten minutes to quitting time, "I need two more close-ups, Harry." And you'd get two more close-ups. He could do anything at any speed. Harry loved what he was doing abundantly.

Why the need for so many cuts?

The material always dictates the style. Here we had all kinds of physically big scenes with lots of extras. You just can't light everyone in a mob as if each were posing for a portrait. They're not going to be on screen that long. I wanted a slam-bang style, and I didn't want to be held up by a lot of fussing.

Let's go back to the narrative. Marcia gets Lonesome to do her radio program. He does a country-boy routine, and while he's doing it, you keep his voice going and cut to people listening to the show and responding to what he's saying. Later, Lonesome does a broadcast where he tells all the townspeople that the sheriff would make a good dog catcher; you cut to the sheriff's house with five hundred dogs on the lawn. In Memphis he does his first TV broadcast and again, it's a country boy up against the city slickers. In New York there's a broadly played audition scene in which Lonesome confronts the advertising executives and their client. You do it again when he sells the senator and gets involved in politics. In each of the scenes, the structure is almost identical. It is the outsider against the establishment. He has to win them over, and he does so by attacking or making fun of them. How do you play essentially the same scene so many times and avoid it feeling repetitive?

First of all I tried to make sure they were all funny and amusing. But the main thing was to make sure that it wasn't just plain repetition, that his behavior changed, that he got bolder and bolder and more and more destructive of the advertising and business customs from one confrontation to the next. The progression was based on Lonesome's increased awareness of his growing power and the pleasure he got from wielding it. His personality becomes increasingly synthetic. It comes to resemble more and more a kind of hayseed fascism: "know-nothingism," in effect.

Did you work with Schulberg on the script?

I worked with him all the time on the conception and on the ordering of the scenes, but I never wrote a word. My contribution was not in the verbal language, the dialogue, but in the language of film, especially in the language of sequence and climax. They are as much the director's prerogative as the writer's, so they have to be determined in collaboration. We worked out the basic movement of the story—what they used to call the continuity. Then I disappeared, and Budd wrote a complete first draft. Then I reappeared, and we worked over it.

Once you get into working over and over a script with the writer, how do you then separate yourself enough to be objective?

You begin to lose your objectivity immediately, but you no longer want to be objective. You want to be personal and egocentric. You become as one, and it can be a wonderful relationship. I would always speak absolutely candidly to Budd, just as I would later try to be candid with myself. It's harder to be objective when I work alone because I have no one to challenge me.

How do you keep your sense of invention from being exhausted?

Partly by involving myself in another project so desperately that I couldn't think of anything else. Also, you assert a will not to think of it, forget it, walk away from it. I did a play while Budd wrote the script. Objectivity can be a problem. You deal with it one way or another, the best you can. When you get a script finished, if you trust a couple of people, you can let them read it. You get very egocentric by that time. You have to be. Directing is an exertion of your will. That's why you've got to be steel inside as to your goal. Fortunately, I have had good relationships with authors. I protected them. I never picked up a pen. That's important. Don't scribble. Don't write lines. The director mustn't take away the screenwriter's identity as the "author." You try to get the best out of screenwriters by liberating them. Have them deal with the real problems rather than have them deal with pleasing you. I'm very strong and insistent so I have to be particularly careful that I don't say, "Do it my way." Indirectly, subtly, I eventually make my will known. But really and truly—I mean this—you do it as a suggestion. It's a subtle relationship. You don't want a writer just running around aping you and admiring you. You want someone who's strong and helpful. With really good authors it's especially important to deal collaboratively. They're on guard against a "writing director" and for good reason. In the old days in Hollywood the studios or the producers would have an author write a complete scene-by-scene scenario, and then they'd say, "Now that the structure is good, we need someone to do the dialogue." They'd fire the writer and get someone else to "dialogue it."

For all the big scenes in the film, there are many extremely intimate ones as well, for example when Lonesome tells Marcia about his childhood. It's the real beginning of his winning her over. How did you work through those intimate moments?

I always started very quietly in a scene like that and had the actors just talk and listen to each other. It's very important. She was always trying to see the good in him. I would give him the very simple action of just winning her or boasting. The main thing is to make the audience believe that these two people are interested in each other and that he wants her as much as she cares for him. Whether he does or not, I don't know. I never was convinced that Lonesome really wanted her, but he wanted everybody, whoever happened to be at hand.

What was the essence of his character?

He'd spent his life as an outsider, and that was the way he thought of himself. But when he gets down to it, he wants the same things the "in" people want. He's a very seducible guy with a very tough front. He's typical of many show business types. They look like rebels, but they're really not. That whole world is very seductive. Money and fame often come very quickly, but they're unstable. So you grab what you can as fast as you can. Lonesome is typical of a lot of actors, directors and writers who go into this very difficult profession. Show business people find themselves showing off a lot, selling themselves constantly. When you're uncertain of yourself, you're dependent upon other people to like you. Comics do that, clowns do that, politicians do that. They're all related to each other because they live by the approval of others. What Lonesome really seeks from Marcia is her approval even though he goes after it in a huffy, arrogant way.

She says that she likes the way he laughs. He replies that he puts his whole self into it just as he puts his whole self into everything he does.

He's really saying, "Go to bed with me, I'll put my whole self into that, too." And he's just gotten a first taste of power. He's gotten people to bring their dogs to the sheriff's front lawn, and Marcia asks him, "How does it feel to have the power to do this?" And "she" equals the audience. They're wondering about the same thing. You feel him liking it, enjoying it. And as soon as you enjoy it, power begins to corrupt you. It becomes power for its own sake. His ego is justified, and he says, "Ah, I've got them." He has a certain vengefulness because he's been on the bottom of society his whole life and all of a sudden he's on top. He enjoys that. We all suffer in this public relations civilization. The taste of our civilization is determined by columnists. And most of the critics are columnists. They're on a head trip, showing off their egos. So the whole thing is a big public relations ego competition.

Shortly thereafter an agent arrives who wants to take him to Nashville, who likens him to Will Rogers. You see him begin to wield another kind of power. He makes a pass at Marcia.

He does something that's absolutely typical of comics and singers. They combine their career push with a sexual push, directed at anybody who happens to be there for conquest. Getting a better deal for himself allows him to wink at Marcia, showing off to her.

In the scene at the train station, as he and Marcia are leaving Piggott, Arkansas, we see the worm in the apple. He's all smiles to the public, but privately he slams the locals.

By this time, the audience has gotten the idea; they know what he's likely to become, but that scene is Marcia's first big and maybe last good chance to pull away from Rhodes. He says, "Boy, am I glad to shake that dump." She is shocked, she should walk, be saying to herself, he's a phony, I made a mistake. But she does not. Instead she feels, "I can fix him." She's sick, you know—a little masochistic. She takes more abuse than any woman should all through the picture.

Did you give Neal that to play?

No, the script does that. You have to play against it. I made her really feel that she was in love with him, which is what women do. They rationalize. The word "love" is an umbrella. It covers a multitude of sins. It disguises what's really happening. You say you "love" someone, but you may want to dominate him, encourage him, or you may want his favor. When a man says he loves a woman, it may mean he loves to brutalize her, or it may mean she's got his conscience, as was the case here. Both women and men kid themselves sometimes. They use that word "love," and it excuses everything they do.

In getting her to play the scene, did you use an "umbrella" term or were you more specific?

I told her, "You do love him, you feel he has so much good in him that you've got to see him through." It's got to be absolutely sincere. You do not direct the actress with the result you hope to get from the script. You give her something that will produce, combined with the script and the situation, the results you want. You don't tell Pat Neal he's going to destroy your life, but call him back. That's called "playing the result."

The film keeps you guessing because you're never quite sure about Lonesome.

There's always some element of honesty in him. He's a truthteller in a hypocritical civilization.

In the first scene at the Nashville TV studio, Lonesome is terribly uncomfortable and you sympathize with his bewilderment. Then he makes a touching speech about being lost in the big city. It's done with an openness and innocence that's moving and intriguing because it plays off a moment of arch nastiness in which he calls Mel Miller, "Vanderbilt '44." When you have a complicated scene in which a character, played by an untrained actor, moves through different levels or pitches of behavior, what do you do?

I told Griffith the whole thing is a fraud, and then I cast a real phony to play the director of the TV show. I always tried to make Andy feel that he was telling the truth, and that Lonesome's strength came from that. The whole problem with Andy was to make him more sincere, more believable and direct. The phoniness is created by the story as it develops and by the scenes as they're directed and laid out. Within that context of falseness, you make Andy believe that he alone sees and tells the truth. Even when Lonesome explains to Marcia why he married Betty Lou later in the picture, there is some element of truth in it.

But in that scene you're describing, he goes to Marcia. She doesn't come to him. He calls and barges into her room. Obviously, he needs something from her; he's not just being a decent guy.

He needs her to believe in him. For a lot of men, the woman they are with when they first get successful becomes the talisman of their success. They have that woman connected with the idea "I made it with her." In this case Lonesome believes that his success is related to his worth, and Marcia has become not only his talisman, she's the container that holds success through a demonstration of conscience. He believes that if she thinks he is a good person, then he must be a good person. So it's very important to him that she continue to believe in him. But he's a complex being. He has very anarchistic and disruptive feelings too.

One of the ways he succeeds is by knocking the establishment. He knocks his sponsor, and they threaten to pull his contract. He goes back on the air and knocks them even more. Anthony Franciosa plays Joey, a flunky who works for the sponsor. He totally agrees with his boss to his face, but in the next breath goes behind his back and sets up a deal to sell Lonesome to national television in New York. When the sponsor does fire him, Lonesome goes back to say goodbye to Marcia. I guess he really goes back to spend the night with her.

No he doesn't. He really is a very complex character and is never totally insincere. In the first place, he does a very honest thing when the sponsor says, "I'm going to fire you if you tell the truth about our product." He tells the truth even more. You've got to admire him for that. He really means, "I don't want any part of this, and I'm going back to my old life." And that's the moment when Marcia realizes that she can only hold him by going to bed with him. She feels that there's something terrifically truthful and alienated about his wanting to go home. But she calls him back, and what she says in a sense is, "I believe in you and anything I have is yours. You're worth more than I am, and I'll put my life on the line with yours." That's what a pure girl does. That's a beautiful scene. I also like the scene in the ad agency in New York that comes soon after. I thought it was hilarious. In the end what it came down to is that what you sell in America is not what's in the product but what's in the ad.

I disagree with you about that scene. I didn't think you did it very well.

It was too broad?

Yes. It seemed to me that you were glib in the handling of those small parts. The people were reduced to clichés.

Possibly so. The whole advertising world does appeal to my sense of the ludicrous. Sometimes when I think something is amusing, I let it go on too long or I go too far with it.

In a series of transitions you show Lonesome's rise and the sales of the product he's selling go up. It ends with an extreme close-up of his mouth in a big grin. You then cut to an enormous wide shot of a country estate in Connecticut—the General's house. The General owns the sponsor, Vitajex, and he knows he's got a valuable tool in Rhodes.

Lonesome's gone on to a new plateau. He sold himself so well that now he's useful in a different way. New horizons of power are opened up.

It's a second-act curtain in a way. There's another set of transitions. Lonesome makes the cover of Life, Look *and the* Journal American. *It ends with him being given a penthouse suite. He's made it to the top.*

And you feel that his latest success is the work of a bigger PR man, namely General Haynesworth. The General's plan is to give Lonesome political power and influence, to make him into a person who creates public opinion. It is sort of an anatomy of American power.

Again, as you said, Lonesome intertwines his career with his relationship with Marcia. He asks her to come over—he's desperate to see her, despite the fact that while he is talking to her, his assistant is hurrying another woman out of his apartment.

That's exactly the point. Marcia is very hip. She knows about the other woman right away, and still she's tempted to be with him. Putting that other girl there was a brilliant idea on Budd's part. Lonesome's behavior is truthfully the way someone like him feels after he's had a night with a girl that he's found to be terribly boring. He may want another girl, the same type, three nights later, but there are moments of self-disgust and loneliness in that kind of screwing, and he thinks, Marcia's my real identity. I've got to have her.

He asks her to marry him. He says, "I need you...I'm in mighty tall grass...You're my lifeline to the truth." She responds, "Don't hurt me."

That's her way of accepting. She knows she's going to get hurt. That's why she says it, of course. Many women who go into that kind of marriage know that. They're not fools. After she accepts his proposal, he shows her the lights of the city from his penthouse windows. We had much more in that scene which we cut. Budd had a great idea—that Lonesome would have a garden on his penthouse balcony. He says, "You can't keep anything alive up here. Dust in this city kills everything." It was his attempt to get back to the best, most honest part of him.

Why did you cut it?

It didn't seem to work. Maybe we thought we'd said enough about how he was feeling. Throughout the picture Budd and I contrasted Lonesome's obvious enjoyment of manipulating people with his genuine reactions to the corrupt elements around him. Self-disgust is the most characteristic and typical reaction.

It's very believable that he wants to marry her, and that's why the next scene works. Marcia is sitting in his penthouse when in comes a woman who introduces herself as Mrs. Rhodes—Lonesome's wife whom he had never di-

vorced. If she doesn't receive $3,000 a month, she's going to make it plenty hot for both of them.

That's a classic scene in women's lives. Marcia conceals her pain. She has too much pride to let it show.

How do you approach a scene where actors have to conceal their feelings?

I did two things in that scene. First, I told Pat, "Don't give her the satisfaction she wants." And I told the other dame, "That prim little bitch sitting there is a phony." I made her believe that Pat Neal herself is a phony. So you deal in reality. It made the scene fun for the other woman.

Do you have to get them to feel the pain first, and then conceal it?

An actor is going to jump at feeling that. The problem is to get her to conceal it.

When Marcia comes to confront Lonesome, we see the nastiness in him. Lonesome and Joey are demonstrating a laugh machine to the General. What an idea that was.

That's Budd. I didn't tell Andy, "You're nasty now." Instead I said, "You're showing this machine off, it could put you at the top. And this bitch is being sour and making nasty cracks. You want to kill her." So he behaves as if she were actually disloyal. All the time you give the actor justifications for what he does. He's right to be sore at her, but she's also right. Drama is the opposition of two sides that are "right," or else the conflict doesn't amount to anything.

Lonesome Rhodes is now becoming a power freak and losing touch with the little people whose laughter made him. He replaces them with a machine, his artificiality has a correlative.

When you use an obvious symbol like that, you're walking a tightrope, and you've got to protect it in every way you can. One thing that helped a lot was that I played the antagonism between Lonesome and Marcia so the audience's total concentration wasn't on the business with the machine. She's resentful and thinks he's become a phony. She even looks at him differently. The scene could have been just a rather far-fetched gag. So it was essential to find a way to relate it to the central story. That's always important to remember. You should never say, "Now we're taking a hiatus and just having some fun." If there's a scene about an applause box it should mean something to the protagonist. As soon as you do that, you cover a multitude of sins because you're always on the main line and everything else is ornament, comment, device. The heart of this scene was the machine and the boss's reaction to it, but even more importantly it was about Rhodes showing off and trying to win him.

The text of that scene doesn't directly tell the main story.

So I interwove a subtext even if it was only expressed by the way Neal and Griffith looked at each other or the way she tagged along behind him. You don't have to have dialogue all the time to keep the story flowing. You tell the actors what's really going on underneath while they're doing whatever the hell they're doing. That happens all the time in life. When you're angry with somebody you avoid the anger. You don't run out and scream. You do something else. I avoid a confrontation unless it has to be settled or you just can't hold it in anymore so you blurt it out. I always give the actors something else to do if possible, otherwise you just get people talking to each other. The more you make it indirect, the more interesting the final explosion or confrontation is.

You keep changing about how much and/or how directly you tell things to the actors.

It depends on what you're getting from them. Their intuitions might be exactly right. There was an interesting article by Liv Ullmann in the *Times* the other day. She said Ingmar Bergman doesn't tell his actors much. He says you can talk a goddamn scene to death. A lot of young directors, who are aiming high, tend to do just that. I used to do it. The point is that to get what you want you may have to just say a single word. You may have given the direction the night before. You may have given it as you said good morning or as you shared your Danish pastry with them. You may do it in some indirect way that leaves them thinking. Or you may do it by explaining that the business they're doing is somehow redolent of the conflict. But you even try to give that direction indirectly because otherwise they're trying to satisfy you, whereas the point is to deal with their partner in the scene.

In the next scene Marcia goes into the writer's room where everyone is trashing Lonesome.

That scene is really about the intention of the girl. What is she going to do? She is confronted with the fact that these guys are saying terrible things about Rhodes that she completely agrees with. She doesn't know what to do, and it dramatizes her inner conflict. You don't see it directly. She doesn't protest. She even joins in knocking him to a certain extent but you know that she's also committed to the guy.... Why are you laughing?

I'm laughing at the precision of your recall. That scene was shot a very long time ago.

It's not just recall. It's a principle of directing. The way I see things, as I said, is that every scene in some way or other should deal with what's happening at the core of the story, or else don't have the scene.

The film shifts gear when we return to Piggott, Arkansas for the cheerleading contest.

One big decision we had to make when we went down to Piggott was how to shoot this huge scene. I decided to build a tower from which we photographed the high school band spelling out "We love Lonesome Rhodes." That cost a lot of money, but I decided the picture needed that kind of opening up. The spectacle also let you see things from Rhodes' point of view—how seductive it all is. Everyone is at his feet, and they really like him. That's America. Everything is PR. Also, it is tempting. Lee Remick, who played Betty Lou, was twenty-one and in perfect physical condition, really a bloom, just a perfect little bud of a girl. She's open and available to him. How could any man resist? Why should he? Of course it's easy to say he's being untrue to Marcia, but that's what makes life complicated and interesting. His appetite for adulation is without bounds. He's starved, like a lot of guys who have spent most of their lives at the bottom. They've been down so long that when they get up, they can't stop climbing.

Throughout the baton contest, Lonesome and Betty Lou keep giving each other the eye. Joey, now his manager, watches it happening. You can see him trying to figure an angle.

I was trying to show that Joey is jealous of anyone moving in on his hold on Rhodes, above all Marcia. What you have is a triangle with Rhodes in the middle. The temper of the times as expressed by Joey is on one side, and Marcia, the girl that thinks he's the only fellow that's saying certain truths out loud in public, is on the other side. He's pulled between the two so Joey is delighted to see him get locked in with Betty Lou. He sees it as a way of cutting Lonesome away from Marcia's influence. He's like some agents in Los Angeles who get between their clients and their wives and yet at the same time send their wives presents and do everything they can to flatter them. You see them slowly break up a marriage. You see, even in the baton scene, you're trying to say something that relates to the central story. Lonesome's a victim of the system. That's putting it in rather corny terms but that's what he is.

But isn't Marcia the real victim? In the following scene, she and Mel sit in a bar, drinking. An advertising man gives her a wire saying that Rhodes is off to Mexico, ostensibly to get his divorce in order to marry her. Despite all the things she knows bad about him, she's still hooked on him—we see it in her face.

I think what Budd did with Marcia there is immense. She's absolutely in agreement with every criticism made of Rhodes, and still she's loyal. It must be like a cold blade on her heart. If that's the result of psychoanalysis, it's unhealthy. It would be better if she killed him. She's killing herself this way. You see the same thing on the faces of Hollywood wives who have husbands like that. You see the cost.

When she goes to meet him at the airport, expecting him to marry her, he has his new wife with him. You shot Patricia Neal pushing through the mob to get to him in a way that she literally becomes a face in the crowd.

I didn't do that consciously, but if the basic idea of a film is valid, it will create those sorts of images again and again. The point of the shot was to show he wanted to hit Marcia as hard as he could. He needed to hit her pretty hard in order to make a final break with her.

Then he goes to Marcia and says, "I was afraid to marry you."

He visits her. That's important because it shows he has the guts to face her. He doesn't try to avoid it. I think that's Andy's best scene in the picture. That scene is essential because it saves Lonesome Rhodes from being just a sneaky, double-crosser. This way the audience can understand his feelings and why he married Betty Lou. I mean, who needs that idealistic busybody, which is what Marcia is, always telling him what he should be. Saving his life is really none of her damn business. He just wants to enjoy himself. Suppose he doesn't want to be the great savior of the American people? At the same time, Marcia's right, too, because he double-dealt her. That's the essence of the whole Stanislavsky system. You justify everyone's point of view. Drama is best when you're dealing with opposing feelings within the audience and they don't know who's right. Conflict doesn't mean a thing if it's mechanical and physical. It means something when the conflict is general, when it's not only between two forces but between values. That's what we face all the time in life. When you decide in favor of "A" you are not deciding in favor of "B." You're losing something when you decide. That's what makes a decision difficult; that's what drama is about. There's a loss and there's no way of getting out of it. There's no perfect solution. A wonderful thing happens in that scene. Again, I've got to give Schulberg a lot of credit. It's the most unusual, unexpected thing in the film. After Lonesome gets all through explaining himself, he says he'll take care of her. "I'm gonna give you a healthy slice of our whole operation...say ten percent of my end...." And she explodes, "Giving me. Giving me! You're not giving me anything. A Face in the Crowd was my idea.

The whole idea of Lonesome Rhodes belongs to me. I always should have been an equal partner. Well, now I'm going to be an equal partner....And I want it on paper." Instead of being the nice, clean girl that crawls back to Piggott, Arkansas, she holds on even then. It comes out of the pain and desperation of his betrayal. It's a way of attacking him while still holding on to him.

Despite this personal setback, Rhodes continues gaining public power. He takes over the presidential campaign of right-wing Senator Fuller. To him it's just like selling any other product.

He's fully enjoying his power, now. When the General, who is again his sponsor, warns him to play it cool, he brushes him off, saying, "I'm a force."

He demands to have a new TV program, The Cracker Barrel Show*—as a platform for his ideas and he gets it.*

What's good is you think, "God, this is ridiculous, the satire is too much." But at the same time you have a feeling, maybe it's close to something that could really happen. It makes you think about it more than it would if it were less extreme. On the other hand, I could have made the Senator nicer and smarter and it wouldn't have hurt.

Marcia and Mel watch a broadcast of the new show on a TV set in a bar.

I was trying to dramatize the scorn that Rhodes by this point had for the people, which is what fascism really is. Democracy depends on some basic, indissoluble intelligence and goodness in people. It assumes that if you tell people the facts, they'll come to the right decision, which is part superstition and part hope. Here he's just manipulating them.

When Lonesome discovers that his manager has been screwing his wife, the confrontation is played out in front of a built-in soda fountain right in his living room.

I don't know who the hell it was Budd and I read about who had an ice cream fountain in her house where she made her own sodas and sundaes. We did the same thing with Betty Lou, and the image is obliterating—it reduces her to nothing. He kicks her out. He was getting isolated. He turned against the General, he turns against Joey. He's all alone.

So he runs right back to Marcia. He's literally taking off his clothes as he comes through the door, claiming that it was her he wanted all the time.

I hoped the audience wouldn't know how she would treat his overture. I wanted to keep it a surprise, so at the end of his long appeal to her, she goes into the closet—you think she's gone to put on a nightgown. Instead, she suddenly comes out with a coat on. She runs out of the building and it's raining. She hails a cab. The first one won't take her—a mundane detail about New York City, which keeps things rooted in reality. The next night at the TV studio, Lonesome behaves like a raving maniac, blowing his stack at everybody while Marcia watches silently from the control booth. We began to shift the focus away from Lonesome and onto Marcia. The audience begins to wonder what she'll do. It was very, very important to reveal the technology of the broadcast because we had to make Marcia's final act real and believable. As the credits begin to come up at the end of the show, she opens the sound pot so that the audience hears the scornful things Rhodes is saying about the American public. The others in the control room try to drag her away, but she holds on. It was a way to have her bring him down single-handedly.

With a sweet smile on his face he says, "Aren't they all stupid, just like sheep." While he's doing that, you cut to people all around the country watching him and reacting.

It's just like at the beginning of the film when he was in the station talking about homemade pie, and we showed the woman cleaning the inside of her oven and cooking a pie, only in reverse. That's worked in with another symbolic mechanical thing which is him going down on the elevator. We intercut between the shots of the numbers on the elevator going down and the shots of everyone, behind his back, taking him apart. The elevator boy says, "Lonesome Rhodes express, going down."

Then he goes to his own party. Nobody has shown up. He's all alone. Then you cut back to the control room. Marcia's still there. Mel persuades her to tell Rhodes that it was she who did him in.

I wanted the audience to feel her pain. She feels guilty. She's done a terrible thing. She's killed her man, her child.

Mel is very supportive, and he's obviously in love with her, but I began to dislike him.

A little bit. I tell the audience that he's absolutely right, he's strong and she should go with him, but at the same time there's a smugness about him. It's a little bit of my feeling about intellectuals leaking through, but his smugness was also essential to the story. If Mel hadn't been so absolutely sure of himself and his values and, thus, a bit pompous, we might only have felt disgust for Lonesome. We might not have seen that something good went down with Lonesome Rhodes. Without that ambivalence, the whole film wouldn't be worthwhile.

In the final scene, Rhodes is reduced to insanity.

I got Andy drunk to play it. We couldn't get it any other way. I wanted him out of control. He had to be a screaming and yelling maniac, ready to be taken away in a wagon. I didn't know how else to do it. It required a really great actor, and Andy had never acted before.

Granted he needs to be out of control, but you also gave him a lot of precise dialogue. He's raving and ranting up on the balcony until he quiets down. Then he races to Marcia, and starts raving again, until she says, "It was me." And he snaps. Instantly calm, Rhodes wishes her luck with Mel. It was very touching. Isn't it risky having an actor drunk when he has all that to do?

Those things were not all shot in the same half hour. He was only drunk when he was up on the balcony. After he played that scene a few times, he was conditioned by it. It was hard, but we did it. The picture ends as they drive off, and you hear his voice calling, "Come back." That was really walking a tightrope. Lonesome's all wrong. Everything the opposition says is true, and still in some way you maintain a modicum of sympathy for him.

I suspect that works partly because you, personally, have enormous affection for him.

I suppose having a thorough acquaintance with elements of corruption and things in myself that I don't totally approve of and admitting them helps. It's very important that a director doesn't within his own soul take a superior stance. I hate smugness, and anytime I can take a shot at it I do.

WILD RIVER
(1960)

IN A PROLOGUE, black and white documentary footage depicts the Tennessee River wreaking havoc. A voice-over narration explains that the Tennessee Valley Authority was set up to dam the river, but some of the people owning homes on the river's banks and islands refused to move.

Chuck Glover (Montgomery Clift) arrives from Washington to persuade Miss Ella Garth (Jo Van Fleet) to relocate. The old lady lives on Garth island with her sons and a village full of black farmers and their families. She knows the island will be flooded, but she would rather die than leave it, and that's what she tells Glover.

Glover also meets Miss Ella's widowed daughter-in law, Carol Garth (Lee Remick), and asks her to help persuade Miss Ella to move. Carol, on her own with her two kids, has withdrawn from life. The two fall in love and through Carol, Glover comes to understand and love the old lady.

Walter (Frank Overton), Carol's fiancé, leads Glover into a trap, and Bailey (Albert Salmi), the worst of the town's racist bullies beats him up for paying equal wages to blacks and whites. Despite this incident, a quart of moonshine later, Glover and Walter become friends, and Glover turns up at Miss Ella's completely drunk. He understands her irascible nature now. "It's her ever-lovin' dignity."

20th Century-Fox presents
ELIA KAZAN'S
Wild River
STARRING
MONTGOMERY CLIFT / LEE REMICK
CO-STARRING
JO VAN FLEET
PRODUCED AND DIRECTED BY ELIA KAZAN
Screenplay by PAUL OSBORN
Based on novels by William Bradford Huie and Borden Deal
CINEMASCOPE
COLOR BY DE LUXE

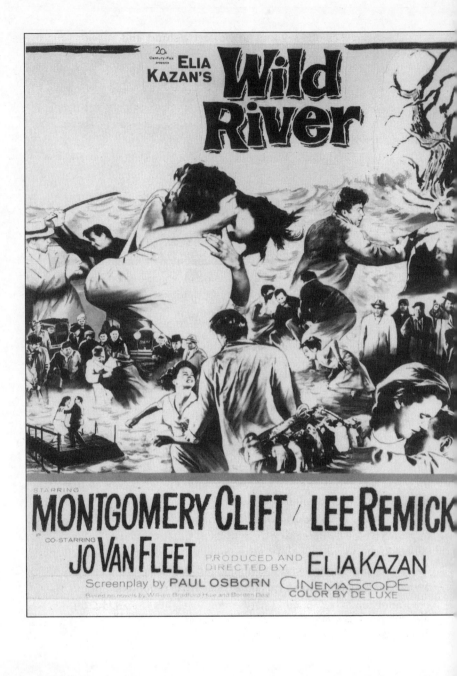

Carol senses she's going to be left behind and pleads to Glover to take her with him. Under pressure from Washington, Glover gets a federal marshall's order to evict Miss Ella the next day. He begs her to leave voluntarily, but again she refuses.

Back at Carol's, she throws herself at him. The town's thugs show up and start a riot. Glover is again badly beaten, but rises far enough to ask Carol to marry him, and she accepts.

The next day the eviction papers are served, and Miss Ella leaves her island. After her relocation, she sits on her new porch staring blankly at nothing. A cow nibbles on the lawn. An old black friend remains at her side. Miss Ella knows that her life is all over.

As Glover oversees the torching of Miss Ella's old house, Carol arrives to tell him that the old lady has died. She reassures him that it could not have gone any other way.

Miss Ella is buried in the only bit of her island still above water, the graveyard: Glover, Carol and her two children fly over the island, the river, and the dam to face the future together.

In Wild River *you start with a character who is almost smug, and during the course of the movie he grows and changes.*

What do you mean, almost smug? The whole point is that Glover is a guy who thinks he knows all the answers, the typical Depression-era liberal, the liberal who did wonderful things, the liberal who saved this country. I worked for the Department of Agriculture for a while, and I got to know a lot of guys like him. I admired them and I liked them, but at the same time there was something of a know-it-all quality in them that I found very false.

You seem to suggest that the "country folk" are better people. But in Wild River, *some of them are pure rednecks.*

I think I romanticize country people a little but I do like them. And with Miss Ella, I wanted to take the most reactionary person I could think of and show that there's a lot of good in her. I'm not here on this earth to say that the tradition of ruggedness and individualism is not even reasonable. She loves her home and doesn't want to lose it. I really love that character. I'll never stop being grateful to Jo Van Fleet for creating her the way she did. I think the best thing in that film is the last two or three reels, when they take her off the island. The cow is rowed across in a rowboat and put in her new front yard. She just sits there. She won't have it. She'd rather die than give in. That's my feeling too. She had to make a difficult choice. There's something good going down. I felt that all through about civilization, about improvement. I think our cities are monstrous. I think our civilization which has been improved and improved and improved has been dehumanized. In many ways I don't think it's as good as the way it used to be. I made Miss Ella as reactionary as possible. She is against all progress. She considers blacks chattel.

On the other hand, you gave her great dignity.

Not gave her, I believe she has it. I believe in land and in folks caring for land. I don't think it's just a counter you can move around. I think Miss Ella's right to want to stay on her land. I think Glover is right, too. That picture, with all of its faults, is the epitome of what I feel more clearly than any other, except maybe *America America*.

In what sense?

Both sides are right. There's a need to do things for the good of the majority, which in this case is to establish inexpensive electric power and to control the erratic, devastating flooding of the Tennessee River. It's obviously important. But when you do that, some individuals are just ruled out, and I think that's a loss. It's necessary. I'm not saying it's not. But it is a real loss and should not be ignored. I think *Wild River* is the picture I did where the right on both sides is revealed at its best. Glover finally feels for Miss Ella and likes her, and for a moment he almost throws up what he's doing in her favor. She's fated to be overwhelmed and she dies for him.

There's a scene early in the film which puts these ideals squarely into opposition. Miss Ella, in the most abusive, bigoted way imaginable, tries to force Sam, an old black man, to sell his beloved dog. He refuses. She then uses his arguments to defend her refusal to sell her land. Glover, who has been watching, matches her arguments step for step. It's kind of breathtaking.

That establishes the main theme of the picture, like the beginning of a symphony. Glover thinks he's doing something right and so does Miss Ella. The film is structured like a love story between the old lady and Glover with Carol, her daughter-in-law, sort of in the middle. He finally comes to love the old lady, and it turns him around, makes a man out of him, because he also comes to understand a point of view that he could not have imagined sympathizing with at the beginning. He loves her at the end, and gradually, as he gets to love her, the audience, who are mostly liberals, do what I make them do. They just adore her too.

Why did you cast Montgomery Clift?

He wasn't my choice. I wish I had been able to cast someone more masculine, someone stronger would have been better. It's hard to cast an intellectual. I would have preferred Brando, but then I always prefer Brando. He was unavailable, so I kept postponing the picture and postponing it, trying to find somebody I liked. I liked Monty Clift personally, but he was in very bad shape. He had had an auto accident going down the hill from Liz Taylor's house. He was banged up. His face was almost a different face. He was also very shaky and on liquor and drugs, just quivering with doubt. It was a tough, tough thing to deal with. He was also unmasculine, which hurt the love story. I think I could have done better, but I didn't know with whom. I still don't know.

Why do you begin the film with documentary stock footage of a flood of the Tennessee River?

You can't stage that stuff without spending millions of dollars. But more importantly, it anchors the film in reality. We were telling the audience, "It actually happened, folks. We're not kidding." It put a terrific burden on the rest of the picture. It had to be as real as the documentary footage. That material creates a sense of emergency and tells the audience at the outset that what the TVA was doing was necessary. That was very important because it keeps the film from becoming a dry, intellectual argument. The TVA had set up land-purchasing offices all through the South, which were regarded as an arm of Washington, and therefore looked on with some hostility. But people were so poor, then. They were getting food and money from the federal government. I think the great thing that was done in the New Deal was persuading the country to believe in and accept the principle that the government of the people has the responsibility of seeing to it that all the people have jobs. The TVA was the first noble and worthy attempt that I remember though I never believe that anything is all good. It doesn't work out that way. And that is the problem posed in *Wild River*. There's a cost for doing what is best for the majority. You record the loss and try to protect against it as much as you can. I don't know what the TVA should have done with a woman like Miss Ella, but you don't just move her into the street.

Lee Remick is another woman in white. She awakens the male hero, on a kind of non-intellectual, sensual level, and that allows him to be opened up in other ways as well. It cracks the rigidity of his assumptions.

She's also smart enough to stay in the middle and not take sides. She knows there's something valuable in what he's trying to do, and still her affection for her grandmother is basic and human. She's a very plain, straightforward, affectionate woman, like the picture itself. It's affectionate and very human. I guess that's why I like it. It turns around a lot of accepted stereotypes.

Baby Doll *and* A Face in the Crowd *were shot in black-and- white. Then you went back to color and CinemaScope for this film. All three films are in one way or another about the South.*

Thematically, *Baby Doll* had a lot to do with being washed-out white. *A Face in the Crowd* looked like it was going to be very expensive and in those days, shooting color really added a lot to the cost of making a film. Also, I had a distrust of color. Still, I thought *Wild River* should be in color because the country wasn't just the setting for the story, it was the essence of the story. It was an outdoor picture, autumn cornfields, rivers, fires, country people's faces.

You've done a lot of pictures in the South, but you're a northern city boy.

When I was a kid I used to hitchhike around a lot. I had a close friend in Chattanooga, a Communist organizer, whom I visited. I spent a lot of time down there, and when I thought about it closely, I realized that the social conflicts in this country were often most visible in the South. *On the Waterfront* and *Panic in the Streets* are city pictures, but I've done both kinds. I've always been interested in country life. I tried to give *Wild River* a legendary quality, a feeling of something that happened long ago, that's now part of our history. I felt very affectionately toward that picture when I made it, and I guess as I got older I feel even more affectionately. *Wild River* was a melancholy picture. Its themes—that there's a cost for everything, that good things die and should, that change is painful but necessary—are ideas that I believe in more and more. History is full of that. But I'm old-fashioned in certain ways. I think what our prosperity has achieved for us is very questionable. It's not very pleasurable. Supposedly, we're a hedonistic society, but there's very little hedonism anywhere. You can't even eat lunch comfortably in New York anymore. Progress and loss feature strongly in my next picture, too.

Whether you live in a small town the way they do, or in a city, maybe this is happening to you right now. . .maybe (if you're older) you remember. . when suddenly the kissing isn't a kid's game any more, suddenly it's wide-eyed scary and dangerous.

No one under 16 will be admitted unless accompanied by an adult.

ELIA KAZAN'S PRODUCTION OF

SPLENDOR IN THE GRASS

THE FIRST PLAY ESPECIALLY WRITTEN FOR THE SCREEN BY WILLIAM INGE

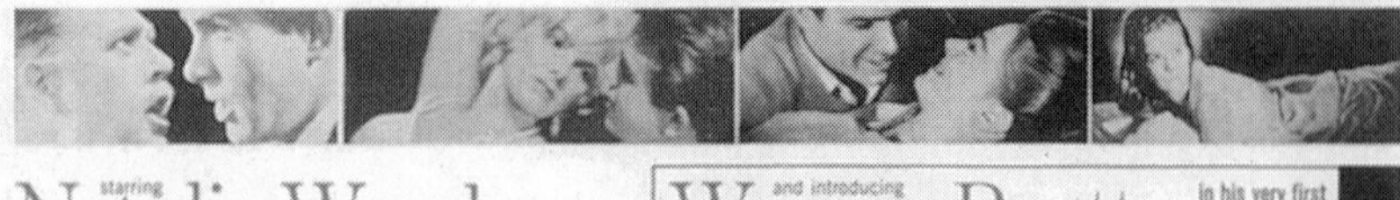

starring Natalie Wood with PAT HINGLE · AUDREY CHRISTIE

and introducing Warren Beatty — in his very first picture--a very special star!

written by WILLIAM INGE · produced and directed by ELIA KAZAN · TECHNICOLOR® From WARNER BROS.

SPLENDOR IN THE GRASS
(1961)

KANSAS, mid-1920's. Teenagers Bud Stamper (Warren Beatty) and Deanie Loomis (Natalie Wood) are madly, obsessively in love. Bud's father, Ace Stamper (Pat Hingle), the richest man in town, is against an early marriage. He wants Bud to go to Yale and follow in his footsteps. Deanie's much poorer family, especially her mother (Audrey Christie), is strongly in favor of their romance. Between Deanie's own virginal but awakening sexual longings, Bud's increasing sexual demands and her mother's rigid, puritanical morality, Deanie is literally driven mad and hospitalized when Bud leaves her and takes up with a girl who is more "accommodating."

Bud goes to Yale, but does his best to flunk out, and gets involved with a waitress, Angelina (Zohra Lampert), who treats him kindly.

Bud's father goes to New Haven determined to straighten his son out. He takes him to New York for a night on the town, hookers and all. But instead of sorting Bud out, Ace kills himself when he learns that the stock market has crashed. Bud returns home married to the waitress and becomes a farmer, which is all he ever wanted to be.

Deanie recovers and comes home. She's agreed to marry a former patient who had been kind to her, though it is clear that she still loves Bud. Her mother claims not to know where Bud lives, but her father tells her where to find him. She goes to visit and while stunned by the discovery that Bud is now married, she is not overcome by it. Though Bud and Deanie still love each other, they accept the compromises they have made. They may never again feel the ecstasy of high romance, but neither will they be shattered when it goes wrong.

Splendor in the Grass is about the collapse of the values of a business civilization and how those values crushed the most tender and human parts of people. Bud Stamper and Deanie Loomis are a really nice couple at the beginning of the film but as the story progresses, they get torn apart. The values of business are forced into their personal lives, by Bud's father, Deanie's mother and a pervading puritanism, which is the ethical arm of business. Bill Inge told me this story. I liked it. Then he wrote a novel and I made a screenplay of it. Then I sent it to Bill and he worked on it. Again, it's historical, which was a way, like in *Wild River*, of saying that these are the values of the American tradition and they're wrong. What I like about *Splendor in the Grass* is the last reel, when she goes to visit him and he's married. Both of them are the children of businessmen. Her father is a shopkeeper and since he's poorer he appreciates her more, but her mother is the kind of woman who is business-minded and drives her husband. It's an awfully simple-minded picture. It's not complex or subtle, but it's truthful.

Was there an aesthetic problem you set for yourself?

Yeah, tenderness. It was the easiest picture I ever made because the script was good. It was pure and simple.

I didn't like the script. I thought it was too simple, and it uses a number of dramatic devices that surprised me. For instance, when Deanie's in the mental hospital, you do a scene in a psychiatrist's office that had an on-the-nose quality which you pretty successfully avoided in other pictures. But here the psychiatrist says things like, "You have to learn to accept your parents as people." And I thought, "Oh come on, you can do better than that."

But what he says is true.

I know it's true. So what? What is factually true is not necessarily what's dramatically sound. You do things better than that. You make them more complicated.

I may, but this is a story about two kids, and the problem is not a complex one. I think the subtlety of the picture comes only at the end.

And that's where it struck me as being inconsistent. The end of that picture is loaded with texture. To me that's the only real tenderness in it. Most of the rest of it is cheap sentimentality. There's only one other scene in the picture that I liked—when Ace goes to Yale to straighten Bud out. He takes him to a nightclub and figures, as a lot of fathers of that sort do, that all the kid needs is a piece of ass. He makes a preposterous fool of himself, setting his son up to get laid. You evoke a fullness in that character, his father, that I thought was lacking almost throughout in Deanie's mother.

I don't agree with you. I think the scene where her mother unpacks with her when she comes back from the hospital and explains herself is wonderful. I'm going to defend the picture now. I don't think there are any characters in our time like that mother. She is absolutely wrong and still she's able to say what she does at that moment and you pity her. Bill Inge had a very shaking quality, or virtue. He wrote what seemed like *Ladies' Home Journal* literature. Then all of a sudden he'd do something, usually toward the end, that took you just a little deeper than you expected, and it's disturbing. You think that the mother is the cliché of clichés, and all of a sudden she says something which is terrific. All of Bill's plays were written like that. Bill was like that. He was the Midwest. He was Kansas. He set in motion the clichés, but then plunged further. I love the end of the film.

Then let's talk about the end. What were you after?

That you accept the cost of disaster. Deanie still has hope when she gets out of the hospital. She puts on a white dress and goes out to visit Bud. She doesn't know what his situation is. She finds him married. The marriage is not what you would call an ecstatically happy one. But it's not an unhappy one either. He's sort of satisfied with it. He doesn't want to give it up. His wife sees that he's still kind of in love with Deanie, and she says a really profound thing, "Yes, he was in love with her." Bill was very deceptive. He was deeper than you think all the time.

The preceding scene was interesting. Deanie wants to visit her old boyfriend. Her mother lies and say he's not around. Her father, who has been sitting there doing nothing through the whole scene, tells the truth. It seemed to me that there was more sympathy with the fathers than with the mothers in this picture.

No, I think the mother is very sympathetic. After all, she had to be the man in the family. They are all sort of equal. The picture's very simple, even simple-minded.

There's such an overstated, simplistic sexual puritanism about it. It was hard to take it seriously when her mother goes through long tirades about how dirty sex is. What she was saying was either funny or neurotic, yet you played it all very straight. All that business with Deanie in the bath declaring she hasn't been "spoiled."

I think most American people feel like you. The picture had a great vogue in France, and I think it's because France is so middle class. They still have the problem that's in the picture. Middle-class kids are brought up that way. Their parents still try to keep their daughters virgins until they marry.

The picture was quite popular here too when it came out, wasn't it?

A lot of people liked the picture, but a lot of guys like you can't stand it.

My objection was not solely on the level of content. In some places the behavior was very rich and interesting, but in so many others it seemed one-dimensional. Did you follow Inge's pattern? Did you intentionally do things very simply, then pull the trap door on all the clichés?

No, I tried to do it like a small story of the heartland of America with affection for everybody, including Bud's father played by Pat Hingle, whom you could say is often a very clichéd character. I tried to make him human even when he is being horrid—like in an early scene when he tells Bud all of his plans for him and in doing so it is clear he wants to totally control his son's life.

Did you have any problems shooting the film?

It was a lark. I shot it all in New York in the studio and in locations around here.

You, in the studio?

Kansas was not like it was in the period depicted in the film. Still, I could have shot it in Kansas, but if you look at the script closely, you'll see that a lot of the film takes place inside the two families' houses. The interiors of both would have had to have been sets, regardless of where I shot the film. I wanted it to seem somehow as if the story took place a long time ago. I did a lot of research on the picture. I went out to Kansas and hung around high schools to watch the kids' behavior. I went to the Menninger Clinic for a while and saw how it worked. It was very interesting to me that the first mental institution of its kind was located in mid-America—almost an acknowledgment that mid-America was cracking up, that its values were not working. I had known a lot about the midwest. I had been there a lot, and I had done Bill's play, *The Dark at the Top of the Stairs*, and gotten to know him very well and like him a lot. But *Splendor in the Grass* isn't only a story about the midwest, it's a story about all of "middle America." What we call "middle America" is not only Kansas, it's North Carolina, it's New Jersey, it's Queens, it's Connecticut—anywhere you find the proper, established, indubitably "good" business class. One of the things I've harped on all my life is that we live in a business civilization, and that the business orientation determines every value. Every time there's a conflict between values, what's good for business is what resolves it. I know the film is simple and simple minded, but I like it. I think the end is worth the whole picture and unless you have the first part you can't have the end.

Where did you find Warren Beatty and Natalie Wood?

Most Hollywood producers, even the studio, had already given up on Natalie Wood. She was washed up...she was twenty-six. I met her and liked her and we got her inexpensively through Warner Brothers on an old contract. Warren Beatty was introduced to me by Bill Inge. I liked Warren right off, so I took a chance on him. Warren had never been in anything before. He had been a high school football player, uncertain but charming. He still is.

Splendor in the Grass *concludes another period of filmmaking for you. With* America, America *and* The Arrangement *you turned to deeply autobiographical material.*

That's why there were lapses of several years between films. I started working directly out of my own experience. I started writing. It was a big revolution for me when I stopped doing what I was used to doing—getting authors to write scripts which I would then bring to the stage or screen—and started writing myself. I started thinking about myself. I really changed my life in 1963. It had to do with things that are personal, involved with my wife's death.

Why did you choose to go into autobiographical material?

I found that the plays or scripts I had been doing, like Arthur Miller's *After the Fall*, did not reflect my point of view. I'm not putting Miller down. I have a great deal of respect for him. And I revered Tennessee Williams. I liked them all, but as I got more and more into myself, I wanted to express my own experience. Also, I had been feeling an increasing strain in dealing with playwrights for a long time. As far back as the last Williams plays, Tennessee complained that I was trying to get my own voice in. I was criticized for distorting plays so that they became more my work than the authors. I used to resent such remarks, but there was some truth in what was said.

Why did you wait so long to make the change?

Self-doubt—about writing. I'm certainly not a stylist and I don't write with ease. My books are rewritten and rewritten again. I used to think that that was bad, but then I read somewhere that Hemingway said he was lucky if he got two good pages a day. He apparently wrote and rewrote. I realized then that rewriting is part of the craft. Writing was hard for me, and somehow I always thought it was supposed to be easy. I should have known better. I had watched Steinbeck several times. God, he was always rewriting every page. A book took me a year and a half to write. That's a long time to be alone on one project. I never realized that it was that kind of a trade. It didn't come naturally to me, but I felt if I didn't stick with it, I would always be doing the work of other authors who don't see life as I do. It finally gets down to the result of my psychoanalysis. What is the point of psychoanalysis—that you like yourself, that you respect yourself, that you value yourself, and in my case, you are able to say: "I'm going to be heard from in my own voice, on my own themes, in my own way." That's a bold step, or at least it was for me, because words had never been my tools. Finally, writing got to be a sort of a desperate act, because at Lincoln Center I found that I was directing plays I didn't give a damn about. Writing became a matter of necessity and self-respect.

ELIA KAZAN'S
"AMERICA
AMERICA"
is the "best
American
film of the
year!"

NEWSWEEK
HOLLIS ALPERT, SATURDAY REVIEW
JUDITH CRIST, HERALD TRIBUNE

"AMERICA AMERICA", written, produced and directed by ELIA KAZAN, introducing Stathis Giallelis with Frank Wolff, Harry Davis, Elena Karam, Estelle Hemsley, Gregory Rozakis, Lou Antonio, Salem Ludwig, John Marley, Joanna Frank, Paul Mann, Linda Marsh, Robert H. Harris and Katharine Balfour—music by Manos Hadjidakis

PRESENTED BY WARNER BROS.

AMERICA AMERICA
(1963)

HIGH ON MT. AERGIUS in Anatolia, Stavros Topouzoglou (Stathis Giallelis), a Greek, questions his Armenian friend, Vartan (Frank Wolff), about America as they chop ice to sell in their village.

After stopping to see his family, Stavros rejoins Vartan, who gets killed by the Turks in an uprising. Stavros is arrested.

As soon as his father (Harry Davis) secures his release, Stavros races to his grandmother to get money to go to America. She scoffs. Returning home, he meets Hohanness (Gregory Rozakis), a boy so determined to get to America, he's walking there. Stavros gives him his shoes. At home his father announces that Stavros is to be sent to Constantinople to earn enough money to bring the rest of the family there.

Soon after he leaves home, Stavros is befriended by Abdul (Lou Antonio), who proceeds to swindle, rob, and then goad him to the point that Stavros kills him.

Stavros arrives in Constantinople penniless. He goes to his uncle in shame, but leaves in disgust when told he should marry into money. Instead he becomes a hamal, a human beast of burden who fights dogs for food and saves his meager earnings for a ticket to America. A series of horrifying incidents leave Stavros broke again and almost dead.

He returns to his uncle and agrees to court a rich girl. He meets Thomna (Linda Marsh), who falls in love with him, and he's taken in by her family. Life becomes pleasant until he runs into Hohanness. Stavros extracts the price of a ticket to America as a dowry and is going to run off after the wedding. But some vestige of decency forces him to tell Thomna the truth.

He meets Mr. and Mrs. Kebabian (Robert H. Harris, Katherine Balfour), a rich couple visiting from America. Stavros becomes her lover and is invited to go with them to America, under Mr. Kebabian's sponsorship. But he discovers their affair and withdraws as Stavros's sponsor. Hohanness, also aboard ship, is dying. He leaps overboard, returning to Stavros his shoes. Stavros takes his name and place as a shoeshine boy, reaches America, and starts making good on his promise to send for his whole family.

Just how autobiographical is America America*?*

Very. A lot of it came from stories I was told as a kid by my grandmother. It's my family's legend—about how my family came to this country. It's all true: the wealth of the family was put on the back of a donkey, and my uncle, really still a boy, went to Constantinople with it and was supposed to start a little business and to gradually bring the family there to escape the oppressive circumstances in the middle of Asia Minor. It's also true that he lost the money on the way, and when he got there he swept rugs in a little store. Naturally, I dramatized these events, but the essential story is all true.

So when young Stavros left Anatolia, he was not planning on going all the way to America?

His instructions were to go to Constantinople. His father was ready to settle for a limited relief from the oppressive Turks, which a move to the city would provide, but the boy had far greater dreams and ambitions. I used to say to myself when I was making the film that America was a dream of total freedom in all areas. I made two points about that. One was that America had a responsibility to the dream; the dream has a responsibility to the dreamer. And furthermore, what these people availed themselves of when they got here, what they turned the dream into, was the freedom to make money. Money became their weapon; it was a symbol of strength. The last thing you see in *America America* is Stavros being given a quarter tip, which he tosses in the air and catches. You feel he's on that track.

There is a scene near the end of America America *that nobody could sit still for had the rest of the picture not prepared us for it. When, at last, Stavros gets through customs and immigration, he kisses the ground, and we see the Statue of Liberty and the American flag.*

I hesitated about that a long time. A lot of people, who don't understand how desperate people can get, advised me to cut it. When I am accused of being excessive by the critics, they're talking about moments like that. But I wouldn't take it out for the world. It actually happened. Believe me, if a Turk could get out of Turkey and come here, even now, he would kiss the ground. To oppressed people, America is still a dream.

The film opens with a very studied wide shot of the beautiful Anatolian countryside featuring Mount Aergius.

I tried to make the film feel like a legend. That's why Stavros and Vartan are on a mountain, cutting ice. The "clean" mountain was a symbol of their aspirations. Ice is a clean thing; snowfall is a clean thing. A brook runs down from the melting ice, and that's a clean thing. All of this contrasts with the hot, dirty, fifteenth- or sixteenth-century town below where the Turks were not only oppressing the Armenians and Greeks, they were oppressing their fellow countrymen. One of the first things you see is a Turk crawl up on his hands and knees and kiss the hand of the little governor.

You tried to make it like a legend. How?

First of all, by the selection of events—piling the family's jewels on a donkey has a legendary quality. The fact that the whole clan walks to the outskirts of town and watches Stavros go off down the hill has, to me, the quality of something that's told to you from out of the past. I also tried to "essentialize" every character and issue. For example, Stavros' father was what the Jews call a "get-alongnik." He says, "Let's be quiet and not make trouble." Stavros has to decide whether to be like his father or fight for his dignity. I tried to dramatize the issue directly and pushed it to the point where Stavros has got to either kill a man or be killed. It gets as essential as that. In addition, in certain parts of the film I didn't make things strictly "realistic." On shipboard, when the first-class passengers went slumming in steerage, the fact that they brought a little band and danced on deck is not quite true. It's realism raised to the point of legend. That's one nice thing about dealing with the past. You can do that. Look at *Moby Dick*. It's full of accurate detail, but Captain Ahab is not a guy you'd ask to sit and have a cup of coffee. "What will you have, a Danish, a tuna on rye, Captain Ahab?" You're dealing with a legendary figure. Right?

What was the essence of Stavros, the central character?

Sheer ambition born out of desperation. I don't believe that people who are not made desperate by their circumstances would do anything like what he does to get to America. Part of it is pride. Part of it is just animal rebelliousness and the need for a sense of dignity. Part of it is hunger. Part of it's humiliation. I have always believed that a person of spirit can become either an artist, a gangster, a prize fighter, or a radical. The impulses are very related. "I'm going to push up. I'm not going to take it the way it is." When you see an artist's face, there's often something threatening about it. They look at you and they're tough. An artist—I mean a good one, not a hack—makes his loved ones pay. The same thing with a fighter. He looks half-scared as if all he's got is his fists. A gangster's the same way. He's proud. He's going to live well. And a radical will do anything to change things. Stavros is like that, too. He'll do anything to change his condition, and the symbol for that was to get to America. It was a false symbol in part, but only in part.

Structurally, the film is quasi-novelistic. It's almost told in chapters.

That's because I had to cover a lot of ground. I followed the example of Brecht, who wrote what he called "epic" theater. What he meant was we should break up the tiny, tidy, traditional three-act form—the form which says, "It's about this, end of act one. Introduce the conflict, end of act two. Come to a climax, end of act three." He felt that the movement of people in the world was much broader, more sweeping and theater should reflect that. In *Mother Courage* he leaps ten years and you have to jump with him. He breaks up the action into significant "chapters." I did the same thing here. As you know, I like unity. It means a lot to me, and Brecht clings to the unity of subject and above all the unity of theme. But he throws over the constrained Ibsenesque unity of time and action. He opened everything up and made us all think differently. Actually, Shakespeare did the same thing. All his great historical plays and even some of his nonhistorical plays, like *Othello*, contain great leaps. If you're dramatizing the entire, big experience of a person's life, you have to weigh his life as a whole and still point events toward the culmination, the final resolution of that experience. In order to do that with Stavros' life, I chopped it up.

In the film's first chapter you set up the circumstances of Stavros' life and his desire to change them. After Stavros and Vartan, with whom he has brought ice to the village, discuss the dream of going to America, Stavros' mother drags him home, and we meet his family.

His father takes him into another room and slaps him. Then he offers him his hand to kiss—the quintessential gesture of authority. You must accept my hegemony. That tells you what the situation is. Stavros is rebellious, but he also accepts it. Like all of my central characters, he's in inner conflict. He loves his father. It would be very simple if he didn't. He even loves his tradition, and the implication is that he'll probably become traditional someday himself.

Vartan is killed at an uprising. You staged it so that his death was almost lost in the excitement of the church burning down. Why?

I wanted to say to the audience, "Don't follow him; he's not a central character." It's very bad, I find, if you develop too much emotional interest in a character that's going to disappear. He's only in the story to serve a purpose: to illustrate the Turks' ruthlessness.

He also served as a role model for Stavros. It seemed odd that Stavros didn't witness his death directly.

But you got the point.

Yes, but like the psychiatrist's scene in Splendor in the Grass, *the way in which the idea was dramatized didn't measure up to the idea itself.*

Often, my problem is being too clear. It is important to avoid duplication and the temptation to make more of something than it's worth. In the next scene Stavros sits by the body of his dead friend. That image accomplishes what killing him on screen would have done and it's much purer. In addition it solved the narrative problem of getting into the next action, where Stavros gets into a fight with the Turks, who are disposing of the bodies and is locked up.

While Stavros is under guard, you reveal his father in a nearby office paying off a Turkish official.

Just as he does so, Stavros is brought into the room. He sees the money change hands and his father kiss the Turk's hand. The ultimate self-betrayal is to kiss the hand of the man that's killing you. Later his father tells Stavros, "My honor is safe inside me," but Stavros' emotional drive comes from seeing his father kiss the hand of the man who killed his best friend.

Stavros' first attempt to leave the village involves getting money from his grandmother, who lives up on a hill. The establishing shot is very wide—reminiscent of the way in which you introduced Aguirre, the Joseph Wiseman character, in Viva Zapata!

She had made a house out of rocks and lived like a savage. I wanted to show the stark landscape. By the way, the actress I cast, Estelle Hemsley, was a black woman. I couldn't find a white woman who was that tough.

He puts a knife to her throat and threatens to kill her if she won't give him the money to go to America. She calls his bluff, and he drops the knife. "You're just like your father," she says.

That's fantastic, that scene. He's not that tough yet.

Why did you cast Stathis Giallelis, a nonprofessional, in the central role? I'm afraid his limitations began to be apparent in this scene.

He's better than the actors I could have gotten. I looked everywhere, including France and England, but everyone I saw looked too actorish. They wouldn't fit in with the scenery. Stathis looked like he came out of it, and, in fact, he did. His father had been killed by the right wing during the civil war in Greece by being beaten around the kidneys until he hemorrhaged internally. It took him three days to die. Stathis stayed on the bed with him, taking care of him and holding him in his arms until he passed away. At age fifteen he became the head of his family. I think that story won me to him. I knew he had been through hardship and understood it well. He was a beautiful boy and worked heroically with what talent he had, but there was a loss no doubt to the film. One of the ways I dealt with his shortcomings, in this scene and in others, was to shoot him in long shots. I pictorialized in order to take the burden off of his performance.

On his way down the mountainside, he meets Hohanness, a boy who serves as his alter ego. Hohanness is so determined to get to America that he is willing to walk there barefoot.

I shot it from a distance so you could see the boys and the landscape. I gave Hohanness a cough and he walked as if he were on his last legs. I cast the role with an actor, Gregory Rozakis, who was all shook up. I wanted to say to Americans, "Look what people gave up to get here. Look what this country meant to the world. People would give up their lives to get here."

Stavros is so ashamed of his own weakness and so moved by Hohanness' determination that he takes off his shoes and gives them to him.

Shoes are legend among poor people. When women go out on a battlefield and start cutting clothes off the dead, they always take the shoes off everybody. You can put anything around your middle or over your head—a cloth or a skin will do—but shoes are precious.

When he gets home, his father announces that all of the family money is to be put in Stavros' hands, that he's to go to Constantinople set up a business and earn enough to bring the rest of the family.

The father in that type of family is part-god. He does not discuss this kind of thing with his wife. He's in communion with his soul and he announces the revelation.

But the mother grows increasingly agitated. She wails that it is foolish to trust the irresponsible Stavros with everything.

It makes the audience wonder whether Stavros will be worthy of his task? The father says, "If we haven't made him worthy by this time we deserve to go down." Legend. It's all like that, as if it's been translated from another language. Not only the words but the thoughts and the actions are like from another world and another era. The only pictures that are like that are the Russian films made in the '20s and '30s about their own past.

As Stavros leaves home, the second chapter of the film begins. Despite the need for exposition, I felt that the opening section was too long.

I have a thing about length. I like it. Films often go very fast now, and, as a result, they feel shallow—not gone into enough. I've often thought there may have been one incident too many in the film, but I didn't know how to cut it.

The trip to Constantinople is a classic rite of passage.

Stavros had to be toughened up. In the beginning he was very mild mannered and inhibited. In order to accomplish what he set out to do, he'd have to sacrifice some of his belief in his own goodness. He had to become ruthless. I dramatized this by introducing a character, Abdul, who initially appears to befriend him. But then Abdul cons him out of all of his possessions, then tells the officials that Stavros is a thief. He continues to goad and threaten to the point that Stavros kills him.

Why did you stage the murder offscreen?

It lends the scene a legendary quality to suddenly see Stavros pull his knife and jump on the praying Turk. I let the two men struggle and roll down the hill, moving out of frame, and I held on the vast space. Otherwise it would have merely looked like a fight. This way it's like Stavros suddenly becomes a man; he is now capable of doing anything required to accomplish what he set out to do.

After the murder, there's a short transitional scene that begins on a poster of the steamship Kaiser Wilhelm.

That's to show that Stavros wants more than to just go to Constantinople. What he wants is the ultimate—America. Also, I was trying to give the sense of "I'm going to get there." The steam whistle's blowing and everybody's jumping on the train. It has a certain gaiety to it, doesn't it?

Yes, and it carries through another transitional scene which takes us to Stavros' arrival in Constantinople. He's at the docks, looking at the ships.

He sees an American man on deck, wearing a straw hat: a real American. A real American flag. America exists; it's not just a dream. This scene takes America, the symbol, and makes it concrete.

At the end of the scene a hamal, a porter carrying a huge load on his back, drops dead, and his body's just pushed aside by the other hamals, who keep right on loading.

It shows the brutality of that civilization and the way the Greeks accepted their humiliation as a fact of life. This scene and the incidents that follow were intended to make you more and more want Stavros to accomplish what he set out to do.

You cut back to his family reading conflicting letters. One is from Stavros, the other from his uncle.

Since I intended the picture to end on a shot of the family, I had to keep them alive in the mind of the viewers. I also wanted to suggest the legendary feeling that the destiny of a civilization was riding on Stavros.

His uncle offered to introduce him to the daughter of Aleko Sinnikoglou, a wealthy merchant.

Had Stavros married for money at this point of the film, without going through real hardship, he would have never grown as a character and would have remained a crummy kid. Instead, he works as a hamal and eats garbage in order to save money. He won't even buy a prostitute so a man offers to treat him. It turns out to be the guy's daughter, which is the essence of degradation. The daughter steals his money and he can't get it back. Everyone laughs at him. The whole idea was to show that in that society you could not realize your dreams purely through honest labor. He joins a group of anarchists and gets shot. He's piled onto a wagon with the dead. The bodies are thrown off a cliff into the water without a Christian burial. He's saved only by falling off the wagon and, with his last strength, he crawls back to his uncle.

And now he's ready to marry for money. The next section of the film begins with him dressed up in church attracting the attention of Thomna, the daughter of a rich merchant.

By now I think that the viewer can forgive him anything he might do to get out of that place. The irony is that though he starts his courtship as a tactic, he begins to fall in love with the family and with their idealized middle-class way of life. He faces a series of temptations. As the women serve them dinner, his future father-in-law vividly describes the bourgeois life he'll lead, and I think there are nights and days when he almost gives in to it.

While he is becoming involved with that family, his old friend Hohanness shows up.

He doesn't even recognize Stavros in his business suit.

Stavros takes him to a restaurant.

He feels guilty about being rich, which is true of a lot of poor kids who marry out of their class or who have had some stroke of good luck. Seeing Hohanness makes him remember his goal and reminds him that getting married was only meant as a means to an end. He also sees in Hohanness a reminder of his own weakness. So when he says, "Don't give up, don't give up. We're going to make it," he's saying it to himself, too. I wanted him to be genuinely tempted by the prospect of marriage, by being part of a wealthy family. That's legendary, too, in that it is a romantic statement of the middle-class ideal, what the Greeks call *fayghast*, which literally means a man who eats a lot. That's why so many of them are fat. To all minority people, a pot belly means you're wealthy. It shows you have plenty of food.

Then the final temptation of middle-class life is offered. The family shows Stavros and Thomna the apartment they've bought for them.

I did that in a wide shot so that you could see that the new apartment is just down the street. Families are very tightly knit geographically and emotionally there for a good reason. They're the only friends you've got. He's so tempted by this generosity and by the sweetness of his fiancée that he's driven to tell her the truth which is, "Don't trust me." He says it out of love and appreciation of their goodness. He's saying he knows himself. That's the deepest, truest line I ever wrote.

It was also the best acting Giallelis did in the film.

Well, you see, the director was clever enough to put the burden of the acting on the girl, and to give Stathis the dramatic task of not revealing anything. It fit his nature. His face became a mask.

The next section of the film begins when he gets involved with Mrs. Ke-

babian, the wife of a rug importer from the United States. A mutual seduction takes place, first at the store and later at her apartment.

I never intended it to seem as if she had gone to bed with him already. In those days, people weren't as quick to jump on each other as we are today. Mrs. Kebabian is lying there thinking about Stavros. In a way he reminds her of her lost youth, her lost dreams, of things she's denied herself. It's not until the next scene that she makes up her mind. There's a moment just before the end of the scene where she sees him standing in front of a mirror trying on a straw hat. The straw hat becomes a symbol of America. Later it becomes her last gift to him.

When Mrs. Kebabian says to Stavros, "I've never known a young man," you cut to a close-up of him kissing her hand. Then you cut to her face, and it changes from tears to a smile.

That's the best kind of close-up. It penetrates a thought and records a transition. There's another beautiful moment at the end of the scene. The cafe has emptied out. There's no one there, except one musician who diddles around by himself and her husband, who is asleep. At the moment she decides she is going to go to bed with Stavros, she is kind to her husband. She leans over, takes a strand of his hair and strokes it. You know she has made her decision.

The very next scene is in the ticket office where they buy the tickets to go to America. One is for Stavros.

But the joy is short-lived, because he meets Hohanness again with a group of shoeshine boys, and it's a moment of great regret and shame for him because he realizes that he could have gotten to America without having become a male whore. I wanted him to lose some of his sense of dignity because of what he had done. I wanted it to be at a cost.

Which is paid off in the next scene where as he packs, his fiancée comes in. He says to her, "I hate this respectability. I don't want it."

"I don't want to be your father. I don't want to be my father." And he's right about that, God, he's so right! He dislikes the hypocrisy and so do I. It's so phony. That idea is all through every picture I ever did, even when it's sterile like in *Gentleman's Agreement.* It's disgusting to me. I was a waiter while at Williams College, and I saw what those kids were, the elite of America. They are now all either dead or in brokerage houses down on Wall Street. The whole middle-class civilization is hypocritical.

At the end of the scene she asks, "What do you think will happen in America?" And he says, "I believe I'll be washed clean."

I cut to the front of the boat with spray hitting the bow.

And with that we move to the penultimate section of the film, on shipboard, bound for America. While Stavros is hanging out with Hohanness and the other shoeshine boys, Mrs. Kebabian's maid summons him to his mistress.

I never put it on a service level. I always meant to suggest that the affair satisfied some deep longing of hers that had always been unfulfilled. I think that's one thing I do well. There's always some human quotient. It's the way I feel. I think people simplify and make convenient, self-serving judgments about other people in order to bring themselves up. For example, "He sold out," or "Oh, he's just gone commercial," like they'll say about you when you have a hit. If you really know people and just deal with them as humans you understand that everything's a mixture. I pick people up, all kinds of people, and talk to them. It's amazing how often you find something that's very deep, very typical and above all very much like yourself. You suddenly want to put your arms around them, "I understand you, brother." That's what Dostoyevsky did. He embraced the scum of the society and understood them. That's why I say don't make your villains psychos and criminals. If a guy has to do something bad, explain it. There's a terrific danger in that you may sentimentalize people, and make them better than they are. I'm accused of that all the time.

The maid enters the husband's room. He makes her tell him what's going on next door. There's a brief series of shots on deck where Hohanness and the others see land. Stavros sees the shoreline from a porthole.

He's thrilled, while the old man Kebabian says, "Oh-hum, Long Island. I think I'll take a nap."

Stavros runs up on the deck. He throws his fez into the water and says, "Tomorrow I'm going to buy a straw hat." There's a hard cut to Mr. Kebabian's cabin, and he says to Stavros, "Tomorrow, without a sponsor, you won't be let into America."

Then Mrs. Kebabian comes into the room. Her husband says, "If a woman is forced to choose, she'll always take money." That's the middle class on the nose.

At that point Stavros says, "My honor is safe inside me." The same remark he had despised his father for saying earlier in the film.

He's aware of the fact that he's been corrupted, and he's fighting it off. The husband of the woman he's been with says, "What would your father think of you now?" And that's the thing that cuts the most, because he realizes that his father would totally, violently disapprove. But he was willing to give up anything, including part of his soul, to get to America. That's the point of the picture. In some terrible way, he had grown up.

Why did you have him repeat the very same line that his father had said?

Corn or legend, take your choice. There's no middle ground; it either works or it doesn't. High risk. High gain.

The next scene is in the hospital. Hohanness is in the hospital, too. Stavros says, "What I'd like to do most is start the trip all over again."

He feels soiled. I can't explain to you because I don't think your generation understands how strong a paternal, authoritarian figure can be. These people from the nineteenth and eighteenth centuries were all wrapped up in satisfying their father's hopes for them, including father Jesus and all the rest of it. Even when he's defying it, the very intensity of the defiance indicates that he still reveres his father's love.

Hohanness is concerned because health department officials are coming on board, and he's afraid that because of his cough he won't be allowed into America. Stavros tells him what to do to relax. "When you're tense, think about your mother and father."

Subconsciously he wishes they'd catch him. He's considering turning him over so that he can take his place among the shoeshine boys, but when it gets down to it, he just can't go that far. But the temptation was there. Stathis didn't have to act it, thank God. If he did, it would have been too obvious. All he had to do was say those lines and the ambivalence was there. I stayed on Stavros' face while the inspector checked Hohanness. Then Hohanness runs out, tells him he's passed and disappears coughing. Stavros never makes a sign.

That takes us to the conclusion of the boat "chapter." Stavros and Hohanness are on deck. Stavros says, "I'm going to swim. Nothing is going to keep me from it." Hohanness says, "Don't be crazy. You'll never make it. If you jump, I jump and I don't know how to swim." Their conversation is interrupted by the appearance of some first-class passengers with their band. Stavros flips out and goes into a wild, frenzied dance. The sequence cuts between Stavros dancing, the first-class passengers watching, and Hohanness moving over to the rail and taking off his clothes. We see him jump. We hear a splash. The last shot is of his shoes with a note tucked inside. Why did you structure the scene that way?

I learned that from [Roberto] Rossellini's film *Paisan*, the last sequence of which had a big effect on me. When he gets to the climax, as the partisan fighters are being massacred, the camera leaps in a non-realistic sequence from crag to crag, faster and faster. It's all over before you know it. The scene is shot as if it were a silent film. Silent filmmaking climaxes allow the audience's emotions to work. They make you engage yourself with the material in order to figure out what's happening. In effect, you tell part of the story to yourself. The act of surmising, the act of suddenly understanding, is very evocative. It's part of good storytelling for me. One of the great strengths that film has is that you're dealing with symbols.

The pair of shoes just sitting there on the edge of the boat tells it all. The shoes that Stavros gave him way back in the interior have been returned.

How do you integrate that kind of storytelling when you're dealing with dialogue?

Wherever possible, if you don't need the words, throw them out. If you have to have dialogue, try to find words that are off the nose, that have overtones, that have poetry. Anything that's suggestive, that opens up the audience's processes is good. I try to create images to tell the story, and sometimes I find that as a result I can use fewer words. Ideally you should be able to visualize and understand the whole picture, even be able to guess what words are being spoken even if you couldn't hear them. One kind of thing you can't do without language, however, is a scene like Paul Mann's speech in *America America* where Mr. Sinnikoglou idealizes middle-class life. That has a value all of its own. The words there evoke images which when imagined are much stronger than they would be if you saw them. Watching Paul's face your fantasy is increased by empathizing with the pleasure that his memories give him. The words there are like an aria.

Except for that kind of scene, words are best when they're non-informational. If possible the words should add something that you cannot get or do not get in the pictures. They should contrast or be ironically related to what's being told to you visually. That gives a scene several dimensions.

Did you shoot much coverage for the scene when Hohanness jumps overboard?

No, just about what you saw in the finished film.... There was one girl among the first-class passengers who was particularly touched by Stavros. She felt something that was terrifying about him, that wasn't just amusing. She went up to him and offered herself to him in effect. She felt his pain. That was important because it kept your feelings in focus.

The next scene is the arrival in New York. It starts with a big hoopla, a band playing, crowds milling.

That's a good cut because it goes from the shoes to the band. Tight shot, big shot. Silence and grief are contrasted with elation. It's a classic editing technique.

At the end of the scene, Mrs. Kebabian's gives Stavros a fifty-dollar bill and a straw hat.

He puts the hat on and by now the audience should be entirely on his side and think the whole trip was worthwhile.

Inside the immigration center Mr. Agnostis sponsors all the shoeshine boys. Stavros assumes Hohanness' identity and, renamed Joe Arness, he fulfills the dream for both of them. Agnostis pays off the immigration man under the table.

America America. When Stavros sees it, he thinks this is just as bad as Turkey. The first American he sees is taking a bribe. Nevertheless, the next thing Stavros does is kiss the ground.

Over that shot you hear Stavros' father reading a letter in which Stavros had enclosed Mrs. Kebabian's fifty dollars. "How did he make so much money so fast?"

The letter said, "While things are not entirely different in America, you have a chance in this country to do better." And I feel we do. Then the Turkish cavalry rides by. They're not as afraid of it now.

The last time we see Stavros is in the shoeshine parlor where a man tips him a quarter.

He takes the money and we feel sure he's going to put his quarters together one by one and bring his family here. And then I cut back to the family in Turkey and you hear his voice saying: "Next, people are waiting, people are waiting."

The final shot is exactly the same image of Mount Aergius with which you began the film. Your voice is heard on the soundtrack, "And so he did bring the whole family over, all but the old man who died where he was born."

Saying that someone died makes the story retreat into history at the same time it looks ahead. That's legendary too.

Why did you choose to both introduce and close the picture with your own voice saying, "I am Elia Kazan."

It anchors it in reality. *America America* may be a legend, but it's not a fairy tale. This is the truth. Nobody makes pictures about that class of people, about their way of thinking and their values. *America America* really captured another civilization. It's my favorite of all the pictures I've made.

THE ARRANGEMENT
(1969)

EDDIE ANDERSON (Kirk Douglas), a top Los Angeles advertising executive, and his wife Florence (Deborah Kerr) are stuck in a polite but icy marriage. They have all of the trappings of success and she seems satisfied. He wants out.

Driving to work, Eddie lets go of the steering wheel and gets mangled. For a long time afterwards, he is unable or unwilling to speak. All efforts to bring him around fail. He slips in and out of often painful childhood memories of his father (Richard Boone) bullying his family. He slides into revery and remembrance of his affair with Gwen (Faye Dunaway). She's sexy and supportive, and she nourishes his creative side, the part of him that always wanted to be a writer.

When Eddie finally recovers from the accident, many still worry for his sanity. He goes to New York, where his father is hospitalized. He's dying and delusional, but he persuades Eddie to take him to the bank for a loan so he can start his business again. Soon, his father turns ugly and reverts to being the bully Eddie knew as a child.

While in New York, Eddie starts up again with Gwen. She now has a baby whom she insists is not his. She lives with Charles (John Randolph Jones), a man of such infinite patience, he even waits out her affairs with other men.

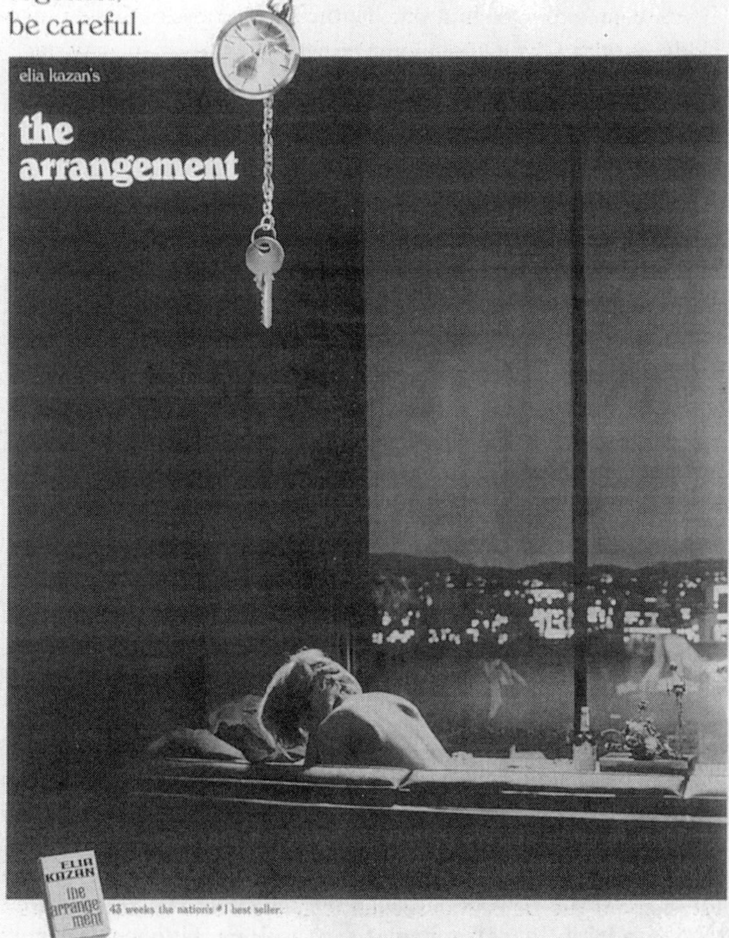
If your
wife insists
you see it
together,
be careful.
elia kazan's
the
arrangement
ELIA
KAZAN
the
arrange
ment
43 weeks the nation's #1 best seller.
elia kazan
kirk douglas · faye dunaway · deborah kerr · richard boone · hume cronyn
charles maguire · elia kazan
technicolor® panavision® from warner bro

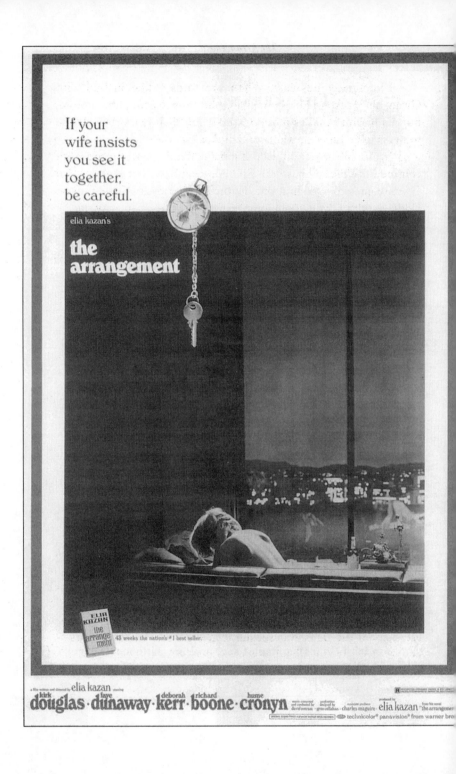

Florence comes east. When she finds Eddie in bed with Gwen, she's certain he's gone mad. She tries to bring him around, but his insanity makes more sense to him than her sanity. All he wants is to be himself, whoever that may be.

In a fit of frustration, Eddie sets the family home on fire. He's confined to a mental hospital. Eddie likes it there but is glad when Gwen comes to take him out. Eddie's father dies. At his funeral Eddie is with Gwen and Florence with her lawyer. It may not be high romance, but they all seem to be where they belong.

The Arrangement *was based on your bestselling novel. Many people said it was autobiographical. Was it?*

Only in part. I'm really not very much like Eddie, the central character. I've never been suicidal. I've never felt that I took the wrong turn. I've always wanted to be a director and—somewhere in the back of my head, a writer—so in that fundamental way it's not autobiographical although a lot of the details came out of things I've been through. One of my criticisms of the film is that, for better or worse, Eddie doesn't have more of the qualities that I do have. I think he could have been deeper that way. A lot of my friends see themselves in certain characters, but that's not so, either. Actually, there's a little bit stolen from everybody I know. But what else do you do? I once thought I'd make the book about a research chemist, who instead of becoming a scientist became a salesman for a big chemical manufacturer. It might have been more interesting had I done it that way. One of the things that was criticized about the book was setting it in the world of advertising—people said it was a cliché. There's a certain truth to that, but it's also one of the most central and apt images of America. It typifies the split between what we profess and what we are. It was a difficult choice, but I made it. I thought it worked well in the book. But the problem with the goddamn movie was the script. I never solved it properly. The ideal length of literary material to be adapted for a movie is a long short story or a novella. My novel had just too much material, and finally after grinding it down to manageable size, what I had left was a rather conventional plot. What's unconventional in the book are the small things, the observations, the little bits, all the minor, erratic details. I couldn't find a way to include them in the film. I don't know what I would do differently now, except not make it probably. A perfect example of what I mean is an incident that occurs in one of my favorite chapters in the novel. Eddie wakes up in his house in Beverly Hills. He has $64,000 in the bank. He and his wife and secretary go over the bills and document their expenses. An hour later he is $400,000 in the hole. That's what affluence is in America. A guy living in an expensive house is just as shaky as anybody else. I love that chapter, but it didn't work nearly as well on film.

Why not?

Because there's so much story to cover. Early on I had decided not to write the script myself. I hired a very good screenwriter. We saw eye-to-eye a lot, but in the end I didn't like his screenplay, so I decided to do it myself. I really struggled with that job. I must have done four versions, but I don't think it really ever got any better. It seems like in life you keep learning the same lesson over and over. I should have sold the book and let someone else make the movie. I work out of obsessive enthusiasm and concern. I only do one thing at a time, and I can't think of anything else while I'm doing it. It's very hard to get going more than once on something at that level of intensity. Never again will I do anything twice. Another thing which hurt the picture badly was losing Brando, who was supposed to play the lead.

What led you to Kirk Douglas as the alternative?

Somebody suggested him, and I said no. But then I met him. He was out to sell himself to me, and he did. I'm not immune when

I feel something good and true is coming out of someone. In the first place his name is Issur Danielovitch. He told me about his relationship with his father and how he was dissatisfied with his own life. He's not at all like people imagine. He's a hard worker and a decent man. I really respected and liked him. I talked to him about a week before I agreed to cast him and found a lot in him that was very much like the character. My working experience with Kirk was excellent. I think he gave a good performance, but there's something about his nature that he can't control. When you look at him, you know that no matter what he's up against, he'll get through and triumph. No matter how hard he tries, you never feel the character he plays is really, really bewildered. Kirk does not suggest the vulnerability that the character had in the book, and as a result the damn picture didn't jell. A lot of the French critics, however, saw in it the essentialization of the American problem, which is what I intended.

Would you explain that?

Everyone becomes a salesman here. If you don't sell anything else, you sell yourself. Ours is a society dominated by business, and the economic pressure even at the upper-middle-class level is fantastic. The epitome of this business civilization is the advertising industry. Everyone feels some degradation, some violation of self, when they spend their lives selling.

Your heroine, Gwen, starts out as part of the industry, yet she stands out from the crowd.

Within the "system" Gwen is a revolutionary on a personal level. She's doing a job to make a living, but it disgusts her. Though she has accepted the fact that the world is ruled by men, she's in private, silent revolt against it. She doesn't think much of men, even the men she sleeps with. She sort of lives through antagonism. You see a lot of women like that in the magazine and media world. There's nowhere else for them to go. They don't want to just become housewives and raise children, and still they don't respect what they're doing. Women like Gwen have come to a very uneasy and crippling compromise. They believe their lives are about as good as they can make them. The men they settle for are no worse than any others—generous with money, decent, kind. They lie a little bit, but everybody does. It's a cynical viewpoint and one without hope or future. Gwen, however, because she's knowledgeable and sharp, is able to say things that disturb Eddie Anderson. With all the faults the film has, I think it was an important picture, because it deals with the present not with something in the past or the future. It doesn't hide behind allegory.

What were the major virtues of the film for you?

It dealt directly with the problem of a man who does something that he is good at but which he despises. Instead of just thinking about it, he does a revolutionary thing. He throws over everything including his money. He turns against his whole life. That subject had never been treated in films, though it is a daydream common to us all. I was pleased with the way we moved in and out of his memories—his mother at the hospital and other things in his past. Some of the scenes of Gwen and Eddie horsing around I thought were well done.

In what way do you think it failed?

It lost many of the sensitive, erratic, unexpected, surprising, original bits that were in the book. I tried awfully hard to make the wife more divided and less of a cliché, but I'm not sure that it worked. I was trying to encapsulate in miniature a whole way of life in the big cities, in the big arenas of this country. On a tough road, when you fall short—even a little bit—you fall very far. If I had done the picture on a much smaller scale, it would have been better. But my book had been a huge bestseller, and I got a big price for it. Once a project starts out on that scale, everything follows from it. I should have shot the picture in the streets of New York instead of at Warner Brothers. It's not that good pictures can't be made in a studio. It's just not where my best talents lay.

Your personal experience making the picture sounds like a precise analogue to the problem that Eddie faces in the film. In being untrue to your instincts, you did the very thing he felt had wrecked his life. You sold out.

Right, and I got drawn into it, knowing all the time that bit by bit I was being misled. You make a few sort of one-third errors and before you know it, you're deep into a process, which is not at all the way I like to make films. In hindsight I think I was so unconsciously repelled by the process and the studio mechanism that my next film, *The Visitors*, was made on a minimum budget and scale. But even now I look back and think, "I'm glad I got all that money from my book, so I don't have to do films or plays I don't like." After *On the Waterfront* and *East of Eden*, which were fairly successful, I didn't have a hit until *Splendor in the Grass*, which was six years later. Then there were quite a few more years before the book came out. I know I'm not going to produce huge moneymakers. It's not my nature. So I'm glad when I hit a vein just right. I never could have done *The Visitors*, and I couldn't have written *The Assassins*, and I wouldn't be in the position I'm in now to do what I want to do. I don't have any regrets about *The Arrangement.* I just wish I had done it better.

It seemed to me you could draw a line right through from East of Eden *to* The Arrangement *in terms of the relationship between father and son.*

I don't think I'm a very catholic filmmaker. I only have one or two themes. I hope sometimes I go deep, but I don't think I've made a great variety of pictures. I don't see why it should be expected of anyone. Hopefully, in one way or another, I'm making a developing statement.

The film opens on Eddie and his wife. They sleep in the same bedroom, but they have very separate lives. They get up in quite routinized fashion, go into separate showers, and don't share much in the way of conversation or affection.

The mechanism of separation in luxury is something that hadn't been shown before in American films. You've seen alienation, but here it is without antagonism. Eddie and Florence always like each other. Neither of them fully recognizes the trouble underneath their marriage, though he senses it. That's where I think I made the first mistake in the film. The first sentences in the book are "I still don't understand my accident. A hand came out of the blue and turned the wheel." In the film I changed that. He tries to commit suicide. Both approaches are valid, but the book is more interesting. The novel becomes a psychological mystery story. When you take the mystery away, the story becomes clearer and stronger but also much more obvious. I think that was a loss.

Why did you change it?

I don't know. It seemed like a good idea at the time. I was obsessed with how to capture the essence of the book in the script. It was frustrating as hell, because I knew in my gut that I was reducing something that's value was nonplot into nothing but plot. There were things I wasn't able to capture in a subtle, original way. For instance, at one moment in the film Eddie looks at himself in the mirror, and he sees someone else. He's going through a complete change like an insect does, and he catches himself in the middle of it. But when I put it on film, something was missing. Eddie's loss of identity wasn't as rich as it was in the book.

After his attempted suicide he is sent home to recuperate. Through a series of flashbacks you show moments from his life before the accident and introduce his mistress, Gwen. Why did you choose that particular narrative tool?

In my notebook for *The Arrangement* I wrote that we live on three levels at once. The future is part of the present and the past affects the present directly. We are constantly dealing with the past. So one of the notes I wrote was, "Make the past present." I do that all through the film, but I probably should have done it even more. As he walks through the hospital, for example, he sees his mother. It was one of my favorite shots, because he sees her through glass, and the reflections of white hospital figures are imposed on the glass too. He stops and looks at her, and then he remembers her back home, protecting him against his father's rage.

You used flash cuts in two different ways. One is like the scene you just described. The other is when Eddie sits by the pool and sees Gwen bringing him grapes. It was confusing as to what was remembered and what was pure fantasy.

They are really the same thing, they just have different kinds of visual cues.

I'm not sure that I agree.

There's a rule in using flashbacks. When you go back in time, what occurs in the past should affect the next thing that happens in the present. If you do that, the flashback is organic and necessary. If you don't, it just seems like you're dragging in additional information.

You used several nonrealistic devices in this film. When Eddie decides he's going to leave his wife for good, he hops on a plane and goes to New York. He calls Gwen from a phone booth across the street from her apartment, looks up, and sees that another man is with her. Then you cut to a Pop art, comic-book image of him beating the guy up and throwing him out the window.

Then I cut to Eddie, back on the street, laughing. He's amused at how silly his fantasy was. I think that's honest. He thinks, "If I were Superman, I'd be able to break in and beat that guy up." But here I am. I'm not Superman and I'm stuck on the outside. What am I going to do?

I'm not questioning the emotional validity, but it was such a campy choice that it stopped me from watching the film and made me aware of the technique.

I think it did with most people. I thought it was good; the critics hated it.

When Eddie's boss visits during his convalescence, you cut to the pool-side television. A wildlife program is showing a scene of animals tearing each other apart. I wondered why you chose such an obvious metaphor for the advertising world.

Underneath our patina of culture and politeness I've seen a lot of people being torn up even worse. The fact that blood doesn't flow and that the wound isn't visible doesn't mean that it's not deep. It's a desperate world. I saw my father's back broken in the Depression much worse than if he'd had a knife stuck in his side. I saw him killed. I don't know any other metaphor for it. Let some other guy make it, but the others don't tell what's happening in this world, this country, this city. Maybe the image wasn't subtle, but it was exactly the way I feel. Animals have more pity. They kill quickly, and at least you die with your blood hot. Still, what you say is true. The shot is too obvious and excessive, but to have put it more mildly would have offended my sense of truth.

One of the scenes I like best is when Gwen is with her current boyfriend, Charles. He's in love with her and makes no demands—including sex. Eddie comes and tries to get her back, and she throws them both out. Later that night Eddie goes back to her, and they make love. A baby is in the crib. We never do find out who the father is. What were you doing there?

I was just telling the truth, which is that a lot of women get to the point where what they really want is a man who's a servant, just as men throughout history have wanted a servant in women. The militant woman is coming out of her sexist cocoon. Gwen takes her own personal way to do that. The baby is a true, complicating factor, that's all. As far as she's concerned, the fact that they make love doesn't mean she's back with him.

But he doesn't know that. His assumption is that if she sleeps with him it means that he's won. That's a major defining part of his character. I also liked the scene at the end when Gwen collects him from the mental hospital.

In the end, Gwen stays with Eddie because she feels some real humanity in him. He's sacrificed something; he's paid his dues, and taken a loss. If a man will go that far, he's worth something, and she respects his struggle. It isn't sexual or romantic. It's the sign of a true relationship between two people. The person you want to be with is the person for whom you have some regard, who helps you and for whom you can do something. It blends in with the old-fashioned idea of marriage, where you're helpmates. You can see their rapport at the end of the film, in the way he stands at his father's grave. Gwen has a complete understanding of his faults, difficulties, weaknesses and erratic behavior. Yet, she's with him—by his side. He stands with her, with an equal recognition that she might someday leave him, that she can be very unstable. Florence is with her lawyer, and they fit like a hand and a glove. I meant it to be a happy ending. But no one thinks so. They look at it and say, "This is miserable. People who hate each other are together." There's some hatred in every marriage. The moment you're dependent upon somebody for anything, there's an element of antagonism or resentment. But that doesn't mean you break up with them. The most neurotic thing you can expect in life is perfection in a human relationship. There's no such thing. Of course, they don't tell you that in the movies.

Speaking of neurosis, you have alluded several times to your own psychoanalysis and said that it was very rewarding. Why then, in a number of films, but most particularly in The Arrangement, *is the psychiatrist and the whole analytic process treated with such scorn?*

I think most psychiatrists deserve it. I once had an analyst that was just like Florence's Dr. Lieberman, and I've known a lot of others who have treated friends of mine. They did very little. The analysts I don't like are those that say, "Adjust." They cripple the rebel. A man is insane if he says this way of living, this society is worth adjusting to. He should be in rebellion; it's healthy. A lot of analysts say, "Now, calm down, boy. You've got it pretty good." In the meantime you're dying inside. The analyst I had whom I liked was himself a rebel and a really great man. I said to him, "I want to be a writer. I know I'm a successful director, but I want to express my own themes. Something's stopping me from saying what I feel. That's what I want you to help me with. I don't want you to tell me to be happy, that I'm a good stage and screen director. I'm not going to direct in the theater anymore. I'm through.

And for the moment I'm not going to make any films. I want to become myself." He really changed my life. He enabled me to write. I think psychoanalysis can be a great thing, but there are a lot of frauds in it.

There was a suggestion in The Arrangement *that Dr. Lieberman is on the make for Florence.*

Furthermore, she liked it. I've seen that a lot. Women whose husbands were slowly being alienated from them who were looking for someone that cared. What they're paying their shrinks for is that "care," not for the unpleasant truth. A lot of doctors don't pay you the respect that is involved in saying, "I believe in your pain, in your disaffection, in your rebellion, and it's valid. Let's do something about that." They're also venal; they charge too much, and I don't like that.

As you're talking, you're revealing something which is unfortunately never squarely dealt with in the film—the anger of the central character.

It would have been good, for example, if Eddie had confronted the analyst and unloaded on him, if he said, "You know, I'm drunk, and I'm in bad shape, but would you get the hell out of my house."

Do you wish you had a second chance to do The Arrangement*?*

I've wished there were a second chance with many of my films. With every piece of work, after I've finished it, I sit down and figure out what I should have done differently. Then it's digested, and I can forget about it. But this film is still an undigested hunk of meat in my belly. I'll have to look at it again some day and study it, because aside from the fact that it's hard to do anything twice, there's something wrong with the way I told that film. Maybe I should have been bolder with it. Or maybe I should have just taken one little hunk of it. I really don't know. There are things I'm very proud of in the film—I love the funeral scene. Eddie's father, who was born on the other side of the world, is buried next to an American freeway with cars rushing by, blowing their horns. The picture starts on a thruway and ends on a thruway. I like that. I've come to the conclusion that not every novel should be made into a film. Unfortunately, we have the psychology of the "big property." Certain material works as a series of words which evoke images that appeal to the ideas and awake feelings in a reader, but which simply can't be filmed. My book affected a lot of people. The film not. There must be a reason why. I'm not the kind of guy who makes a film that nobody likes and says, "They'll see it twenty years from now." If the film is good, it affects people. Clearly this didn't.

Every one wants to
turn his back on violence
until it knocks at his front door.

A Film by ELIA KAZAN

"THE VISITORS"

Produced by
CHRIS KAZAN and NICK PROFERES
Directed by ELIA KAZAN
Original Screenplay by CHRIS KAZAN
COLOR

R RESTRICTED
Under 17 requires accompanying Parent or Adult Guardian

United Artists
Entertainment from Transamerica Corporation

THE VISITORS
(1972)

AN UNMARRIED COUPLE, Bill and Martha (James Woods and Patricia Joyce), live with their baby on property owned by Martha's father, Harry (Patrick McVey), a once promising but now drunken writer of western novels. Their rather bleak isolation is broken when two young men pay a visit.

Sarge (Steven Railsback) and Tony (Chico Martinez) were in the same platoon as Bill in Vietnam. Sarge, Tony and four other soldiers raped a sixteen-year-old Vietnamese girl and then Sarge killed her. Bill not only refused to participate, he turned the others in and testified against them. Sarge and Tony have been locked up for the past two years, but have recently been released on a legal technicality.

Tony tells Bill he, for one, has no hard feelings. But something is about to happen. Harry immediately takes to the visitors. They get drunk, shoot a neighbor's dog and carry on like real men—not like the wimp Harry's daughter's had a child with.

Bill and Martha's already strained relationship disintegrates during the course of the drunken evening. Sarge flirts with Martha, who flirts back, and things turn steamy. Bill sees this, and a brawl ensues in which Sarge beats Bill almost to death. He proceeds to smack Martha around, then rapes her.

Finally, the visitors leave. Bill and Martha sit on opposite sides of a room. He asks her, "Are you all right?" She does not answer.

How did The Visitors *come to be? It's utterly unlike your other films, with its stripped-down, naturalistic look.*

It all began in a casual conversation with my son, Chris. I had just read Daniel Lang's essay "Casualties of War," a piece published in *The New Yorker*. I thought, "My God, it would be interesting to speculate about what those two boys that had been turned in by their fellow soldier for raping and killing a young Vietnamese girl would do if when they got out of jail, they came to visit the person who turned them in." That's about all I said to Chris. He didn't say much in response, only that he thought it would be an interesting subject for a film. He had never directed a film and was wary of attempting it. So he said he'd write it and urged me to direct it. I was really flattered and pleased when he asked me. I think most kids want to get their old man out of their lives as quickly as possible and forget him, or recover from the wounds the old man has inflicted, psychic and physical. And here was Chris including me in his project. I thought it over and said I'd direct it. I like cold weather, and the whole idea of doing the film in Connecticut in the snow, with absolute beginners, was very intriguing. Also after the technical over-elaboration and fantastic cost of *The Arrangement*, I wanted to get back to the simplicity of filmmaking. With the new fast films, lights, and cameras, filmmaking can be a basic and easy process. A couple of years ago, I was involved with my wife's film, *Wanda*. I didn't direct it, because I didn't want to make a film without a union crew, and my efforts to get the stagehands' union to cooperate and allow us to use very few men had failed. So I urged my wife, Barbara, to direct it. As I watched her work, I was envious, because it was such a pleasant process, working with a few friends on something you like and doing your best with it. When *The Visitors* came up, I said, "The hell with it. I'll use well-trained technicians who are not union members and make the film for the love of it," which is after all the best way to do anything in art. It turned out to be a delight. We all lived and worked together. The two houses shown in the film are my home and Chris's home. Except for two actors we all slept in the sets at night. We ate every meal together. The kids who played the central roles were under my constant surveillance. I kept them in good shape and away from any influences except my own.

Why did you cast players who had no real film experience?

If the audience saw a familiar face in any of the roles, they'd know how it was going to end. It would have given the story away. This picture had to be so real, so plain, so homely and honest, that I was almost forced to use unfamiliar faces. Apart from that it's a great joy to work with people who are doing something for the first time. They are hungry. They come to work. They don't come to fool around all day.

Did working with your son present any unique problems?

Of course, we were both very aware of that possibility, but we immediately fell into a very good relationship. In a gentle, friendly way he was critical of certain aspects of me. I asked him to watch every final rehearsal. He'd watch and then come up to me and say, "You already said that. You don't have to repeat it." Or "You stressed that enough. It doesn't need to be underscored." I always try to get someone around with an objective viewpoint when I shoot. Usually it's the writer. Schulberg did it on *A Face in the Crowd.* Williams did it for a little while on *Baby Doll.* It's very helpful to have someone around whom you like and trust and who is involved with the fate of the picture to say, "No, you haven't quite got it." One of the reasons I feel so loyal to this picture is that it was the product of a good relationship between me and my son. The irony was that we had more artistic freedom with a nothing budget than I had with all the studio's resources on *The Arrangement.*

What is the picture about for you?

The picture is about the price of the Vietnam War on the soul of the American people. It's an antiwar picture. If you teach a generation of young people to think life is cheap and that the answer to problems is violent confrontation, that's the way they are going to turn out at home as well as on the battlefield. The film makes this point in almost primal terms. The important thing to me was to try to make the villains, the two visitors, not heavies, not psychos, not criminals, not bastards, not monsters, but absolutely typical and characteristic young American boys. What so shocked the American public about My Lai was that for the first time we saw that butchery and monstrosity committed in war can be done by someone as ordinary and familiar as Lieutentant William Calley. I think that other pictures that had been dealing with violence have had something unconsciously hypocritical about them. I don't mean that the people who made them are hypocrites. They are fine artists, but they work inside a show-business tradition which says that violence is somehow entertaining. They make the perpetrators of violence psychos or heavies, thereby giving the viewer an out. The audience can sit there very smugly and think, "Oh sure, they're monsters, so naturally they do bad things." The fact is that many of the terrible savage things that were done in Vietnam were done by familiar kids.

So you tried to make the pair of "visitors" look like everyday kids.

Sarge and Tony arrive at Bill's house not knowing what they're going to do. You first watch as they find out what they feel, and then you find out what they're going to do, and then you wait for it, and it happens. There was no problem with any of that. A lot of viewers, however, have said, "Why does Martha suddenly start to flirt with Tony?" She was dissatisfied with her relationship with her lover. A person caught in that sort of dilemma very often does something violent and terrible when they don't know a polite or civilized way to get out of a personal situation that has gone wrong.

Is Bill, the character played by Jimmy Woods, the true protagonist of the film?

No, he's just part of the story. There's no protagonist in the film. It's about a situation—not about one person who gets into difficulties and then solves them. A lot of my films are that way. That's why some of them are hard to take. Despite all the violence and emotion, there's often a certain coolness or objectivity. In nearly all Hollywood films you root for or against somebody. The director organizes your emotions so you know what you're supposed to feel. I try to get the audience bewildered.

The Visitors, *probably more than any of your other films, reflects that sensibility.*

In *Wild River* we're really not on any one character's side. You admire the old woman, but you disapprove of her. Monty Clift's character is weak and fumbly. He's full of illusions. If the audience roots for anybody, it's for Lee Remick—a little. I don't even know if you're entirely for Marlon Brando in *Waterfront.* You follow him emotionally, but I never intended to say, "God, he's right." I'm violently against anything that says, "This person is right, that person is wrong." What I'm for is something which says, "This person is partially right and partially wrong." I think the true dramatic state at this moment in world history is an attempt to confront problems that are insoluble. That leads to a certain amount of bewilderment. What is noble is the effort to solve the problems despite the pain and difficulty and not the solution reached. That's what I try to reflect in my films. Joe Losey was head of the jury at Cannes when *The Visitors* was screened there. He said that he admired my direction, but he didn't know what I was trying to get at. What he missed was my saying, "These guys are bastards and Jim Woods is a good guy." They're not, and he's not. They are all just human beings in a dilemma. That's my idea of what to do in art.

Did you set an esthetic problem for yourself?

I sure as hell did. I had to retrieve something after *The Arrangement.* I'm faced with a situation where it's increasingly difficult for me to get money for the films I want to make. In that sense I'm a young filmmaker all over again. It's not easy, and the more personal I get and the more I get into my own material, the harder it is to get financed. So I had to find a way to make a film far less expensively than in a studio, and that was the challenge I set for myself. It was a great experience to feel that I was not going to be crippled just because they don't want to give me money. I have a project now that I'm trying to get off the ground. You'd think that Columbia Pictures, having made a fortune on *On the Waterfront*, would say, "For a million dollars we'll go with the guy, even if we don't see the values in the script, yet." No, they turn it down flat. They won't even return my phone calls. Maybe they're embarrassed to say no to me, but whatever it is, it's insulting.

When you do a picture on a very low budget, the studio has a minimal investment to protect with all its potential advertising dollars. What do you do about the fact that if the picture isn't an immediate hit, it's not likely to be seen by many people?

That's a very kind understatement about what happens. The studio puts it right in the trash barrel and puts the top on it—very tight. It's very black and very dead in the barrel. It happened on *The Visitors*. It played for nine days at the Little Carnegie. They jerked it and put *The Yellow Submarine* in for the umpteenth time. Then they forgot about it. I urged them to reconsider, and they agreed to screen it at Cannes. We got terrific write-ups in the French papers, and when it opened in three theaters in Paris, it did very good business. Also, it played all over Spain and Denmark. I was able to do that much, but I don't know the answer to your question. It's a bad situation. Even with a picture that costs millions, you're up against exactly the same problem. It's a little better, because they have a bigger investment to protect, but if the front office thinks it's a flop, they'll throw it away.

The opening shot of The Visitors *tells us almost all there is to know about the relationship between Bill and Martha. It's a very wide shot of the exterior of the house. You see them at the window. There is snow on the ground. The audience is placed at a distance from the couple just as they are placed at a distance from each other.*

That was the intention. Bill and Martha are together because it's warm inside, not because there's any passion between them.

The first thing you feel is the tension. You see that she's a jumpy, dissatisfied, high-strung girl—slightly spoiled, too. At one point when he caresses her breast, she pats his hand. It is a castrating, if gentle, gesture. She resents always having to take care of the baby because he works. He resents living in her father's house. There's a moment later on when she hands him the phone, and the expressions on their faces say it all.

Harry, Martha's father, is introduced. He's extremely arch.

I was trying to make him and his irritation toward Bill understandable. Throughout the film, but especially in the drunk scene, I tried to make him seem like a lonely figure at the dead end of an outdated philosophy. He does the best he can by writing Westerns. I was trying to create a person that you rejected intellectually but emotionally would find rather pitiful and touching.

Once the visitors arrive the picture falls into focus.

From then on you wonder what they are going to do; you wonder what happened in the past—in Vietnam. Gradually the characters bring each other up to date, and at the same time we can see that they're feeling each other out, testing each other.

Shortly after their arrival there is a long expository scene between Bill and Tony.

It opens up the sense of ambivalence. Tony says that he has no hard feelings toward Bill, and he means it. But he's just spent two years in jail, and you can't simply brush that aside. He has feelings even if he's unaware of them or wishes he didn't, and Bill knows it. Also, this scene focuses Bill's attention onto Sarge. Sarge, he thinks, is the one who will or will not do something. Bill will not initiate any action. He will only react to whatever Sarge does. So the audience begins to watch him as well.

One great difficulty I had with the picture was that Woods's character is so passive that when he ultimately has to react, there's almost no way he can do anything of consequence.

That was not the actor's fault; it was mine. I should have given Jim a moment when the urge to act was made very clear. At one point I actually did go for that quality, but I let it slide by kiddingly. The problem was I was trying to get across the complexity of Bill's character. He says to himself, They did wrong, but they were my buddies. Did I do wrong? Why did I do it? As soon as both sides of an issue are expressed like that, it creates a stasis of indecision. Bill didn't know what the hell to do. Events had to pile on so thick and become so threatening that he finally had to do something.

Why was the picture almost all shot in wide angle?

We had very little equipment, so everything was shot with low-key lighting. When you have to work with a low light level, you can focus much better with a wide-angle lens. It also allows a much greater depth of field.

Did it also help solve the technical problem of having nonpros hit their marks?

Oh, they hit their marks perfectly. I don't draw many marks on the floor anyway. You put a prop here or there, or you tell them to go to the end of the sofa. You try to make the solution to the problem nontechnical.

You have said that when characters are in conflict they'll come out of it changed. How did that operate for you in this picture?

I didn't write the script. So I can't say that particular proclivity of mine is as strong here as in some of my other films. I think Martha changes a lot. She's by far the most interesting character. She goes through hell, and I think at the end she is a very tough and bitter person. She's by far stronger than Sarge. He didn't change much—he only confirmed what he already felt.

The ending reminded me of Splendor in the Grass, *in that Bill and Martha seemed resigned to accepting their relationship, whatever its shortcomings.*

I meant the opposite. I intended to show a final alienation.

She's not connected with him, sexually or otherwise. From the moment she dances with Sarge, it's clear that she no longer admires Bill at all. In that last shot they're apart, indifferent to one another. He's looking at her, but she doesn't even look back; she just sits there. Then he says that really absurd line, "Are you all right?" It's fantastically insensitive to what she's been through. Like a lot of Chris's work, the line has a double meaning. It's like saying to America the Vietnam War never happened: we lost 55,000 men, wiped out a civilian population and spent billions of dollars—but it never happened. We cancel our experiences. But it did happen, and there was a price. She slowly turns and looks at him as if to say, are you kidding? It's a very bitter tough ending. I admire it a lot.

The central confrontation takes place after Bill finds Martha dancing with Sarge. He starts a fight in the house. They move outside, and the bulk of the mayhem is played behind a parked car—off camera.

An outdoor scene at night is the hardest kind of scene to light, especially if there's nothing to put light on. There was nothing out there but an empty field, and we had only four lighting units. So the way I did it was sort of a necessity.

You could have left it inside.

All fights between men take place outside. "Let's step outside." It's the right place to play it. Once we decided to go that way, the solution to the technical problem also made the scene more effective. It allowed you to imagine what happened, like Stavros' murdering Abdul in *America America*. I wanted to make the scene strong, but I didn't want to make an entertainment out of bloodletting. So I had the car fill three-fourths of the screen and built up the sound of the fight. Then I cut to the door of the house, where Martha was struggling with Tony. I used a lesser act of violence to suggest the much more savage violence that was going on behind the car.

I don't think it's fun to get bashed around, I don't think men recover from a punch in the jaw very quickly. Steve Railsback, who played Sarge, did a most creative thing—something which I never would have thought of myself. He played the first part of the fight groggy. When Woods clipped him, he got up staggering. His head only cleared as the fight went on.

Was there any difference in your approach to working with actors all of whom had such little experience?

The youngsters are far more flexible. They don't come to you with any fixed ideas in their minds, and therefore they are more open to suggestions. You can get them going and see what happens. They're there to do what you want with. They're not protecting their screen image or their professed sexuality and all that nonsense that's unconsciously in the mind of everyone who's made a few pictures. Also, they had far better training than most stars. Railsback was very well trained, and I used his training. He prepared for scenes beautifully.

In what way?

He was actually living through the feelings and the intentions that were in the part. I would tell him what I wanted out of a scene and what he was thinking of while the scene was happening. I told him that his character was often mysterious, not explicit. He had thoughts that were not expressed. For example, when Sarge is folding the blanket after he's taken a nap, he laughs inexplicably. That was Steve's contribution, and it was the kind of thing I encouraged.

What about the others?

The others were less trained. The girl, Patricia Joyce, had been very badly trained at Yale. It took two or three weeks before she could just walk across the room without being self-conscious, but she got better and better as I got to her more and more.

When you say "got to her," what did you do?

The first thing was to get her to relax. The fact that she slept in the house and got to know us helped. She became unconscious about me as a possibly dissatisfied critic. Then I would tell her what she wanted, and I would drive her towards that. I would give her things to think about during a scene that were real, that made her reactive, so that she couldn't just say the lines in a preset, determined way.

Did you try to use the actors' own personalities?

Oh, yes, a lot. For example, I kept Railsback and Martinez away from the girl for weeks. I also told them to stay away from each other, so there would be a certain sense of mystery. On the other hand, I got Jimmy Woods close to Patricia Joyce. I was able to control all that, because I had them living there in the house. I also did some diabolical things behind the scenes that made the off-camera life continue when they were on-camera. It's a valuable thing to do. For example, if you sense an antagonism between actors who are going to have to be antagonistic in front of the camera, don't smooth it out. It's sort of mean to encourage it. But don't heal it—leave it alone. Don't make everybody chummy. Clubbiness is not helpful.

The basic material is very low-keyed and gritty. The look reinforced that. Was that a conscious choice or financial necessity?

There are no absolutes, Jeff. A highly polished look isn't always wrong. It depends on the material. It would have been disgusting in relation to this kind of conflict in this kind of setting. It would have looked like drama. I mean that pejoratively—"drama." *The Visitors* shouldn't have looked enacted. It should have looked like it really happened. Nobody's too pretty or too noble or too brave.

What are your feelings about this approach to filmmaking? Does working independently, off on your own with a very small crew, appeal to you?

Not only is it appealing, it's exhilarating. It's marvelous.

Is that the way you'd like to go from here?

Not necessarily. It depends on the kind of picture and the scale required. But I certainly want to work that way sometime again. It's terrific. Throughout the shooting, I was rearranging the furniture, and Chris was cooking pancakes for the breakfast scene. I was carrying the tripod, and the actors were bringing in firewood. We were all friends, and everybody was making a picture together. What could be better than that? It's ideal.

THE LAST TYCOON
(1976)

THE FILM OPENS WITH Monroe Stahr (Robert De Niro) demonstrating the skills that have made him a legendary Hollywood studio chief. He's intelligent and decisive, and everyone jumps when he speaks. We meet his boss/colleague, Pat Brady (Robert Mitchum), and sense that there's going to be a battle for power somewhere down the line. Brady's daughter, Cecilia (Theresa Russell), has a college-girl crush on Stahr, but he treats her like the kid he still thinks her to be. Anyway, "Movies are his girl." At least until an earthquake causes a flood on the back lot, and Kathleen Moore (Ingrid Boulting) literally comes floating into his life, riding on the head of Siva, the Hindu god of destruction.

He is immediately obsessed by her, and in between teaching writers how to write, directors how to direct, and actors how to act—all of this while fending off a run by his enemies at the studio to render him powerless—he uses all of his resources to track down the beautiful Kathleen.

Moore shows no interest in his overtures. She's not impressed with his stature in the movie business, the esteem in which he is held by others, his power, his money, or his interest in her. She doesn't even like the movies. But he is persistent and obviously sincere, and she finally gives in. They fall deeply in love. We learn that she had held him at a distance because she had been very damaged by an affair that ended badly. Later we learn that despite

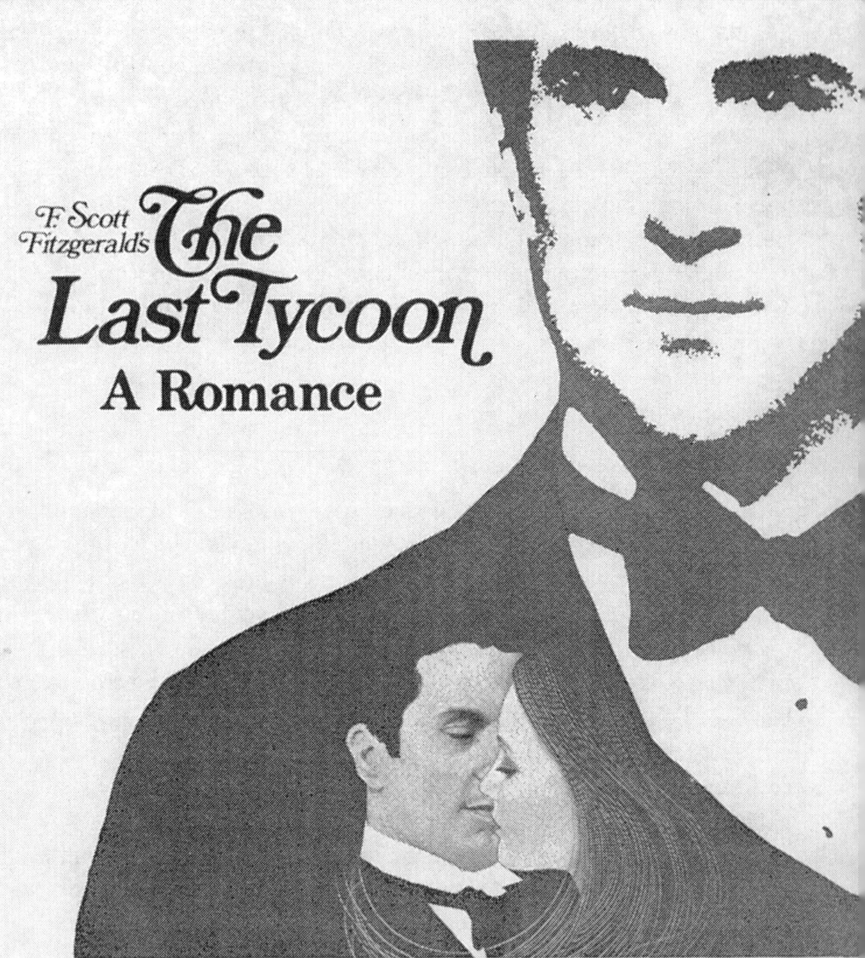
F. Scott Fitzgerald's
The Last Tycoon
A Romance
Paramount Pictures Presents A Sam Spiegel-Elia Kazan Film
starring Robert De Niro
Tony Curtis Robert Mitchum Jeanne Moreau
Jack Nicholson Donald Pleasence
Ray Milland Dana Andrews and introducing Ingrid Boulting
Screenplay by Harold Pinter Produced by Sam Spiegel Directed by Elia Kazan
Music by Maurice Jarre Production Services by Tycoon Service Company
PG PARENTAL GUIDANCE SUGGESTED
SOME MATERIAL MAY NOT BE SUITABLE FOR PRE-TEENAGERS
Read the Bantam Paperback Technicolor® A Paramount Release

her obvious feeling for Stahr, she has promised to marry the man who had rescued her from her disastrous affair. He is due to arrive at any moment.

In the meantime, the cabal intent on destroying Stahr at the studio, gathers its forces. He could care less. He's a man obsessed, and Kathleen had agreed to go off with him. An odd and artificial turn of events occurs, and instead, she marries her fiancé.

Stahr gets outrageously drunk and attacks Brimmer (Jack Nicholson), a Communist who's trying to organize the writers at his studio. It's a flimsy excuse, but in Stahr's wounded state, it is all the cabal needs, and the wunderkind is forced out of the studio that he had helped build.

When the production of *The Last Tycoon* was announced, it engendered incredible expectations from the film community, the critics and the public at large. And with good reason. The source material was the final, though incomplete novel by F. Scott Fitzgerald. Not only was Fitzgerald one of our most highly esteemed novelists, he was writing about material he knew well—Hollywood of the '30s. And Hollywood of the '30s was by all accounts the most glamorous and romantic time in one of the most glamorous and romantic places in the world.

The screenplay was by Harold Pinter, among the most highly regarded playwrights in the English language. It was to be produced by Sam Spiegel, who had not only given us *On the Waterfront* but *The Bridge on the River Kwai* and *Lawrence of Arabia*, as well as many others. The lead role was to be played by Robert De Niro, who was already a big star and thought by many to be the best young actor in America. To top it off, the film was to be directed by Elia Kazan, whose previous work had by then placed him in the pantheon of living filmmakers. In Hollywoodese, the "elements" of the "package" were unbeatable. The picture had the "buzz," and the hype machine was churning it out full bore.

But there was a whole other side to the story. Kazan said about *Tycoon*, "It began as a conveniently timed job, one I'd not have undertaken except for Mother's debility." Kazan's mother was terminally ill. Shooting in Los Angeles would provide a way to get her out of the cold Eastern winter, which she could no longer abide, and it would allow him to have her under his roof where he could look after her.

Once he got involved in the project though, he threw himself into it with all of the obsessive-compulsive concentration that he had brought to all of his other work—as much as caring for a dying mother and living in a shredded marriage would allow for. But Kazan had once told me, getting a scene to play properly has a lot to do with getting it started right. The same holds true for a film, and this is a film that at best got off on the wrong foot.

I think many people, certainly the critics, expected and longed for (though perhaps unconsciously) a film by the master that would be a kind of summing up—of all that he knew about filmmaking and all that he knew about Hollywood. It would unravel and lay bare the secrets of how America's dreams are forged. That is not what they got. Maybe because *Tycoon* is the least Kazan-like of all of his movies since *Sea of Grass.* The finished film looked and felt as if it could have been made by any number of other talented directors. It is very difficult to connect *Tycoon* to Kazan's body of work, especially those done in the past twenty-five years when, starting with *Panic in the Streets*, he had gone his own way.

The film lacks Kazan's concern with the ambivalence of characters and the situations they are caught up in. Monroe Stahr never has to face a "difficult" decision—one where no matter what he does, there is a loss. There was no inner conflict, which, as Kazan said, was where the real and important drama always takes place. The film is not concerned with "essentialization," taking a situation and rooting it in reality but raising the emotional stakes so that reality becomes transformed into myth. The film begins with self-declared mythic figures and works its way down from there. Most important of all, the film lacks passion, and passion has been at the heart and soul of all of Kazan's films. The lack of passion begins and ends with the characterization of Monroe Stahr. As Kazan put it, he had to "transform a New York Italian kid into Hollywood 'royalty,' a thin, somewhat sickly Jew with erudition and culture." In other words, an intellectual. But what comes across is not just an intellectual, but an intellectual whose ideas are disconnected from his emotions. Even when he is obsessively chasing after Kathleen, it feels like he is more connected to his thoughts and memories of his dead wife than he is to the actual flesh-and-blood girl to whom he is making love. This is a character right out of Pinter—not Kazan. It doesn't ring true. More importantly, it isn't engaging. As Kazan said, after the fact, "...it was clear to Sam [Spiegel] and me that we had a dubious commercial product, and it was clear to me if not to Sam that the reason was that we had fudged on the basic dramatic situation. The film had not gripped anyone; no one was concerned about Monroe Stahr's fate.... Scene by scene the film flowed, but no one could be concerned about De Niro's troubles or respect his pain. Some of the individual scenes were good, it did have tender moments and some amusing ones, but there was nothing to compel an audience to see it." How did all this come to be?

As previously mentioned, Kazan took the job because it gave him a chance to look after his dying mother. That this is true is supported by the fact that he said "yes" to it within twenty-four hours—without even thoroughly reading the script. This was extremely uncharacteristic behavior. He had spent months, sometimes years, working on screenplays. He knew that if the script wasn't right, trying to fix it on your feet was a daunting if not impossible task. He had second thoughts about it, to be sure. After *The Arrangement*, he wanted no part whatsoever of making a studio picture, especially in Hollywood, ever again. And though he was still trying to get an independent feature off the ground, he was almost entirely committed to writing books. Still, the concern for his mother overrode everything else. Besides, he'd been promised by Spiegel that they'd go to London to work on the script with Pinter.

(Pinter was going through marital difficulties and was apparently unable to travel to California.)

And indeed they went to London on three occasions. But virtually nothing came of it. Kazan found that Spiegel and Pinter had grown very tight. They'd worked together for a long time on the script before he'd gotten involved in the project. And now Spiegel, impressed with Pinter's status in the British literary world, seemed to feel that his job was to protect him and his "holy writ" from a dominating director. Kazan finally cornered Pinter and told him that he felt there was a great hole in the center of the script—the love story—and that he felt as if it were all happening underwater. Pinter's response was, "Isn't that where it always happens?" Kazan threw in the towel and determined to make the best film he could out of the material he had. That's the way Kazan tells the story. It leaves a lot of questions unanswered.

What happened to the Sam Spiegel of *On the Waterfront*, who had driven Kazan and Schulberg crazy by insisting that they open it all up again? What happened to Kazan, who for twenty-five years had fought to get his films the way he wanted them before he would expose even a foot of film? They both knew that fundamental story problems can't be fixed on the soundstage any more than you can repair a ship's keel while it is in the middle of the ocean. But they both caved. And they both seemed to miss a story problem that was even more damaging than the weakness of the love story, which is that the love story is not related to the rest of the film.

In fact one can legitimately ask what the hell the film is meant to be about. We are shown that Monroe Stahr is Hollywood royalty, a man with extraordinary power. We are shown that he richly deserves the power he wields. Then he falls in love with a girl who looks like his dead wife. She runs off with someone else; he gets drunk and makes a fool of himself with a union organizer. For this, he is sacked from the studio, his career apparently at an end. It doesn't add up. It doesn't make much sense. And it doesn't feel like an integrated whole. Why should it? The script was based almost entirely on the half of the novel which Fitzgerald had finished, in which the love story predominates. Had he finished the book, perhaps we would have known how the love affair was meant to fit into the overall story. As it is, Stahr lacks any real central purpose, any real goal. Without that we are left with a series of well-executed scenes, but they do not come together to form a satisfying picture. For Kazan, a man who stressed over and over the need for his characters to have an objective, this was a glaring and mysterious failing.

Wasn't anyone paying attention? Why did Kazan, after so many years of artistic freedom, act as if he was suddenly an employee and not the creative center of the movie? One can only conjecture. I suspect that politics—personal and professional—had a lot to do with it. Of course it is also possible that Spiegel agreed with Pinter and that Kazan simply lost the battle of wills. This I think is the least likely explanation.

Having lost the fight over the script, he now had to put the picture together. The casting of the two principal girls was once again fought out in the arena of politics. Ingrid Boulting and Theresa Russell were both Spiegel's choices. Kazan suspected that Sam wanted Boulting for horizontal reasons of his own. He was certain that was the case with Russell, who made no bones about Sam trying to cozy her into bed for months. Kazan was initially against both of these choices but agreed to work with them. As he did, he found possibilities, and as was always his way, he focused on the actors' potential and not on their limitations. Before he knew it, he had become the champion of both women, while Sam took a dubious posture, thus cleverly placing all of the responsibility on Kazan's shoulders.

Russell confirmed to me many of the things that Kazan had told me about how he casts actors whose work he's never seen and whom he doesn't know personally. He called her back five times. The first time they simply talked. In every session thereafter he improvised, moving from a simple situation, where she had to act as if she had forgotten something in his office and had to find it before his secretary returned, to much more complicated situations. Often he would improvise with her. They never once had a reading. She said that she's never been through anything like it in her life. That he was brilliant and relentless. He wouldn't make a decision about giving her the role until he was truly satisfied she had it in her. By that time, she was totally confident she had it in her as well.

If Kazan was taking a chance with the two girls, in some ways he was taking an even bigger risk with De Niro. Once again, Kazan behaved uncharacteristically. He insisted on Robert De Niro for the lead role. Not that De Niro wasn't a wonderful actor and an interesting choice, but Kazan had never met him. Kazan has gone on record repeatedly about how essential it was for him to know his actors inside and out. To spend weeks with them if necessary to gather his material—to find out what buttons to push, how to help them toward a performance. This time he played a hunch. There was another problem. Up until this point in De Niro's career, his screen persona had been that of a tough Italian street kid. He was going to have to fight his own considerable iconography in every frame.

Kazan and De Niro worked very hard at the transformation. De Niro dropped forty pounds. He actually looked sickly and thin. But that was just the external appearance. The internal life was something different. As Kazan put it, "He had to play a person who succeeded because he had a better mind than those around him. There was one acting exercise that I gave him that we worked on again and again, its purpose being to complicate his thinking and give him the necessary quality of thoughtfulness and reserve. I wanted an observer to feel: You never know what that man is thinking. The improvisation, which we called the 'doublethink,' consisted of Bobby retaining some supplementary or contradictory thought when he spoke. Again and again I asked him to actually think one thing as he was saying something quite the opposite. I suggested that he practice doing this in life, and it began to change the way Bobby 'came on.'"

Kazan felt that it had worked well. I agree. I think De Niro captured many of the ambiguities and contradictions of his character beautifully. We see him function believably as a sympathetic "father," a man who knows and understands writers' and actors' and directors' problems from the inside; at the same time we see him manipulate and cut a swath through the power boys. He loves writers, has the highest regard for their talent. But he thinks their brains should belong to him. He thinks nothing of putting a dozen of these men and women, whom he respects so highly, to work on the same project without ever informing them. He has money, power, is single and straight. Women by the score love him, including Cecilia. But he always behaves like a gent, and when it comes time to really making a run at the one woman he loves, he stumbles and loses her. De Niro is very believable whether playing the tough, ruthless studio chief or the extremely sensitive lover.

The only real problem De Niro faced was the same one Kazan faced—the gaping holes in the story. No amount of improvising was going to solve that one.

As the shooting began, Kazan's mother's health deteriorated rapidly. He raced to the hospital at every lunch break to sit by her side. She had an inoperable malignancy and was no longer eating. In the middle of shooting, she died. Kazan was holding her hand as she took her last breath. He knew it was coming, and in some ways it was a relief. But it had to be a terrible blow. She had been his protector as a child, a major source of his sense of self-worth, and now she was gone. By his own account, his marriage was in tatters. There was no comfort or support to be expected from that front. So he soldiered on alone.

At times it was all he could do to stay afloat. For some of the big scenes he resorted to making shot lists, the way they teach you in film school. He even ran them by Sam for his approval and was glad when he got it. This was not Kazan at the top of his game. And still he soldiered on.

Most of the critics disliked the picture, some violently. It was a commercial failure, which by their own lights vindicated their judgment. I disagree. While it is not a great film, in many ways Kazan did a very good job. The acting is excellent despite the fact that Ingrid Boulting came in for a pasting. Kazan predicted that she would. He wrote in his diary, "The scenes with Ingrid Boulting don't come off.... But if something is wrong with those scenes on the screen, it is not Ingrid's fault, it is Sam's and it is Harold's. But who will be blamed? Ingrid."

In all of the technical areas, the film can only be praised. It is perhaps the most beautiful-looking of all of Kazan's pictures. The sound, the costumes, the makeup, the sets, the props, etc. were done with all of the prodigious skill that Hollywood craftsmen bring to their jobs. I believe the central flaw in execution in this case always goes back to the script.

One possible explanation of the script's shortcomings is that they were dealing with such an esteemed novel that they stuck to it quite literally, without thoroughly examining how it needed to be transformed in order to make a successful and believable film. A glaring example is the scene in which Monroe sees Kathleen for the first time. Maybe in a great novel you can just get away with having Stahr meet the goddess who will destroy him while she is clinging to the head of the Hindu god of destruction, which had broken loose from its mooring in the prop department when the studio was hit by an earthquake, which caused one of the main waterlines to burst, which, in turn, caused a flood on the back lot—maybe. Symbol is piled on top of symbol on top of symbol. Or as they say in Hollywood, "It's like stuffing bananas with bananas." In the movie it all just lies there, though we know from De Niro's reaction shots that the entire catastrophe means little compared to the vision of the woman riding the goddess.

Kazan's diary entry reads, "...I suppose it is believable in the book...but as I watched it happen, I didn't believe it, not for a minute. Ingrid is supposed to be clinging to the top of the head. Bullshit!" As a central part of the director's job is to be the audience for each scene as he shoots it, one can legitimately ask why we should believe it any more than he did.

Fitzgerald left a sketchy outline, indicating where he might have gone with the novel once the love story ended. Clearly he knew he had a lot more story to tell before Stahr (who was dying, though this is not dramatized in the film) was forced to end his romance with the real love of his life—the movies.

The filmmakers (including the writer) were stuck. They put together an ending, using scenes Fitzgerald had written between Stahr and Brimmer, a Communist union organizer (Jack Nicholson), in which Stahr gets drunk, makes a fool of himself, and as a result gets dumped by the head office—as if getting drunk in Hollywood were some sort of unheard-of offense. The scenes are well made, but they hardly make a satisfying end to the hopes, dreams, and obsessions of a living legend. As Kazan said about not having a satisfying conclusion to the film, "...it means that something is very wrong earlier in the story."

The Last Tycoon failed to be the great summing up, and it was turned on viciously by those who had decided that that was what it was going to be. I believe they were wrong to overlook all that was good about the film. But that is an old story in Hollywood, as both Monroe Stahr and Kazan knew well.

My own feelings about the film are best summed up in a letter by Raymond Chandler, defending Hemingway and one of his last fully completed novels, *Across the River and into the Trees*. Obviously the circumstances of Hemingway's and Kazan's lives differed, but I think Chandler's observations are appropriate:

"...just what do the boys [the critics] resent so much? Do they sense the old wolf has been wounded and this is a good time to pull him down?...it's not the best thing he's done...there's not much story in it, not much happens and...the mannerisms stick out. Obviously he was not trying to write a masterpiece; but in a character not too unlike his own, trying to sum up the attitude of a man who is finished and knows it, and is bitter and angry about it. Apparently Hemingway had been very sick and he was not sure he was going to get well.... I suppose those primping second-guessers who call themselves critics think he shouldn't have written the book at all. Feeling the way he felt, they wouldn't have had the guts to write anything. I'm damn sure I wouldn't. That's the difference between a champ and a knife thrower. The champ may have lost his stuff temporarily or permanently, he can't be sure. But when he can no longer throw the high hard one, he throws his heart instead. He throws something. He doesn't just walk off the mound and weep."

By the end of the shooting, Kazan probably knew he was taking the last shots he would ever take. Pinter had left him without a final scene. So he invented one. Monroe Stahr, all alone, walks down an entirely deserted studio street. He pauses for a moment looking back at it all, then disappears into the dark shadows of a soundstage. The magician had put all of his tricks back in their box. He'd thrown his heart at the screen. Now it was time once again for him to move on. Or as Kazan might have said, "Where's the next hill?"

A FACE IN THE CROWD

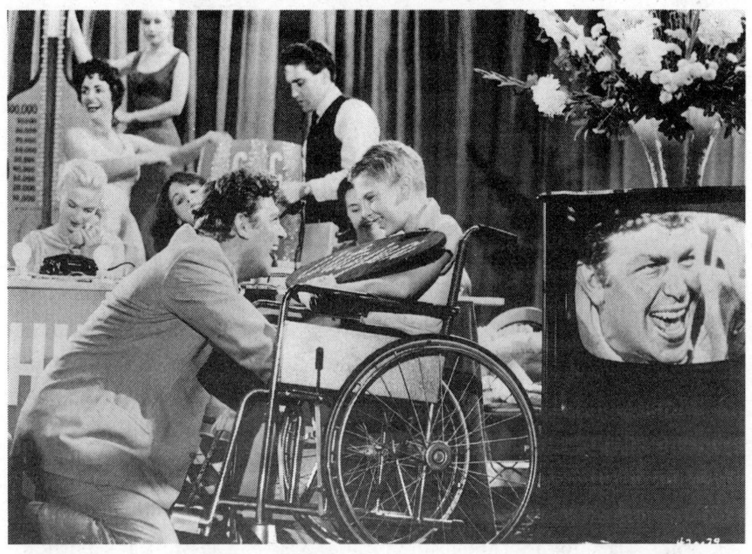

"I had to open up the f-stop on the camera enough so that I could photograph what was happening on the TV monitor and still photograph people and get some sort of exposure on their faces." (Andy Griffith as Lonesome Rhodes)

"The spectacle lets you see things from Rhodes's point of view. Everyone is at his feet."

"It shows he has the guts to face her. . . .It saves Lonesome Rhodes from being just a sneaky double-crosser."

". . . there's a smugness about him (Walter Matthau as Mel). It's a little bit of my feeling about intellectuals leaking through. . . ."

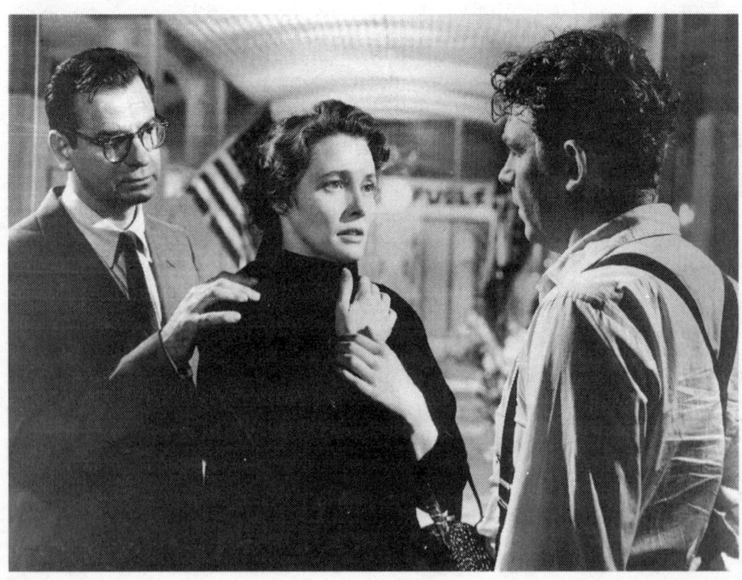

WILD RIVER

"I think the best thing in that film is . . . when they take Miss Ella (Jo Van Fleet) off the island."

"The cow is put in Miss Ella's new front yard. She just sits there. She won't have it. She'd rather die than give in."

"I think Miss Ella's right to want to stay on her land . . . . That picture, with all its faults, is the epitome of what I feel more clearly than any other . . . ."

SPLENDOR IN THE GRASS

Bud (Warren Beatty) and Deanie (Natalie Wood) at the end of the film. They have both accepted the cost of disaster.

Deanie declaring that she hasn't been "spoiled."

"I tried to make Bud's father, Ace (Pat Hingle), human, even when he was being horrid."

AMERICA AMERICA

"It lends the scene a legendary quality to suddenly see Stavros (Stathis Giallelis) pull his knife and jump on the praying Turk."

"Stavros is so tempted by the sweetness of his fiancée (Linda Mash) that he's driven to tell her the truth, which is 'Don't trust me.' . . . That's the deepest, truest line I ever wrote."

Stavros and Hohannes (Gregory Rozakis) just before Stavros throws his fez into the water.

THE ARRANGEMENT

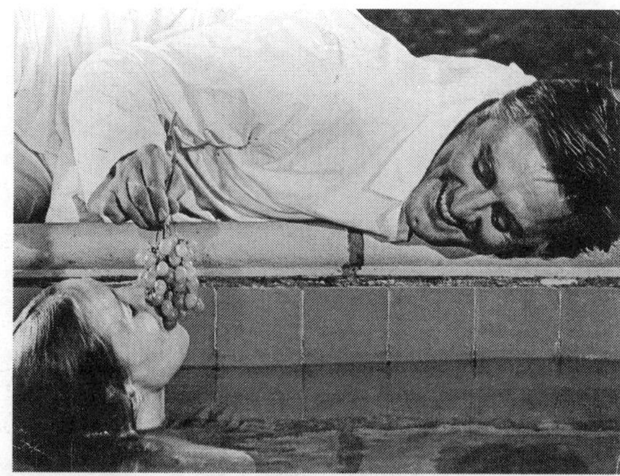

"Some of the scenes of Gwen (Faye Dunaway) and Eddie (Kirk Douglas) horsing around were well done."

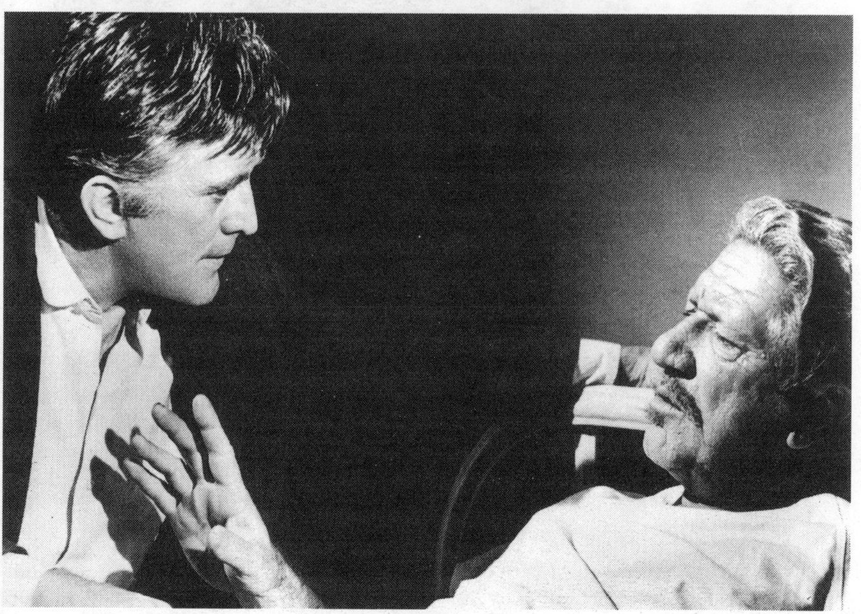

" . . you could draw a line right through from *East of Eden* to *The Arrangement* in terms of the relationship between father and son." Kirk Douglas shown here with Richard Boone playing his father.

THE VISITORS

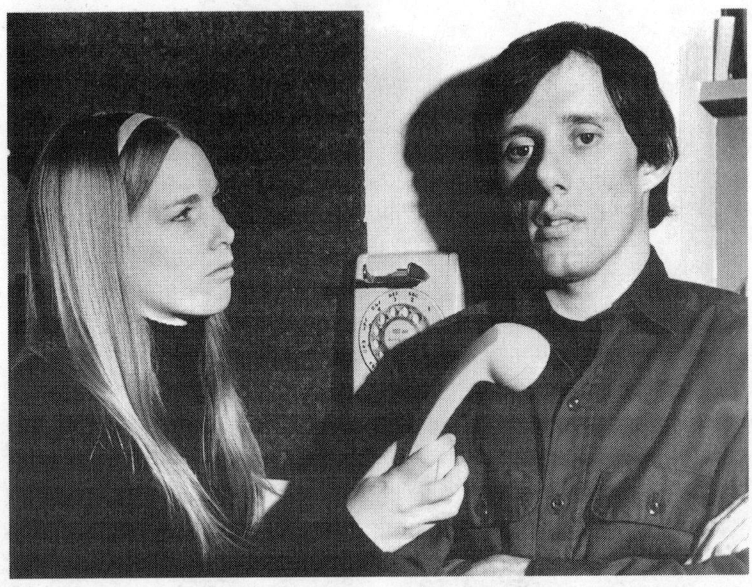

". . . when Martha (Patricia Joyce) hands Bill (James Woods) the phone, their expressions say it all."

THE LAST TYCOON

Even when Monroe Stahr (Robert De Niro) is obsessively chasing after Kathleen (Ingrid Boulting), it feels like he is more connected to his thoughts and memories of his dead wife.

Stahr gets drunk and makes a fool of himself with a union organizer (Jack Nicholson) while Cecilia Brady (Theresa Russell) looks on.

Cecilia Brady flirts with the love of her life, Monroe Stahr. Kazan called Russell, who had never done a film before, back five times before he felt confident she had the role in her.

Afterword: Himself, Undiminished

THE RUSH FOR the four o'clock train to Montauk reminded me why, after four months in L.A., I still loved New York. So many people, and they're all in a hurry. I settled into a seat and wondered what it was going to be like spending a week alone with Kazan. He'd invited me out to his summer place in Montauk at the very tip of Long Island to review my edited version of our interviews.

When I jumped off the train, there was Kazan, hands stuffed in his pockets, a cigar between his teeth, stalking the platform. The collar of his faded blue jacket was turned up against the cool breeze coming off the ocean. Feisty as ever, he yanked me to him as we shook hands. I called and raised by giving him a hug. During the months we'd spent together we had become friends. We knew a lot about each other, knew each other's moves, knew how to bob and weave and evade when it suited us.

This was probably going to be the last chance I would have to go through the material with him, and I came prepared with a list of questions, things I wanted to expand, explore further or clarify. I was determined not to let him off the hook.

Since we had first met, I had done some more directing and had written a couple of scripts. I'd tried out things that I had learned from him. Some had worked. Others hadn't. I wanted to find out why. Had I done something inadequately? Had I misunderstood what he'd meant? Despite myself, I knew in my heart that I was looking for rules. Some secret formula I could always rely on when all else failed. I was sure that Kazan had such a secret, and I was going to make him turn it over.

Also, I wanted to raise again the whole issue of Kazan's informing to HUAC. The House was in the middle of impeachment hearings. Richard Nixon was on the ropes, charged with high crimes and misdemeanors. Because Kazan once had been a friendly witness and Nixon's early political career had been largely built on his red-baiting, he and Nixon had, willy-nilly, become bedfellows. I wondered if the current events had made Kazan rethink his decision to name names.

My guess is that his testimony had probably never been far from his consciousness. In *On the Waterfront*, Terry Malloy testified against his friends to serve what he believed to be the greater good, even though it went against the codes of his community. *The Visitors*, made nearly twenty years later, is about a man who does exactly the same thing. *Waterfront* ended with a note of triumph and hope. *The Visitors* faded out on bleak isolation and despair. What did this change of tone tell me about Kazan? These interviews were never intended to be part of the literature of the McCarthy era. I'd come to Kazan to learn about filmmaking. Still, the HUAC experience had been so central to his life and his life so central to the history of the time, that it would be silly and cowardly not to push him as far as I could. While I had asked Kazan about his testimony when we discussed *On the Waterfront*, I had a few more questions—one in particular—that I was determined to raise.

Heavy foliage blocked any view of Kazan's house from the highway. We turned into a blind driveway and pulled up beside a cottage sitting on a high bluff overlooking the sea. That evening Kazan cooked dinner as we brought each other up to date. At one point he touched my arm and cut the small talk short. "You've changed a lot since you went to Los Angeles," he remarked.

"I have?"

"Yes. You've gotten a lot tougher—embattled."

"Oh?"

"I don't mean that negatively. You've got to be tough and ready to do battle in that world."

"And you think I am?"

"You seem that way to me," he said, smiling and nodding.

"Good. When can we start going over the manuscript? I've got a fight or two to pick with you."

"Eat your dinner first and get some rest. We can start in the morning." He laughed and pushed toward me a plate full of fresh fish cooked in butter and lemon.

As I lay in bed, my mind drifted back over the last eighteen months. Many friends had asked, "What's he really like?" There was no simple answer. Why should there have been? Kazan's an enormously complicated man.

Many have said that he is the most seductive, charming person they had ever met—a master at making you feel as if you were the best and most important person ever to wander into his life. The reason he is so good at it is that for that moment, at least, you *are* the most important person to him. Soon enough, though, he will surely move on and find someone else. Like Lonesome Rhodes, the Andy Griffith character in *A Face in the Crowd*, he is a seductive man of large appetites. Underneath, however, he always tells the truth. Also like that character, he can be thoughtless, deceitful, selfish, and self-serving (as he revealed in his autobiography). He has many of the qualities that one attributes to the Old Testament prophets, and as he got older, he even started looking like one.

Kazan often seems nourished by contradictions that would flatten other people. He's liberal and reactionary. He's seriously macho, yet many of his closest friends and collaborators have been gentle homosexuals. He's both gregarious and shy, openhandedly generous but very careful with money, full of self-confidence yet riddled with insecurity. He is a great believer in family and yet, by his own account, has spent his life philandering.

Kazan carries his body as if he were a street kid, although he was raised in suburbia and has an Ivy League education. He appears to be a man of action, almost contemptuous of intellectuals, yet his library is jammed with books that have been read and reread. He seems casual and offhand but feels things intensely.

There is one thing about which he has been consistent—his devotion to his work. He'd do anything, sacrifice anyone (including himself) to get it right. I can't help but admire that kind of determination. It's infectious, full of enthusiasm and promise. But there's danger in it, too. It can slide easily into believing that the end always justifies the means, a charge often leveled at Kazan. As I drifted off to sleep, I remembered something he once told me: "The real challenge is not simply to survive. Hell, anyone can do that. It's to survive as yourself, undiminished."

At five-thirty in the morning I was awakened by the insistent clicking of a typewriter. Kazan had been up and working for over an hour, making notes for his new novel. "Don't you ever sleep?" I asked.

"Sure," he answered without looking up. "I do like the animals do, take little ten-to-fifteen-minute naps during the day. You wake up and you feel fresh all over again." I trudged to the kitchen and quickly downed three cups of coffee in an effort to get my motor to catch up to his. He went back to work.

The questions about HUAC were not going to wait long. Nixon had resigned at noon that day. I kept an eye on Kazan as we watched Nixon's departure on a small black-and-white television set. Nixon looked hopelessly out of sync. His movements and his words didn't match. His arms kept flapping and his face smiling as he mounted the steps to his plane, waving good-bye. It was if he were trying to convince himself that he was setting off in triumph rather than disgrace. Kazan's face revealed nothing as he watched. He'd once told me that it was a very good thing when the central character in a movie has a sense of mystery about him, if you can never quite figure out what he's feeling or thinking. It makes you wonder all the time what he's going to do next. Kazan was the perfect man to play the lead in his own life.

I was a young kid when the political witch hunts took place. Although I had no idea what any of it meant, I sat with my family and dutifully watched the Army-McCarthy hearings. I wanted them to be over so I could go back to *Captain Video*. The one thing I did know was who were the bad guys. The persecution of my uncle left no room for doubt.

I began my questions by turning to *On the Waterfront* and our earlier discussion of how the film paralleled events in Kazan's life. He told me much the same story as before. He named names because he believed that there had been a Communist conspiracy that was trying to influence American policy and the way that Americans thought. Communists, as he remembered it, were in high places both in and out of the government. They were certainly in the theater and movie business. They were trying to control the content of plays and motion pictures. And they were receiving their orders from Moscow. Or as he put it, "They say there was no conspiracy. That's bullshit. There was a conspiracy. I know. I was part of it. I thought I would be doing a terrible thing to pretend ignorance." He reiterated his belief that Communists posed a serious threat to America.

I was going slowly, gliding from question to question, barely pushing beyond what was by now familiar territory, knowing that I had laid a sort of prosecutorial trap for him. Once again he repeated in an offhand way that he hadn't given the committee any names that they didn't already have. He wasn't telling them anything that they didn't already know.

I sprung the trap. "If you truly believed that there was a Communist conspiracy and that it presented a real danger to our country, why did you stop there?" He looked at me quizzically, drawing his knees up into the wing chair in which he sat. "Why didn't you go further? Why didn't you tell them things that they didn't know, give them names that they didn't already have, get rid of all the Red bastards?"

For a moment Kazan looked right at me, alert as a bobcat. He crossed his arms, pulling them close to his chest as if protecting himself from the sea breeze, and spoke very quietly. "I don't have to defend myself to you or anyone else." He held my eyes a moment longer. Then his head dropped forward, and he passed out cold.

I've spoken with dozens of people who had been involved directly or indirectly with the Hollywood blacklist, and I've observed that no matter how honest and clearheaded people mean to be, when they recall that era they tend to remember things in a way that is consistent with the self-image they wish to preserve. From Lillian Hellman—who tried to grab the moral high ground and remembered only playing heroine to the music of her own conscience—to those who cried out for mercy and forgiveness, the pattern is the same. If you push people hard enough, you find inconsistencies in everyone's story. Not that they had lied. But the psyche protects itself in mysterious ways. I hadn't held out much hope that Kazan would prove to be different. In the split second in which he went from bright, clear awareness to unconsciousness, his psyche spoke very loudly. Our exploration of the blacklist and his testimony had come to an end.

During the next few days, our conversations about the rest of the manuscript proceeded smoothly. We usually agreed as to what needed trimming and what could be added. But when I got into certain technical areas and pushed Kazan harder and harder for simple direct answers, he drew back. The temperature in the room started to rise, and no sea breeze was going to cool things off. I was determined to find the alchemist's formula. He knew what I was after, and we butted heads.

Finally, his patience wore thin. "Goddamnit, will you stop trying to pin it all down. You want me to codify, to enunciate principles," he shouted. I yelled right back. "That's right. I do and you keep resisting. Why?"

"I will always resist you when you try to reduce directing to a collection of laws. What will really help is to understand that there aren't any rigid laws. Rules, before they were rules, were the experience of one artist who found that in a particular set of circumstances, certain techniques were of value in helping him achieve what he wanted. Then some academic came along and turned these observations into doctrine, claiming 'Things must be this way or things must be that way.' That's nonsense. I don't believe in any of that. You have to always leave yourself free to experiment.

There simply aren't any absolutes."

He paused for a moment and reflected. "Not even that is an absolute. The point is that, sooner or later, you have to say to yourself, the hell with what anyone says are the rules. I don't care who he is. You have to be able to say to yourself that you are going to go out and do what you want. And part of that is again and again to find the way to make happen what you want to have happen on screen or on stage. You have to do whatever the hell it takes to get for yourself what you are after."

"Yes, but aren't there...?" He cut me off.

"You're looking for generalizations. But when you are on your feet directing, you sometimes get crazy ideas. The only way to find out if they'll work is to try them."

"Oh, come on now. You studied and worked for years. At least on some level, directing is a craft and all crafts are learnable."

He was getting exasperated again, but he remained generous. Perhaps he remembered some moment from his own youth when he, too, had been looking for answers and believed that they existed.

He started again, taking a different approach. "Directing is a craft. But you must always remember you are dealing with human beings in a human situation. There is no single way to do it. You must never be afraid to try anything you feel might help. You meet each situation as you come to it. You read a scene and have your own reaction to it—you feel something about it. Not know—feel. In fact you can't separate knowing and feeling, because everything you do you do as a total person. Your job as a director is to try and get the audience to experience the scene the way you did. A director is a human propagandist, who says, 'This is the way I see life.'

"How you go about doing that will vary all the time. You have an idea of what a scene should be, then you have to deal with whatever problems arise in getting that across. You work and work and fool around until you find the solution to your problem. If you watch children at play, you'll notice that when they make up games, they have a lot of fun. Directing is not unlike that kind of play. There should be fun in art."

Kazan had rooted his technique deep in the human heart. His advice to go your own way without fear, to stop wasting time and energy looking for rules that guaranteed success, to solve problems as they arose—bringing to bear all that you know about the human psyche and the particular people you are working with in a particular situation—was not limited to the art or craft of filmmaking. This was advice for life. But I was still not willing to let it drop.

"Do you mean to tell me that in all of your years of directing theater and film, you never acquired a set of techniques that were transferable from one experience to another?"

"Of course I have. But it's different for everybody. The important thing is to not become rigid, to always allow yourself chances to change and to grow. Directing is a human craft. Your tools are human beings; you're working with human values in the service of other human beings. You develop your own methodology each time out. And if you really are any good, each time out you feel as if you are learning the craft all over again."

I had no further questions.

POSTSCRIPT

In a meeting held on January 9, 1999, of the Board of Governors of the Motion Picture Academy of Arts and Sciences, Karl Malden moved that Elia Kazan be given an honorary Oscar "in appreciation of a long, distinguished and unparalleled career. . . ."

Malden's speech had been impassioned, and for good reason. In 1989, the American Film Institute refused to honor Kazan because, as one of the board members said, "I don't care about the films he directed. He named names and we just can't honor someone who did that." In 1995, the San Francisco Film Festival Board of Directors did the same. It happened again in 1997 when the Los Angeles Film Critics refused to honor Kazan. But now, before his peers, Kazan's time had come. The vote by the thirty-nine-member board was unanimous. There had not even been any debate, let alone dissent. But the quiet accord didn't last twenty-four hours.

The response was instantaneous and explosive. Those opposed to the award, led by men who had been blacklisted, expressed contempt. As they saw it, the central act of Kazan's life had been to betray his friends. Kazan's supporters ranged from the extreme right who wanted to canonize him for being anti-Stalinist, to those who more moderately believed that it was possible and appropriate to recognize the value of Kazan's work regardless of his political actions.

The media finally had an Oscar story that wasn't about who was going to wear what dress. The controversy made it a sure thing that the central questions of the 71st Oscars were: what was Kazan going to say and what would his detractors do?

When the moment finally arrived, and Kazan, nearly 90, was led onto the stage by Robert De Niro and Martin Scorcese, he thanked the Academy, then for a brief second flashed a trace of his old defiance. He congratulated *them* for their courage in giving him the award.

For the billion people who saw the Oscars on television, it looked as if most, though not all, of the glittering audience had risen to their feet to give the traditional ovation. Those inside the hall saw a different picture. Upwards to half the audience sat on their hands.

Kazan has been a controversial figure in the performing arts for nearly seventy years. In what may well have been his final public act, he remained true to himself. He had once again aroused a strong emotional response in his audience, and once again he kept them guessing until the very last moment as to what was going to happen next.

CREDITS

FILMOGRAPHY

Features

A Tree Grows in Brooklyn (1945)

Production Company	20th Century-Fox
Producer	Louis D. Lighton
Director	Elia Kazan
Assistant Directors	Saul Wurtzel, Nicholas Ray
Script	Tess Slesinger, Frank Davis Based on the novel by Betty Smith
Director of Photography	Leon Shamroy
Editor	Dorothy Spencer
Art Director	Lyle Wheeler
Set Decorators	Thomas Little, Frank E. Hughes
Special Effects	Fred Sersen
Music	Alfred Newman
Orchestrations	Edward B. Powell
Costumes	Bonnie Cashin
Sound	Bernard Fredericks

Dorothy McGuire (Katie Nolan), Joan Blondell (Aunt Sissy), James Dunn (Johnny Nolan), Lloyd Nolan (McShane), Peggy Ann Garner (Francie Nolan), Ted Donaldson (Neeley Nolan), James Gleason (McGarrity), Ruth Nelson (Miss McDonough), John Alexander (Steve Edwards), B. S. Pully (Christmas tree vendor), Ferike Boros (Mrs. Rommely), J. Farrell MacDonald (Carney), Adeline DeWalt Reynolds (Mrs. Waters), George

Melford (Mr. Spencer), Mae Marsh, Edna Jackson (Tynmore sisters), Vincent Graeff (Henny Gaddis), Susan Lester (Flossie Gaddis), Johnny Berkes (Mr. Crackenbox), Lillian Bronson (Librarian), Alec Craig (Werner), Charles Halton (Mr. Barker), Al Bridge (Cheap Charlie), Joseph J. Green (Hassler), Virginia Brissac (Miss Tilford), Harry Harvey, Jr. (Herschel), Art Smith (Ice man), Norman Field, George Meader (Principals of school), Erskine Sanford (Undertaker), Martha Wentwonh (Mother), Francis Pierlot (Priest), Al Eben (Union representative), Peter Cusanelli (Barber), Robert Anderson (Augie), Harry Seymour (Floor walker), Edith Hallor

Filmed in 73 days. Released in USA, February 1945; GB, April 1945. Running time: 128 min. Distributor: 20th Century-Fox.

Sea of Grass (1947)

Production Company	M-G-M
Producer	Pandro S. Berman
Director	Elia Kazan
2nd Unit Director	James C. Havens
Assistant Director	Sid Sidman
Script	Marguerite Roberts, Vincent Lawrence Based on the novel by Conrad Richter
Director of Photography	Harry Stradling
Editor	Robert J. Kern
Art Directors	Cedric Gibbons, Paul Groesse
Set Decorators	Edwin B. Willis, Mildred Griffiths
Special Effects	A. Arnold Gillespie, Warren Newcombe
Music	Herbert Stothart
Costumes	Walter Plunkett, Irene Valles
Sound	Douglas Shearer

Spencer Tracy (Jim Brewton), Katharine Hepburn (Lutie Cameron), Melvyn Douglas (Brice Chamberlain), Robert Walker (Brock Brewton), Phyllis Thaxter (Sarah Bess), Edgar Buchanan (Jeff), Harry Carey (Doe Reid), Ruth Nelson (Selena Hall), William "Bill" Phillips (Banty), Robert Armstrong (Floyd McCurtin), James Bell (Sam Hall), Robert Barrat (Judge White), Charles Trowbridge (Cameron), Russell Hicks (Major Harney), Trevor Bardette (Andy), Morris Ankrum (Crane), Nora Cecil (Nurse), Pat Henry (Brock as a baby), Duncan Richardson (Brock at 3), James Hawkins (Brock at 5), Norman Ollestead (Brock at 8), Carol Nugent, William Challee, Paul Langton.

Filmed in 75 days. Released in USA, April 1947; GB, January 1947. Running time: 131 min. Distributor: M-G-M.

Boomerang (1947)

Production Company	20th Century-Fox
Executive Producer	Darryl F. Zanuck
Producer	Louis de Rochemont
Director	Elia Kazan
Assistant Director	Tom Dudley
Script	Richard Murphy Based on a *Reader's Digest* article, "The Perfect Case," by Anthony Abbott [Fulton Oursler]
Director of Photography	Norbert Brodine
Editor	Harmon Jones
Art Directors	Richard Day, Chester Gore
Set Decorators	Thomas Little, Phil D'Esco
Special Effects	Fred Sersen
Music	David Buttolph
Musical Director	Alfred Newman
Orchestrations	Edward B. Powell
Costumes	Kay Nelson
Wardrobe Director	Charles Le Maire
Sound	W. D. Flick, Roger Heman

Dana Andrews (Henry L. Harvey), Jane Wyatt (Mrs. Harvey), Lee J. Cobb (Chief Robinson), Cara Williams (Irene Nelson), Arthur Kennedy (John Waldron), Sam Levene (Woods), Taylor Holmes (Wade), Robert Keith (McCreery), Ed Begley (Harris), Leona Roberts (Mrs. Crossman), Philip Coolidge (Crossman), Lester Lonergan (Cary), Lewis Leverett (Whitney), Richard Garrick (Mr. Rogers), Karl Malden (Lieutenant White), Ben Lackland (James), Helen Carew (Annie), Barry Kelley (Sergeant Dugan), Wyrley Birch (Father Lambert), Johnny Stearns (Reverend Gardiner), Guy Thomajan (Cartucci), Lucia Seger (Mrs. Lukash), Dudley Sadler (Dr. Rainsford), Walter Greaza (Mayor Swayze), Helen Hatch (Miss Manion), Joe Kazan (Mr. Lukash), Ida McGuire (Miss Roberts), George Petrie (O'Shea), John Carmody (Callahan), Clay Clement (Judge Tate), E. J. Ballantine (McDonald), William Challee (Stone), Edgar Stehli (Coroner), Jimmy Dobson (Bill), Lawrence Paquin (Sheriff), Anthony Ross (Warren), Bert Freed (Herron), Royal Beal (Johnson), Bernard Hoffman (Tom), Fred Stewart (Graham), Lee Roberts (Criminal), Pauline Myers (Girt), Jacob Sandler (Barman), Herbert Rather (Investigator), Anna Minot (Secretary), Brian Keith (Demonstrator), Mayor Charles E. Moore, and the people of Stamford, CT.

Locations filmed in Stamford, Connecticut. Filmed in 49 days. Released in USA, February 1947; GB, January 1947. Running time: 88 min. Distributor: 20th Century-Fox.

Gentleman's Agreement (1947)

Production Company	20th Century-Fox
Producer	Darryl F. Zanuck
Director	Elia Kazan
Assistant Director	Saul Wurtzel
Script	Moss Hart
	Based on the novel by Laura Z. Hobson
Director of Photography	Arthur Miller
Editor	Harmon Jones
Art Directors	Lyle Wheeler, Mark-Lee Kirk
Set Decorators	Thomas Little, Paul S. Fox
Special Effects	Fred Sersen
Music	Alfred Newman
Orchestrations	Edward B. Powell
Costumes	Kay Nelson
Wardrobe Director	Charles Le Maire
Sound	Alfred Bruzlin, Roger Heman

Gregory Peck (Phil Green), Dorothy McGuire (Kathy), John Garfield (Dave Goldman), Celeste Holm (Anne), Anne Revere (Mrs. Green), June Havoc (Miss Wales), Albert Dekker (John Minify), Jane Wyatt (Jane), Dean Stockwell (Tommy Green), Nicholas Joy (Dr. Craigie), Sam Jaffe (Professor Lieberman), Harold Vermilyea (Jordan), Ransom M. Sherman (Bill Payson), Roy Roberts (Mr. Calkins), Kathleen Lockhart (Mrs. Minify), Curt Conway (Bert McAnny), John Newland (Bill), Robert Warwick (Weisman), Louis Lorimer (Miss Miller), Howard Negley (Tingler), Victor Kilian (Olsen), Frank Wilcox (Harry), Marlyn Monk (Receptionist), Wilton Graff (Maitre D), Morgan Farley (Clerk), Robert Karnes, Gene Nelson (Ex-GIs), Marion Marshall (Guest), Mauritz Hugo (Columnist), Jesse White (Elevator starter), Olive Deering, Jane Green, Virginia Gregg, Helen Gerald.

Filmed in 65 days. Released in USA, March 1948; GB, June 1948. Running time: 118 min. Distributor: 20th Century-Fox.

Pinky (1949)

Production Company	20th Century-Fox
Producer	Darryl F. Zanuck
Production Manager	Joseph Behm
Director	Elia Kazan
Assistant Director	Wingate Smith
Script	Philip Dunne, Dudley Nichols. Based on the novel *Quality* by Cid Ricketts Sumner

Script Supervisor	Rose Steinberg
Director of Photography	Joe MacDonald
Camera Operator	Til Gabbani
Editor	Harmon Jones
Art Directors	Lyle Wheeler, J. Russell Spencer
Set Decorators	Thomas Little, Walter M. Scott
Special Effects	Fred Sersen
Music	Alfred Newman
Orchestrations	Edward B. Powell
Wardrobe Director	Charles Le Maire
Sound	Eugene Grossman, Roger Heman

Jeanne Crain (Pinky), Ethel Barrymore (Miss Em), Ethel Waters (Aunt Dicey), William Lundigan (Dr. Thomas Adams), Basil Ruysdael (Judge Walker), Kenny Washington (Dr. Canady), Nina Mae McKinney (Rozelia), Griff Barnett (Dr. Joe), Frederick O'Neal (Jake Walters), Evelyn Varden (Melba Woolev), Raymond Greenleaf (Judge Shoreham), Dan Riss (Stanley), Arthur Hunnicutt (Police chief), William Hansen (Mr. Goolby), Everett Glass (Mr. Wooley), Bert Conway (Loafer), Harry Tenbrook (Townsman), Robert Osterloh (Police officer), Jean Inness (Saleslady), Shelby Bacon (Bov), Rene Beard (Teejore), Tonya Overstreet, Juanita Moore (Nurses), Herbert Heywood, Paul Brinegar.

Kazan replaced John Ford after a few days of shooting. Filmed in 52 days. Released in USA and GB, November 1949. Running time: 102 min. Distributor: 20th Century-Fox.

Panic in the Streets (1950)

Production Company	20th Century-Fox
Producer	Sol C. Siegel
Production Manager	Joseph Behm
Director	Elia Kazan
Assistant Director	Forrest E. Johnston
Script	Richard Murphy. Based on a story by Edna and Edward Anhalt
Adaptation	Daniel Fuchs
Script Supervisor	Stanley Scheuer
Director of Photography	Joe MacDonald
Camera Operator	Til Gabbani
Editor	Harmon Jones
Art Directors	Lyle Wheeler, Maurice Ransford
Set Decorators	Thomas Little, Fred J. Rode
Special Effects	Fred Sersen

Music	Alfred Newman
Orchestrations	Edward B. Powell, Herbert Spencer
Costumes	Travilla
Wardrobe Director	Charles Le Maire
Sound	W. D. Flick, Roger Heman

Richard Widmark (Dr. Clinton Reed), Paul Douglas (Police Captain Warren), Barbara Bel Geddes (Nancy Reed), Walter Jack Palance (Blackie), Zero Mostel (Raymond Fitch), Dan Riss (Neff), Alexis Minotis (John Mefaris), Guy Thomajan (Poldi), Tommy Cook (Vince), Edward Kennedy (Jordan), H. T. Tsiang (Cook), Lewis Charles (Kochak), Ray Muller (Dubin), Tommy Rettig (Tom Reed), Lenka Peterson (Jeanette), Pat Walshe (Pat), Paul Hostetler (Dr. Gafney), George Ehmig (Kleber), John Schilleci (Lee), Waldo Pitkin (Ben), Leo Zinser (Sergeant Phelps), Beverly C. Brown (Dr. Mackey), William A. Dean (Cortelyou), H. Waller Fowler, Jr. (Major Murray), Red Moad (Wynant), Val Winter (Commissioner Quinn), Wilson Bourg, Jr. (Charlie), Irving Vidacovich (Johnston), Mary Liswood (Mrs. Fitch), Aline Stevens (Rita), Ruth Moore Mathews (Mrs. Dubin), Stanley J. Reyes (Redfield), Darwin Greenfield (Violet), Emile Meyer (Beauclyde), Herman Cottman (Scott), Al Theriot (Al), Juan Villasana (Hotel proprietor), Robert Dorsen (Coast Guard lieutenant), Henry Marmet (Anson), Arthur Tong (Lascar Bay), Tiger Joe Marsh (Bosun).

Working titles: *Port of Entry* and *Outbreak*. Released in USA, September 1950; GB, July 1950. Running time: 96 min. Distributor: 20th Century-Fox.

A Streetcar Named Desire (1951)

Production Company	Group Productions
Producer	Charles K. Feldman
Production Manager	Norman Cook
Director	Elia Kazan
Assistant Director	Don Page
Script	Tennessee Williams Based on his play
Adaptation	Oscar Saul
Director of Photography	Harry Stradling
Editor	David Weisbart
Art Director	Richard Day
Set Decorator	George James Hopkins
Music	Alex North
Musical Director	Ray Heindorf

Costumes	Lucinda Ballard
Sound	C. A. Riggs

Vivien Leigh (Blanche DuBois), Marlon Brando (Stanley Kowalski), Kim Hunter (Stella Kowalski), Karl Malden (Mitch), Rudy Bond (Steve), Nick Dennis (Pablo), Peg Hillias (Eunice), Wright King (Collector), Richard Garrick (Doctor), Ann Dere (The matron), Edna Thomas (Mexican woman), Mickey Kuhn (Sailor), Chester Jones (Street vendor), Marietta Canty (Negro woman), Maxie Thrower (Passerby), Lyle Latell (Policeman), Mel Archer (Foreman), Charles Wagenheim (Passerby).

Released in USA, March 1952; GB, February 1952. Running time: 122 min. Distributor: Warner Bros.

Viva Zapata! (1952)

Production Company	20th Century-Fox
Producer	Darryl F. Zanuck
Director	Elia Kazan
Script	John Steinbeck
Director of Photography	Joe MacDonald
Editor	Barbara McLean
Art Directors	Lyle Wheeler, Leland Fuller
Set Decorators	Thomas Little, Claude Carpenter
Special Effects	Fred Sersen
Music	Alex North
Musical Director	Alfred Newman
Orchestrations	Maurice de Packh
Costumes	Travilla
Wardrobe Director	Charles Le Maire
Sound	W. D. Flick, Roger Heman

Marlon Brando (Emiliano Zapata), Jean Peters (Josefa), Anthony Quinn (Eufemio), Joseph Wiseman (Fernando), Arnold Moss (Don Nacio), Alan Reed (Pancho Villa), Margo (Soldadera), Harold Gordon (Madero), Lou Gilbert (Pablo), Mildred Dunnock (Señora Espejo), Frank Silvera (Huerta), Nina Varela (Aunt), Florenz Ames (Señor Espejo), Bernie Gozier (Zapatista), Frank De Kova (Colonel Guajardo), Joseph Granby (General Fuentes), Pedro Regas (Innocente), Richard Garrick (Old general), Fay Roope (Díaz), Harry Kingston (Don Garcia), Ross Bagdasarian (Officer), Leonard George (Husband), Will Kuluva (Lazaro), Fernanda Elizcu (Fuentes' wife), Abner Biberman (Captain), Philip Van Zandt (Commanding officer), Lisa Fusaro (Garcia's wife), Belle Mitchell (Nacio's wife), Henry Silva (Hernandez), Ric Roman (Overseer), George

J. Lewis (Rurale), Salvador Baguez, Peter Mamakos (Soldiers), Henry Corden (Senior officer), Nestor Paiva (New general), Robert Filmer (Capt. of Rurales), Julia Montoya (Wife), Danny Nuñez.

Kazan started to work on the script in 1943. Working titles: *The Little Tiger, The Angry Earth, Door to a Nation, The Invader*, and *Sudden Death*. Released in USA and GB, March 1952. Running time: 113 min. Distributor: 20th Century-Fox.

Man on a Tightrope (1953)

Production Company	20th Century-Fox
Producer	Robert L. Jacks
Associate Producer	Gerd Oswald
Director	Elia Kazan
Assistant Director	Hans Tost
Script	Robert Sherwood. Based on the story *International Incident* by Neil Paterson
Director of Photography	Georg Krause
Editor	Dorothy Spencer
Art Directors	Hans H. Kuhnert, Theo Zwirsky
Musical Director	Franz Waxman
Orchestrations	Earle Hagen
Songs	Bert Reisfeld
Costumes	Ursula Maes
Wardrobe Director	Charles Le Maire
Sound	Martin Mueller, Karl Becker, Roger Heman

Fredric March (Karel Cernik), Terry Moore (Tereza Cernik), Gloria Grahame (Zama Cernlk), Cameron Mitchell (Joe Vosdek), Adolphe Menjou (Fesker), Robert Beatty (Barovik), Alex D'Arcy (Rudolph), Richard Boone (Krofta), Pat Henning (Konradin), Paul Hartman (Jaromir), John Dehner (The Chief), Dorothea Wieck (Duchess), Philip Kenneally (The sergeant), Edelweiss Malchin (Vina Konradin), William Costello (Captain), Margaret Slezak (Mrs. Jaromir), Hansi (Kalka, the midget), The Brumbach Circus (The Cernik Circus), Gert Froebe (Plainclothes policeman), Peter Beauvais (SNB captain), Robert Charlebois (SNB lieutenant), Rolf Naukhoff (Police agent).

Locations filmed in Germany. Released in USA and GB, May 1953. Running time: 105 min. Distributor: 20th Century-Fox.

On the Waterfront (1954)

Production Company	Horizon
Producer	Sam Spiegel
Assistant to Producer	Sam Rheiner
Director	Elia Kazan
Assistant Director	Charles H. Maguire
Script	Budd Schulberg. Based on articles by Malcolm Johnson
Director of Photography	Boris Kaufman
Editor	Gene Milford
Art Director	Richard Day
Music	Leonard Bernstein
Costumes	Anna Hill Johnstone
Sound	James Shields

Marlon Brando (Terry Malloy), Eva Marie Saint (Edie Doyle), Karl Malden (Father Barry), Lee J. Cobb (Johnny Friendly), Rod Steiger (Charley Malloy), Pat Henning ("Kayo" Dugan), Leif Erickson (Clover), James Westerfield (Big Mac), John Heldabrand (Mutt), Rudy Bond (Moose), John Hamilton ("Pop" Doyle), Barry Macollum (J. P.), Don Blackman (Luke), Arthur Keegan (Jimmy), Mike O'Dowd (Specs), Martin Balsam (Gillette), Tony Galento (Truck), Tami Mauriello (Tillio), Fred Gwynne (Slim), Abe Simon (Barney), Joyce Lear (Bad girl), Thomas Hanley (Tommy), Anne Hegira (Mrs. Collins), Nehemiah Persoff (Driver), Pat Hingle (Waiter), Rebecca Sands (Police stenographer), Tiger Joe Marsh, Pete King, Neil Hines (Policemen), Vince Barbi, Lilian Herlein, Donnell O'Brien, Clifton James, Michael Vincente Gazzo.

Kazan started work on the project in 1951. Working titles: *The Bottom of the River*, *Golden Warriors*, and *Crime on the Waterfront.* Released in USA, October 1954; GB, September 1954. Running time: 108 min. Distributor: Columbia.

East of Eden (1955)

Production Company	Warner Bros.
Producer	Elia Kazan
Director	Elia Kazan
Assistant Directors	Don Page, Horace Hough
Script	Paul Osborn. Based on the novel by John Steinbeck
Dialogue Director	Guy Thomajan
Director of Photography	Ted McCord (CinemaScope)
Color Process	Warnercolor

Editor	Owen Marks
Art Directors	James Basevi, Malcolm Ben
Set Decorator	George James Hopkins
Music/Musical Director	Leonard Rosenman
Costumes	Anna Hill Johnstone
Sound	Stanley Jones

Julie Harris (Abra), James Dean (Cal Trask), Raymond Massey (Adam Trask), Richard Davalos (Aron Trask), Burl Ives (Sam, the sheriff), Jo Van Fleet (Kate), Albert Dekker (Will Hamilton), Lois Smith (Ann), Timothy Carey (Joe), Mario Siletti (Piscora), Lonny Chapman (Roy), Nick Dennis (Rantani), Harold Gordon (Mr. Albrecht), Jonathan Haze (Piscora's son), Barbara Baxley (Nurse), Bette Treadville (Madame), Tex Mooney (Bartender), Harry Cording (Bouncer), Loretta Rush (Card dealer), Bill Phillips (Coalman), Jack Carr, Roger Creed, Effie Laird, Wheaton Chambers, Ed Clark, Al Ferguson, Franklyn Farnum, Rose Plummer (Carnival people), John George (Photographer), Earle Hodgins (Shooting gallery attendant), C. Ramsay Hill (English officer), Edward McNally (Soldier), Jack Henderson, Ruth Gillis, Joe Greene, Mabel and June Smaney.

Released in USA, April 1955; GB, July 1955. Running time: 115 min. Distributor: Warner Bros.

Baby Doll (1956)

Production Company	Newtown Productions
Producer	Elia Kazan
Production Manager	Forrest E. Johnston
Director	Elia Kazan
Assistant Director	Charles H. Maguire
Script	Tennessee Williams. Based on his one-act plays *27 Wagons Full of Cotton* and *The Unsatisfactory Supper* or *The Long Stay Cut Short*
Director of Photography	Boris Kaufman
Editor	Gene Milford
Art Director	Richard Sylbert
Associate Art Director	Paul Sylbert
Music	Kenyon Hopkins
Costumes	Anna Hill Johnstone
Wardrobe	Flo Transfield
Speech Consultant	Marguerite Lamkin
Sound	Edward J. Johnstone

Carroll Baker (Baby Doll Meighan), Karl Malden (Archie Lee Meighan), Eli Wallach (Silva Vacarro), Mildred Dunnock (Aunt Rose), Lonny Chapman (Rock), Eades Hogue (Town marshal), Noah Williamson (Deputy), Jimmy Williams (Mayor), John Stuart Dudley (Doctor), Madeleine Sherwood (Nurse), Will Lester (Sheriff), Rip Torn (Brick), and the people of Benoit, Mississippi.

Released in USA and GB, December 1956. Running time: 114 min. Distributor: Warner Bros.

A Face in the Crowd (1957)

Production Company	Newtown Productions
Producer	Elia Kazan
Production Manager	George Justin
Director	Elia Kazan
Assistant Director	Charles H. Maguire
Script	Budd Schulberg. Based on his short story *Your Arkansas Traveller* from his book *Some Faces in the Crowd*
Director of Photography	Harry Stradling
Associate Director of Photography	Gayne Rescher
Camera Operators	Saul Midwall, James Fitzsimons
Editor	Gene Milford
Art Directors	Richard Sylbert, Paul Sylbert
Music	Tom Glazer
Songs:	"A Face in the Crowd," "Free Man in the Morning," "Mama Guitar," "Vitajex Jingle" Tom Glazer, Budd Schulberg
Costumes	Anna Hill Johnstone
Wardrobe	Flo Transfield
Sound Editor	Don Olson
Sound	Ernest Zatorsky
Technical Advisers	Charles Irving, Toby Bruce

Andy Griffith (Lonesome Rhodes), Patricia Neal (Marcia Jeffries), Anthony Franciosa (Joey Kieley), Walter Matthau (Mel Miller), Lee Remick (Betty Lou Fleckum), Percy Waram (Colonel Hollister), Rod Brasfield (Beanie), Charles Irving (Mr. Luffler), Howard Smith (J. B. Jeffries), Paul McGrath (Macey), Kay Medford (1st Mrs. Rhodes), Alexander Kirkland (Jim Collier), Marshall Neilan (Senator Fuller), Big Jeff Bess (Sheriff Hesmer), Henry Sharp (Abe Steiner), Willie Feibel, Larry Casazza (Printers), P. Jay Sidney (Llewellyn), Eva Vaughan (Mrs. Cooley), Burl Ives (Himself), Bennett Cerf, Betty Furness, Faye Emerson, Virginia Graham, Sam Levenson, Mike Wallace (Extras in bar sequence), Logan Ramsey (TV director), Earl Wilson, Walter Winchell, Vera Walton, John Stuart Dudley, Fred Stewart, Rip Torn, Granny Sense, Harold Jinks, Diana Sands, Charles Nelson Reilly, Sandy Wirth.

Locations filmed in Arkansas, Memphis, and New York. Released in USA, June 1957; GB, October 1957. Running time: 126 min. Distributor: Warner Bros.

Wild River (1960)

Production Company	20th Century-Fox
Producer	Elia Kazan
Director	Elia Kazan
Assistant Director	Charles Maguire
Script	Paul Osborn. Based on the novels *Mud on the Stars* by William Bradford Huie and *Dunbar's Cove* by Borden Deal
Director of Photography	Ellsworth Fredericks (CinemaScope)
Color Process	DeLuxe Color
Color Consultant	Leonard Doss
Editor	William Reynolds
Art Directors	Lyle R. Wheeler, Herman A. Blumenthal
Set Decorators	Walter M. Scott, Joseph Kish
Music	Kenyon Hopkins
Costumes	Anna Hill Johnstone
Sound	Eugene Grossman, Richard Vorisek

Montgomery Clift (Chuck Glover), Lee Remick (Carol Garth), Jo Van Fleet (Ella Garth), Albert Salmi (Hank Bailey), Jay C. Flippen (Hamilton Garth), James Westerfield (Cal Garth), Barbara Loden (Betty Jackson), Frank Overton (Walter Clark), Malcolm Atterbury (Sy Moore), Robert Earl Jones (Ben), Bruce Dern (Jack Roper), James Steakley (Mayor), Hardwick Stewart (Marshal Hogue), Big Jeff Bess (Joe John), Judy Harris (Barbara-Ann), Jim Menard (Jim Junior), Patricia Perry (Mattie), John Dudley (Todd), Alfred E. Smith (Thompson), Mark Menson (Winters), Pat Hingle (Narrator).

Kazan started work on the film in 1955. After finishing a first script called *Garth Island*, he asked for the contribution of Ben Maddow and Calder Willingham. Nine different versions of the script were worked out while the film went through the following titles: *Time and Tide*, *God's Valley*, *As the River Rises*, *The Swift Season*, *The Coming of Spring*, and *New Face in the Valley*. Released in USA, June 1960; GB, July 1960. Running time: 109 min. Distributor: 20th Century-Fox.

Splendor in the Grass (1961)

Production Company	Newtown Productions/NBI
Producer	Elia Kazan
Associate Producers	William Inge, Charles H. Maguire
Director	Elia Kazan
Assistant Directors	Don Kranze, Ulu Grosbard (New York scenes)
Script	William Inge
Script Supervisor	Marguerite James
Director of Photography	Boris Kaufman
Color Process	Technicolor
Editor	Gene Milford
Production Designer	Richard Sylbert
Set Decorator	Gene Callahan
Music/Musical Director	David Amram
Costumes	Anna Hill Johnstone
Wardrobe	Florence Transfield, George Newman
Choreography	George Tapps
Sound	Edward Johnstone

Natalie Wood (Wilma Dean Loomis), Warren Beatty (Bud Stamper), Pat Hingle (Ace Stamper), Audrey Christie (Mrs. Loomis), Barbara Loden (Ginny Stamper), Zohra Lampert (Angelina), Fred Stewart (Del Loomis), Joanna Roos (Mrs. Stamper), Jan Norris (Juanita Howard), Gary Lockwood (Toots), Sandy Dennis (Kay), Crystal Field (Hazel), Marla Adams (June), Lynn Loring (Carolyn), John McGovern (Doc Smiley), Martine Bartlett (Miss Metcalf), Sean Garrison (Glenn), William Inge (Reverend Whiteman), Charles Robinson (Johnny Masterson), Phyllis Diller (Texas Guinan), Buster Bailey (Old man at country club), Jake La Motta (Waiter), Billy Graham, Charlie Norkus (Young men at party), Lou Antonio (Roustabout), Adelaide Klein (Italian mother), Phoebe Mackay (Maid), Mark Slade, Marjorie J. Nichols, Richard Abbott, Patricia Ripley.

Released in USA, October 1961; GB, January 1962. Running time: 124 min. Distributor: Warner Bros.

America America (1963)

[British title: *The Anatolian Smile*]

Production Company	Warner Bros.
Producer	Elia Kazan
Associate Producer	Charles H. Maguire
Production Assistant	Burtt Harris
Director	Elia Kazan
Script	Elia Kazan. Based on his own novel and his unpublished story "Hamal"
Script Supervisor	Marie Kenney
Director of Photography	Haskell Wexler
Camera Operator	Harlowe Stengel
Optical Effects	Film Opticals inc.
Editor	Dede Allen
Production Designer	Gene Callahan
Music	Manos Hadjidakis
Lyrics	Nikos Gatsos
Costumes	Anna Hill Johnstone
Sound Editor	Edward Beyer
Sound	L. Robbins, Richard Vorisek

Stathis Giallelis (Stavros Topouzoglou), Frank Wolff (Vartan Damadian), Harry Davis (Isaac Topouzoglou), Elena Karam (Vasso Topouzoglou), Estelle Hemsley (Grandmother Topouzoglou), Gregory Rozakis (Hohanness Gardashian), Lou Antonio (Abdul), Salem Ludwig (Odysseus Topouzoglou), John Marley (Garabet), Johanna Frank (Vartuhi), Linda Marsh (Thomna Sinnikaglou), Paul Mann (Aleko Sinnikaglou), Robert H. Harris (Aratoon Kebabian), Katharine Balfour (Sophia Kebabian), Dimitris Nicolaides, Leonard George, Gina Trikonis, George Stefans, Peter Dawson, Xander Chello, Carl Low.

Filmed at the Alfa Studios, Athens. Released in USA, December 1963; GB, April 1964. Running time: 168 min. Distributor: Warner Bros.

The Arrangement (1969)

Production Company	Athena Enterprises
Producer	Elia Kazan
Associate Producer	Charles H. Maguire
Director	Elia Kazan
Assistant Director	Burtt Harris
Script	Elia Kazan. Based on his own novel
Director of Photography	Robert Surtees (Panavision)

Color Process	Technicolor
Editor	Stefan Arnsten
Production Designer	Gene Callahan
Art Director	Malcolm Ben
Set Decorator	Audrey Blasdel
Music	David Amram
Costumes	Theodora Van Runkle
Sound Editor	Larry Jost
Sound	Richard Vorisek

Kirk Douglas (Eddie Anderson/Evangelos), Faye Dunaway (Gwen), Deborah Kerr (Florence Anderson), Richard Boone (Sam Anderson), Hume Cronyn (Arthur), Michael Higgins (Michael), John Randolph Jones (Charles), Carol Rossen (Gloria), Anne Hegira (Thomna), William Hansen (Dr. Weeks), Charles Drake (Finnegan), Harold Gould (Dr. Liebman), E. J. Andre (Uncle Joe), Michael Murphy (Father Draddy), Philip Bourneuf (Judge Morris), Diane Hull (Ellen), Barry Sullivan (Chet Collier), Ann Doran (Nurse Costello), Chet Stratton (Charlie), Paul Newlan (Banker), Steve Bond (Eddie at 12), Jim Halferty (Eddie at 18), Joseph Rogan/Joseph Cherry (Gwen's baby), Clint Kimbrough (Ben), Kirk Livesey, Bert Conway, John Lawrence, Elmer J. McGovern, Barry Russo, Dee Carroll, Richard Morrill, Betty Bresler, Virginia Peters, Pat Paterson, Dorothy Konrad, Maureen McCormick.

Released in USA, November 1969; GB, January 1970. Running time: 125 min. Distributor: Warner Bros.

The Visitors (1972)

Production Company	Chris Kazan—Nick Proferes Productions
Producers	Chris Kazan, Nick Proferes
Director	Elia Kazan
Script	Chris Kazan
Director of Photography	Nick Proferes (Super 16, color)
Lighting	Michael Mannes
Assisted by	William Mamches
Editor	Nick Proferes
Music	Bach's Suite No. 1 for lute, played by William Matthews (guitar)
Sound Editor	Nina Shulman
Assistant Sound Editor	Marilyn Frauenglass
Sound	Dale Whitman

Patrick McVey (Harry Wayne), Patricia Joyce (Martha Wayne), James Woods (Bill Schmidt), Chico Martinez (Tony Rodriguez), Steve Railsback (Mike Nickerson),

Shot on location on Elia Kazan's property in Newtown, CT; flashback scene shot in Westchester County, NY. Working title: *Home Free.* Released in USA, February 1972. Not yet released in GB. Running time: 90 min. Distributor: United Artists.

The Last Tycoon (1976)

Production Company	Paramount
Producer	Sam Spiegel
Director	Elia Kazan
Script	Harold Pinter, based on the novel by F. Scott Fitzgerald
Cinematographer	Victor Kemper
Editor	Richard Marks
Composer	Maurice Jarre
Production Designer	Gene Callahan
Art Director	Jack Collins
Set Designer	Bill Smith, Jerry Wunderlich
Costumes	Anna Hill Johnstone

Robert De Niro (Monroe Stahr), Tony Curtis (Rodriguez), Robert Mitchum (Pat Brady), Jeanne Moreau (Didi), Jack Nicholson (Brimmer), Donald Pleasence (Boxley), Ingrid Boulting (Kathleen Moore), Ray Milland (Fleishacker), Dana Andrews (Red Ridingwood), Theresa Russell (Cecilia Brady), Peter Strauss (Wylie), Tige Andrews (Popolos), Morgan Farley (Marcus), John Carradine (Guard), Jeff Corey (Doctor), Diane Shalet (Stahr's secretary), Seymour Cassel (Seal trainer), Anjelica Huston (Edna), Bonnie Bartlett and Sharon Masters (Brady's secretaries), Eric Christmas (Norman), Leslie Curtis (Mrs. Rodriguez), Lloyd Kino (Butler), Brendan Burns (Assistant editor), Carrie Miller (Lady in restaurant), Peggy Feury (Hairdresser), Betsy Jones-Moreland (Writer), Patricia Singer (Girl on beach).

Running time: 125 minutes. Color. Rated PG

Shorts

People of the Cumberland (1937)

Production Company	Frontier Films
Director	Elia Kazan

Script Elia Kazan
Director of Photography Ralph Steiner
Running time: 20 min.

Film Performances

1930s *Cafe Universal* and *Pie in the Sky* (both directed by Ralph Steiner)
1940 *City for Conquest* (as Googie. d: Anatole Litvak)
1941 *Blues in the Night* (as the clarinet player. d: Anatole Litvak)

THEATER

Prior to his professional career, Kazan appeared in several plays at Yale, including *Love of One's Neighbour* (as a Tourist), *Dr. Faustus* by Christopher Marlowe (as Wagner), *The Stepmother* (as Dr. Gardner), *Reckless* by Lynn Riggs, *Andromaque* by Jean Racine (as Pylade), *Thirty Minutes in a Street, Blood o' Kings, Merry-Go-Round* by Albert Maltz and George Sklar (as Joe Zelli), *I Got the Blues* (as Sam), *Until the Day I Die*, and *The Three Sisters* by Anton Chekhov (as Solyony).

Stage Performances

1932 *Chrysalis* by Rose Albert Porter (as Louis; also stage manager. Martin Beck Th., 15 November)
1933 *Men in White* by Sidney Kingsley (as the Orderly; also stage manager. Broadhurst Th., 26 September)
1934 *Gold Eagle Guy* by Melvin Levy (as Polyzoides; also stage manager. Morosco Th., 28 November)
1935 *Till the Day I Die* (as Baum) and *Waiting for Lefty* (as Agate Keller) by Clifford Odets (Longacre Th., 26 March), *Paradise Lost* by Clifford Odets (as Kewpie. Longacre Th., 9 December)
1936 *Johnny Johnson* by Paul Green (as Pte. Kearns. 44th Street Th., 19 November)
1937 *Golden Boy* by Clifford Odets (as Eddie Fuselli and Joe Bonaparte. Belasco Th., 4 November. Kazan toured in the same play during the 1938–39 season and also appeared in London in the role of Eddie Fuselli at the St James's Th., 21 June 1938)
1939 *The Gentle People* by Irwin Shaw (as Eli Lieber. Belasco Th., 5 January)

1940 *Night Music* by Clifford Odets (as Steve Takis. Broadhurst Th., 22 February), *Liliom* by Ferenc Molnar (as Ficzur, the "sparrow." 44th Street Th., 25 March)
1941 *Five Alarm Waltz* by Lucille S. Prumbs (as Adam Boguris. Playhouse Th., 13 March)

Stage Productions

1931 *The Second Man* by S. N. Behrman (Toy Th., Atlantic City)
1934 *Dimitroff* by Elia Kazan and Art Smith (co-director: Art Smith. Group Th.)
1935 *The Young Go First* by Peter Martin, Charles Scudder, and Charles Friedman (co-director: Alfred Saxe. Park Th., 28 May)
1936 *The Crime* by Michael Blankfort (co-director: Alfred Saxe)
1938 *Casey Jones* by Robert Ardrey (Fulton Th., 19 February)
1939 *Quiet City* by Irwin Shaw (Belasco Th., 16 April)
Thunder Rock by Robert Ardrey (Mansfield Th., 14 November)
1941 *It's Up to You* by Arthur Arent (Dept. of Agriculture)
1942 *Cafe Crown* by Hy S. Kraft (Cort Th., 23 January)
The Strings, My Lord, Are False by Paul Vincent Carroll (Royale Th., 19 May)
The Skin of Our Teeth by Thornton Wilder (Plymouth Th., 18 November)
1943 *Harriet* by Florence Ryerson and Colin Clements (Henry Miller Th., 3 March)
One Touch of Venus by S. J. Perelman and Ogden Nash (Martin Beck Th., 14 March)
1944 *Jakobowsky and the Colonel* by S. N. Behrman (Martin Beck Th., 14 March)
Swing Out, Sweet Land by Jean and Walter Kerr (International Th., 27 December)
1945 *Deep Are the Roots* by Arnaud D'Usseau and James Gow (Fulton Th., 26 September)
Dunnigan's Daughter by S. N. Behrman (Golden Th., 26 December)
1947 *All My Sons* by Arthur Miller (Kazan also produced with Harold Clurman, Walter Fried, and Herbert H. Harris. Coronet Th., 29 January)
Truckline Cafe by Maxwell Anderson (as producer only. Belasco Th., 27 February)
A Streetcar Named Desire by Tennessee Williams (Ethel Barrymore Th., 3 December)
1948 *Sundown Beach* by Bessie Breuer (Belasco Th., 7 September)
Love Life by Alan Jay Lerner (46th Street Th., 7 October)
1949 *Death of a Salesman* by Arthur Miller (Morosco Th., 10 February)

1952 *Flight into Egypt* by George Tabori (Music Box Th., 18 March)
1953 *Camino Real* by Tennessee Williams (National Th., 19 March)
Tea and Sympathy by Robert Anderson (Ethel Barrymore Th., 30 September)
1955 *Cat on a Hot Tin Roof* by Tennessee Williams (Morosco Th., 24 March)
1957 *The Dark at the Top of the Stairs* by William Inge (Kazan also produced with Saint Subber. Music Box Th., 5 December)
1958 *J.B.* by Archibald MacLeish (ANTA, 11 December)
1959 *Sweet Bird of Youth* by Tennessee Williams (Martin Beck Th., 10 March)
1964 *After the Fall* by Arthur Miller (ANTA Washington Square Th., 23 January)
But for Whom Charlie by S. N. Behrman (ANTA Washington Square Th., 12 March)
The Changeling by Thomas Middleton and William Rowley (ANTA Washington Square Th., December)

Unpublished Plays

Bloody Ground. Melodrama in one act (date unknown).
The Blood of the Brewsters (June 1931).
Skit Farce in One Act by Elia Kazan (June 1931).
Triangle Seventeenth, A Collegiate Comedy (June 1931).
A Prodigee Genius. A one-act satire (November 1931).
The Failure. A one act drama (December 1931).
Bridegroom (1932).
Saved (1932).
Alumni Day, a play in three acts (1933).
Two strike plays (including *For Bread and Unity*, a class war fairy tale, 1933–34).
College Days (revised version of *Alumni Day*, 1937).
A play by Elia Kazan and Clifford Odets (title unknown).

PUBLICATIONS

Books

America America, 1962: Stein and Day, New York
The Arrangement, 1967: Stein and Day, New York
The Assassins, 1971: Stein and Day, New York

The Understudy, 1975: Stein and Day, New York
Acts of Love, 1978: Alfred Knopf, New York
The Anatolian, 1982: Alfred Knopf, New York
Elia Kazan: A Life, 1988: Alfred Knopf, New York
Beyond the Aegean, 1994: Alfred Knopf, New York

Articles, etc.

"The Director's Playbill," *New York Herald Tribune*, September 1943.
"Beginner's Notes" (diary on the shooting of *A Tree Grows in Brooklyn*, edited by Nicholas Ray, unpublished, 1944)
"Audience Tomorrow, Preview in New Guinea," *Theater Arts*, October 1945.
"Advertisement" (with Harold Clurman; on Maxwell Anderson's *Truckline Cafe*), March 1946.
"About Broadway and the Herring Catch," *New York Times*, 16 October 1949.
"Pressure Problem" (on the enforced cuts in *A Streetcar Named Desire*),
New York Times, October 1951.
"A Statement," *New York Times*, 4 December 1952.
"Playwright's Letter to the World" (on *Camino Real*), 15 March 1953.
"Movie That Had to Be Made" (on *Man on a Tightrope*), 3 May 1953.
"The Director's Notebook" (on *A Streetcar Named Desire*), in *The Griffin*, 1953.
"A Star Will Find Its Sky" (unpublished), 1957.
"Paean of Praise for a Face Above the Crowd" (on Budd Schulberg), May 1957.
"The Writer and Motion Pictures," *Sight and Sound*, Summer 1957.
Preface to *Seen any Good Films Lately?* by William K. Zinsser, 1958.
"Knowing Everything Is Only the Beginning," *New York Herald Tribune*, 5 July 1961.
"Theater: New Stages, New Plays, New Actors" (on the Lincoln Center experiment), *New York Times Magazine*, 23 September 1962.
"Shooting America" (diary of the shooting of *America America*, unpublished), 1963.
"Here's What's Behind America America," *Valley Times*, 2 April 1964.
"Kazan Unbowed by Year of Repertory," Newark *Sunday News*, 2 August 1964.
"On Process Development of Repertory, Or A Team Needs Patience and Years," *New York Times*, 9 August 1964.
"Political Passion Play Act Two" (on the Democratic Convention in Chicago), published in *New York*, 23 September 1968.

Interviews

With Lewis Gillenson, *Harper's Bazaar*, November 1951.
John Durniat, "Amateurs Can Be Great," *Popular Photography*, May 1955.
"A Quiz for Kazan," *Theater Arts*, No. 11, 1956.
Frederic Monon, "Gadge!," *Esquire*, February 1957.
Ward Moorehouse, "Keeping up with Kazan," *Theater Arts*, June 1957.
"An Interview with Elia Kazan" *Equity*, December 1957.
Henri Rode, "Entretien avec Elia Kazan," *Cinémonde*, August 1961.
"Candid Conversation: Elia Kazan," *Show Business Illustrated*, February 1962.
Robin Bean, "Elia Kazan on 'The Young Agony,'" *Films and Filming*, March 1962.
Jean Domarchi and Andre S. Labarthe, "Entretien avec Elia Kazan," *Cahiers du Cinéma*, April 1962.
Donald Stewart, "An Interview with Elia Kazan," *Nugget*, 1963.
James F. Fixx, "Who Cares What the Boss Thinks?," *Saturday Review*, 28 December 1963.
"Arthur Miller Ad-Libs on Elia Kazan," *Show*, January 1964.
Richard Schechner and Theodore Hoffman, "Look, There's the American Theatre," *Tulane Drama Review*, winter 1964.
"Elia Kazan Ad-Libs on *The Changeling*," *Show*, January 1965.
Michel Ciment and Roger Tailleur, "Entretien avec Elia Kazan," *Positif*, October 1966.
Michel Delahaye, "Entretien avec Elia Kazan," *Cahiers du Cinéma*, November 1966.
Claudine Tavernier, "Entretien avec Elia Kazan," *Cinéma 70*, November 1970.
Bernard R. Kantor, Irwin R. Blacker, and Anne Kramer, "Directors at Work: Interviews with American film-makers," 1970.
Stuart Byron and Martin L. Rubin, "Elia Kazan Interview," *Movie*, no. 19, 1972.
Charles Silver and Joel Zuker, "Visiting Kazan," *Film Comment*, summer 1972.

Short Interviews

J. B. Bidgman, *The National Herald*, 4 April 1943.
Murray Schumbach, "A Director Named Gadge," *New York Times*, 1947.
Ward Morehouse, "Kazan Demands Truth in Plays," 1956.
"Kazan Decries the James Dean Myth," *Mirror News*, 25 April 1957.
Mike Wallace, "What About Movie Censorship?," *Congressional Record*, 21 August 1957.

Ernest Schier, "You Can Have Broadway," *Sunday Bulletin* (Philadelphia), 1 October 1961.
Henry T. Murdock, "Elia Kazan Splendid Salesman for *Splendor*," *Philadelphia Inquirer*, 1 October 1961.
John Bustin, "Elia Kazan: Adult Moviemaker," *American Statesman*, 3 October 1961.
Elinor Hughes, "Kazan Describes Working with Inge on *Splendor*," *Boston Herald*, 6 October 1961.
Sinnone Anger, *La Presse* (Montreal), 9 October 1961.
Paul Toupin, "Le Cinema, Je l'Apprends de Film en Film," *Montreal Photo Journal*, 14 October 1961.
Interview in *Newsweek*, 16 October 1961.
"Elia Kazan Talks about His Two Lives," *Times*, 9 January 1962.
George Christian,"A Chat with Kazan," Houston *Post*, 1 March 1964.
Kaspar Monahan, "Elia Kazan Speaks His Mind," *Pittsburgh Press*, 1 March 1964.
George Oppenheimer: "Kazan Answers Critics on *The Changeling*," *Daily Times*, Marmaroneck, NY, 18 November 1964.
"Ella Kazan le Faiseur de Rebelles," *Pariscope*, 12 January 1966.
Guy Braucoun, "Elia Kazan: *l'Arrangement* Fait le Procès de l'Amérique," *Lettres Françaises*, 8 April 1970.
With Kira Appel, *France-Soir*, 8 April 1972.
With Nicole Jolivet, *France-Soir*, 6 May 1972.
With Guy Le Clech, *Le Figaro*, 10 June 1972.

RADIO

★

Elia Kazan appeared on the *Philip Morris Hour*, *The Kate Smith Hour*, and the Group Theatre radio program.

INDEX